Getting Started in

Consulting

SECOND EDITION

Alan Weiss, Ph.D.

WILEY

John Wiley & Sons, Inc.

Published by John Wiley & Sons, Inc., Hoboken, New Jersey.
Published simultaneously in Canada.

For general information on our other products and services please contact our Customer Care Department within the United States at (800) 762-2974, outside the United States at (317) 572-3993 or fax (317) 572-4002.

Wiley also publishes its books in a variety of electronic formats. Some content that appears in print may not be available in electronic books. For more information about Wiley products, visit our web site at www.wiley.com.

Library of Congress Cataloging-in-Publication Data:
  Weiss, Alan 1946–
    Getting started in consulting / Alan Weiss.—2nd ed.
      p. cm.—(The getting started in series)
    Includes index.
    ISBN 0-471-47969-1 (pbk.)
    1. Business consultants—Handbooks, manuals, etc. 2.
  Consultants—Marketing—Handbooks, manuals, etc. I. Title. II. Getting started in.
  HD69.C6W459 2003
  001'.068—dc22   2003059557

Printed in the United States of America.

10 9 8 7 6 5 4

For L. T. Weiss,
who has taught me more about life than I ever thought I'd know,
and who has demonstrated a combination
of support, joie de vivre, and independence
that I will forever admire.

Contents

Chapter 1

Establishing Goals and Expectations
You Will Be What You Decide to Be, Nothing Less, Nothing More

Chapter 2

Physical Space and Environmental Needs
Act Like You Have a Business and You'll Have One   **23**

Chapter 3

Sorting Out the Legal, Financial, and Administrative
First, Let's Kill All the Lawyers

Chapter 4

Fundamental Marketing
Creating a Gravity for Your Business

Chapter 5

Advanced Marketing
Creating a Brand

Chapter 6

Initiating the Sales Process and Acquiring Business
Building Relationships

Chapter 11

The Quick Start

How to Hit the Consulting Ground Running at Full Speed

Appendixes

Introduction to the Second Edition

In two short years this book has become such a mainstay of those entering the consulting profession that the publisher and I decided to revise it so that it contains the most up-to-date information possible. I've also added a new Quick Start chapter to accelerate the start-up for those of you prepared to do so, and a new Appendix entry of 101 Questions that should stand you in good stead in every phase of the sales process.

Since the first edition, the consulting profession has seen increased status for the solo practitioner. Large firms have been damaged by overly optimistic growth goals, excessive infrastructure, and ethical breaches. But independent consultants continue to be responsive, cost-effective, and highly focused resources for organizations seeking assistance.

There is no other profession I know of where the practitioner is paid to learn, increasing his or her value, providing larger fees to learn still more on the next assignment. Once you enter this cycle, there is no limit on your ability to help clients, to grow, and to create wealth.

If that isn't enough encouragement to read on, then you probably should seek out the corporate world. But if it is, then join me on this fabulous journey.

Let's get started.

—Alan Weiss, Ph.D.
June 2003, East Greenwich, RI

Acknowledgments

My thanks to the several hundred people who have participated in my Private Roster Mentor Program. The privilege of working with them to build and grow their practices has enriched my life and immeasurably added to my understanding of the attributes and factors required for success in the consulting profession.

To Dr. William Winter and my friends at the American Press Institute over the past 20 years and 50 appearances. Thanks for great times.

My eternal thanks to Maria, Danielle, and Jason for their love and forbearance.

About the Author

Alan Weiss began his own consulting firm, Summit Consulting Group, Inc., out of his home in 1985 after being fired by a boss with whom he shared a mutual antipathy. Today, he still works out of his home, having traveled to 49 states and 54 countries, published 21 books and over 500 articles, and consulted with some of the great organizations of the world, developing a seven-figure practice in the process.

His clients have included Merck, Hewlett-Packard, State Street Corporation, Fleet Bank, Coldwell Banker, Merrill Lynch, American Press Institute, Chase, Mercedes-Benz, General Electric, American Institute of Architects, the Federal Reserve, and over 300 similar organizations. He delivers 30 keynote speeches a year, appears frequently on radio and television to discuss issues pertaining to productivity and performance, and has been featured in teleconferences, videoconferences, and Internet conferences.

He has a Ph.D. in organizational psychology, and has served as a visiting faculty member at Case Western Reserve, St. John's, and a half dozen other major universities. He has held an appointment as adjunct professor at the graduate school of business at the University of Rhode Island, teaching a popular course on advanced consulting skills. His books have been translated into German, Italian, Spanish, and Chinese.

Dr. Weiss resides with his wife of 35 years, Maria, in East Greenwich, Rhode Island with their dogs Koufax and Phoebe.

Establishing Goals and Expectations

You Will Be What You Decide to Be, Nothing Less, Nothing More

Winston Churchill remarked once that "we build our houses, and then they shape us." He was referring to Parliament. But the statement applies to most of our lives. That is, we create and fulfill our own expectations. When you consider entering the *consulting* field and, intelligently, ask others what to expect and prepare for, you'll probably be told:

consulting the application of talents, expertise, experiences, and other relevant attributes, which results in an improvement in the client's condition.

- ✔ You'll work long hours and travel incessantly.
- ✔ You'll have to work the phones daily to get prospects.
- ✔ You can't make more than $300,000 or so annually as a solo practitioner.
- ✔ Divide your yearly needs by billable days to create a per diem fee.
- ✔ Underpromise and overdeliver.

I run a seven-figure practice from my home, with no staff, no office, and no sweat. If I had believed the preceding advice I never would have entered the field because, as much as I desperately wanted to be my own boss, I didn't want to work for any boss—including myself—who would labor under those adverse conditions. If we're going to take the risks inherent in starting and managing our own business, we ought to at least be able to reap the rewards.

The problem is that if you educate yourself incorrectly at the outset, you're vulnerable to successfully meeting the exact wrong set of expectations. You will have brilliantly achieved a sorry state (which I see all too frequently in my mentoring program in consultants who are burned out, alienated from their families, losing money while supporting staffs, and generally suffering through conditions that they'd never approve for their own clients). There is a plethora of bad advice in the consulting profession, and there are more people pontificating about how to succeed than there are successful independent consultants. That should tell you something.

So, no matter how gray the hair, no matter how many years in the business, no matter what the claimed experience, don't believe anything you hear about this being an onerous and difficult profession. It's actually one of the absolute best in the world, provided you have the resources, the focus, the talents, and the passion for it. You should expect to become successful in assisting clients, to grow personally prosperous, and to create a rich and rewarding life for yourself and your family. If you don't expect those things, why are you considering any future in this business?

STARTING AT SQUARE ZERO: FINANCIAL NEEDS

One of the primary reasons that people who enter the profession fail is not due to contacts, talent, competition, or methodology, but to undercapitalization. While it doesn't cost a fortune to create a consulting practice, there are the minor expenses of letterhead, phone, and postage, and the major expenses of feeding yourself, paying the mortgage, and putting gas into the car. When you start working as a consultant you don't stop living as an individual (and, perhaps, as a family supporter).

If you follow the guidelines in this book, you should begin to generate business in six months from your actual start-up. However, this is dependent on many variables, such as your market, your particular focus, serendipity, and so forth. The stream or pipeline of business won't really be strong until you've been in business for a year or so. Consequently, the ideal starting point financially begins here (which is why I call it "square zero" and not, for example, "square one"; this is the true baseline).

Reduce Monthly Expenses

Reduce your monthly living expenses as much as you reasonably can. This has to be an accurate calculation. You can't reduce rent payments, but you can put off a vacation this year. You can't reduce the heating bill, but you can dine out less often. Arrive at the lowest monthly expenditure level that you (and your family) can reasonably commit to.

Establish a Fund for the Year

Find enough money—real money, not future business or projections—to fund that monthly expenditure for a full year. You might not need all of it if business develops early. If you don't develop any business in the course of the year, you can truthfully say that you gave it a shot but the profession is not for you. However, some of the best people I know have required 6 to 12 months to bring home the initial bacon, and you literally cannot afford to become defocused because of bill collectors figuratively at the door, or believe you're a failure because business literally didn't develop in the first few months of your new venture.

If your monthly living expenses are $4,000, you need to find $48,000 that is available to you, and you need the mentality to be willing to spend it to support yourself while you launch your business. Here are some typical sources that have worked for others:

✔ *Home equity loan.* This is a terrific source if you own your own home and have equity, because it is easy to secure, the interest is fully tax deductible, and can either be withdrawn only as needed or can be withdrawn in a lump sum and the portion not immediately needed can be invested. You can also pay these back without penalty. Overall, this is a very good funding source. As we've all seen, there are times when interest rates dip so low that even the most conservative financial adviser would advocate this route.

✔ *Nonretirement savings.* Take a deep breath and cash in the stocks, bonds, and other investments in order to make a still better use of the money—an investment in yourself and your future. The only penalty here would be applicable capital gains taxes, and there is periodic pressure in Congress to reduce those. However, if you cash in stocks that have lost money, you have the secondary benefit of taking a tax deduction on the loss. If you plan to fund your business this way, therefore, consider selling the losers, not the winners.

✔ *Retirement savings.* This is more problematic, because you will have to pay some penalty for funds that aren't reinvested in a retirement account within 60 days of withdrawal, under current Internal Revenue Service (IRS) provisions. You will also lose the power of tax-free interest appreciation. However, the younger you are, the more viable it is to withdraw funds of this type, since there is all the more time to replenish them. My recommendation: Try not to use this source if you're over 40.

✔ *Credit lines.* Actually, it's not difficult to create a substantial fund using only the credit available on existing credit cards. (I once took the time to calculate that if I maximized every cash advance available on every credit card I owned, I could raise several hundred thousand dollars within 24 hours.) The problem is that the interest rates are usually staggering compared to other sources and the revolving credit actually adds to your monthly expenses, which will now be commensurately higher. These are not a good deal, unless they are for the short term (less than 90 days) and you're confident of business that can be used to repay them promptly. (*Note:* Even an unused credit line causes concern to future lenders because they assume that you may someday access it, meaning your indebtedness could increase, thereby endangering their own loan.)

> **Career Key** If you begin by funding your business correctly, you will create a precedent that will lead to prudent fiscal responsibility and maximum profit. Nothing, absolutely nothing has ruined more consulting careers than concerns about short-term financial pressures. Eliminate them early.

✔ *Investors.* While some new consultants attempt to put together a prospectus and to attract the equivalent of venture capital, such a formality is a waste of time. You're far better off with investors who know you and are willing to help out, even though there is considerable risk. Prepare a brief business plan[1] that reaches out two to three years (after that they are exercises in fantasy) and demonstrate:

equity
ownership of an enterprise. In this case, it is sometimes offered in place of cash compensation for services rendered. Equity can be attractive as a portion of compensation, but should never represent total compensation, especially for new consultants.

- ✔ The nature of your market.
- ✔ How you intend to penetrate the market.
- ✔ What your unique offerings and talents are.
- ✔ The funding necessary to sustain you.
- ✔ The return (revenue and profits) anticipated.
- ✔ Economic conditions that support your theses.

Offer your investors either a payback schedule that provides a decent return on their investment or a very small (e.g., 5 percent) *equity* ownership in your nascent business. Do not offer any investor a major or controlling interest, or that person will be justified in making decisions about how you conduct the business, how you spend your time, and what market you pursue, meaning that you've wound up working for someone else again.

✔ *Family.* For some this is the easiest, and for some this is the hardest source to approach. Even if you were to seek the entire amount this way, a year's stake of $48,000 spread over 5 to 10 family members is only $5,000 to $10,000 each. And you may want to secure only part of the year's needs this way, making it even more desirable. *Hint:* Prepare the same business plan that was recommended for outside investors. The family deserves to see it, you will seem more serious and less on a lark, you will divorce yourself from the person they remember as the kid falling off a bike and become a business professional in their eyes, and you'll feel better about the whole thing. Plan to repay the family with the same rigor that you would anyone else. Otherwise, you are on a lark.

There are other sources of funding, such as selling valuables, a spouse taking on a part-time or full-time job, seriously reducing lifestyle (e.g., taking children out of private tuition schools), hitting the lottery, severance pay from a prior job, selling a second home, and so forth. The alternatives described are the common ones, but the key is to set aside a full year's reasonable (not extravagant and not destitute) living expenses. If you decide to enter the consulting profession full-time (not as a between-jobs stopgap) and create a career, and you do so with only a few months of reserves, you may be lucky and manage it. But the odds will be against you, so at least be cognizant of the dangers.[2]

PERSONAL ATTRIBUTES: THE INVESTMENT FROM WITHIN

I'm asked all the time what skills are required to be a successful consultant. But it's actually the wrong question, since skills can be learned. The more important issue is what behaviors and attributes are required, since these are not usually learnable and our behavioral range is finite. (Learning how to conduct a meeting is a skill set, for example, but the tolerance for sitting through tedious meetings is a behavioral trait that many of us don't possess, myself included.)

Here are the ideal consultant behaviors and attributes as they apply to a solo practitioner, based on my observations of success and failure over 27 years. *Be advised that the greatest danger to the start-up venture in this profession is a lack of self-esteem of the principal.* If you don't believe you can help others, no one else will believe it. And if you don't manifest it, no one else will see it.

Ten Traits

1. *Humor and perspective.* There are few things as important as remaining on an even keel. You shouldn't be as high as the last victory (sale) or as low as the last defeat (rejection). See both the comic and tragic within *client* engagements. You must retain your objectivity—and sanity—which can be easily distorted when you work alone. Humor is also a sign of high intelligence and mental agility. If you can't laugh at yourself and at the world around you, join the corporate ranks or become a philosopher, but don't put out a consulting shingle.

2. *Influence.* You have to be able to speak, either formally or informally, in such a way that you can command a room or persuade an individual. Many consultants are horrid public speakers, which severely limits their effectiveness and their practice. A grasp of proper English, a wide-ranging vocabulary, and a talent for metaphor will serve you well in both marketing and implementation.

 client an organization or individual that engages the consultant to achieve certain results in return for agreed-upon compensation.

Career Key The effective use of language influences a discussion; influencing a discussion influences the relationship; and influencing the relationship controls the business. Language is the most dramatic asset you can utilize.

3. *Confidence and self-esteem.* This is no profession for the faint of heart. Strong and powerful people will stare in your face, and weak and frightened people will nip at your heels. The Japanese have a word for "presence": *sogomi.* They define *sogomi* this way: They know it when they see it, and it's the ability to exude confidence and power. You should be seen as a credible peer by clients and prospects, not as a vendor, salesperson, or subordinate.

4. *Fearlessness.* This is different from confidence. This is the ability to walk away from business you don't want and *buyers* you don't like. It's the ability to say to prospects that their basic premises are incorrect and that you'd be doing them a disservice if you proposed a project based on their current expectations. Nothing increases credibility (and, ultimately, business) like the willingness to stand your own ground, disagree when you have better information and insights, and offer a differing view of a situation. You may get thrown out. Or you may be embraced as an honest person.

5. *Rapid framing.* This is a little-known and little-understood trait that I've identified as one of the keys in differentiating consultants early in discussions with a prospective client. It is the ability to quickly summarize the issues—not to propose solutions, which are premature in early meetings—so that the discussion can focus rapidly on the next steps. For example, "Jill, what I'm hearing is that your customer retention is declining, but you're not really sure why, and you're reluctant to take any corrective actions until you're positive about the cause." Many clients aren't sure themselves how to articulate their concerns and needs, and the consultant who can do so for them becomes a partner and solidifies the relationship.

6. *Value generation.* Most consultants make the mistake of zealously guarding what they consider to be their intellectual property. In reality, there's nothing new under the sun. The ability to provide a prospect with real *value* right from the initial contact will create a subliminal message: "If I'm getting this much from our preliminary discussions, how much would I gain if I

buyer
that person who can write a check (expend budget without further approvals) for the consultant's products and services; also called economic buyer or true buyer.

value
the degree of improvement to the client represented by the achievement of the objectives. These may be quantitative (2 percent increase in sales) or qualitative (there will be much less stress for me).

actually hired this person?!" Smoothly and deftly work into the conversation ideas, books, articles, approaches, references, experiences, and anything else that will create early value and reliance.

7. *Intellect.* There may be no greater asset than intellectual firepower. The more you are able to quickly use examples, paraphrase, cite historical analogies, recognize weakness in an argument, ask penetrating questions, and so forth, the more you will at least be seen as a peer and probably be seen as an invaluable asset to the client's business. Powerful people tend to hire powerful people, and powerful people are the ones with large sums to invest. Weak people are frightened by powerful people, but they are not the buyers you want to appeal to in any case.

> **Career Key**   Continually improve your intellectual breadth. Do not focus solely on business skills, consulting methodologies, or even marketing. Consulting is a relationship business, and the more you are conversant in a variety of areas, the better your chances of building those relationships.

8. *Active listening.* Instead of tuning out and thinking about still another way to tell the prospect how good you are, demonstrate your ability to listen clearly, take part in the conversation through reflective listening (replying "in other words . . ." and paraphrasing, for example), and assure the other party that you're involved in and concerned about these issues. This will do wonders not only in securing business, but in *networking*, dealing with your bankers, resolving confrontations, and so on. Active listening is one of the rarer traits in consulting, since most consultants try to talk too much (and when they're talking they can't be listening and learning).

9. *Instantiation.* I couldn't help it—this is one of my favorite words. It means "making abstract examples and concepts tangible." Consultants tend to talk at 35,000

networking
the activity of meeting others in a systematic manner, particularly those who can buy, recommend, or otherwise support your services. The best networking is accomplished one-on-one by providing value to the other party first.

feet while the client is dealing with problems on the ground. It is a tremendous advantage to be able to say, "By participation I don't mean anarchy, but rather people taking on accountability for the outcome of their work, such as following up the next day with a customer who complained about late shipments." Clients are concerned with the pragmatic improvement tomorrow. You have to take your approaches and translate them into that improved future.

 Talking to Consultants

Q. What one key approach or activity would you do differently today from when you started?

A. I would have included interviews with the target group as a precursor for any and all work that I embark on. I never realized how much value, how many answers to the problem I was hired to help solve, and how much rapport I could create throughout an organization with a dozen well-placed phone calls. I found that the best answers, training, innovation, and ideas almost always come from within. I am just a facilitator to pull it out, keep the project on course, prioritize the solutions, and hold the team accountable to implementation.

Q. What was your biggest surprise—what do you wish you had known that you didn't know?

A. How much money the large organizations have to invest in quality solutions that I can offer and how valuable my solutions can be for the right organizations. Good consultants should never work on any opportunity that they can't quantify and get agreement about having significant potential value. By doing this it becomes much easier to charge six figures for the solutions that have a tenfold return on investment.

—Mark Faust, president, Echelonmanagement.com

10. *Bang-bang responsiveness.* I'm convinced that responsiveness is an innate character trait, because it's so easy, yet done so poorly by so many consultants. I promise a 90-minute response to all phone calls, and I meet that standard 99 percent of the time. Yet many consultants don't get back to people for days. In this profession, getting there first is a major advantage. You must have the disposition to return calls, respond to letters, answer e-mails, and meet commitments faithfully and reliably. If you are disorganized, can't seem to move the piles of papers off your desk, and have a yard of pink phone messages sticking out of your pockets, find a day job. You won't make it as a consultant.

If you have a reasonable chance of performing well in these 10 areas, you've got an excellent shot at making it as an independent consultant. Eight of 10 might do it. Less than that and you may be setting yourself up for high stress at least and failure at most.

TIME USE: THERE'S NO SUCH THING AS NOT HAVING ENOUGH TIME

Every day I work with consultants who don't have time to be with their families, enjoy their hobbies, or even work with all the clients they would like to. In fact, many of them have to schedule coaching calls with me weeks in advance, even though I have the time and my practice is many times the size of theirs. What's wrong with this picture?

Career Key Your consulting practice is a means to an end. The ultimate objective is to provide for loved ones, enjoy life, maximize your contributions to the environment around you, and fulfill your ambitions and dreams. It's counterintuitive, perhaps, but you'll be more successful launching and building your career if you see it as a means and not an end in itself.

Never lose sight of the fact that time is the great equalizer. We all have the same amount of time, man or woman, young or old, wealthy or impoverished, neophyte or veteran. The question, of course, is *how we choose to invest it*. There is no such phenomenon as not having enough time. When we say, "I'd like to, but I don't have time," what we're really communicating in that statement is, "That particular activity is not a priority, so I'm spending my available time on something I consider more important." So if you don't have time to market your services, to write an article, to spend a romantic evening with your spouse, or to attend your kids' soccer games, then you're simply choosing not to. This is a sobering but vital fact to understand as you create and build a professional consulting practice.

As you get organized, get organized. Create lists— folders are effective only if you see them daily and look through them; I prefer lists that sit on your desktop and can be toted along, not computer screen lists that disappear behind screen savers when you're away from the monitor. The lists should establish your priorities for *both professional and personal goals*. Whenever I ask consultants what their current status is and where they'd like to be in two years, they inevitably provide purely business objectives: revenues, number of clients, name recognition, and so on. This is a fundamental weakness, because our professional and personal lives are so intertwined in this profession.

(By the way, paper lists that are constantly in view are far superior to electronic lists kept on a computer or Palm Pilot. A list that takes work to access might as well not be there.)

Here are the 10 keys to effective time investment as you proceed from square zero. They will stand you in good stead throughout your consulting career, no matter how large and successful the business becomes.

Ten Time Investment Tips

1. *Integrate your professional life and your personal life.* You only have a single life. Don't compartmentalize, trying to create 8-, 10-, or 12-hour workdays. If you feel like writing an article on Saturday afternoon, do it. If you want to see your daughter's dance recital on Wednesday morning, do that. A week has an enormous amount of time if it's not arbitrarily chopped up and apportioned. (When you say that you "don't have the time" to see your kids' events, you really mean that other things are more important and you've decided not to see their events.)

2. *Use lists to create forward progress.* At the outset, keep a monthly, weekly, and daily "to do" list. This will not only create an important feeling of accomplishment as you cross off successfully completed tasks, but it will also forge momentum. In other words, you won't be able to say that you're still working on that article 90 days later. (It takes 90 minutes, not 90 days, to write an article.) Integrate personal and professional needs on the lists, so that your life and business are moving forward together, and you're not leaving one behind to advance the other.[3] (These list formats are available in every type of personal calendar product, but I reiterate that I like simple pieces of paper that you can keep in a pocket or purse or on a desktop.)

3. *Don't do things that are easily delegated and/or for which you aren't skilled.* Invest in a graphic designer to do your letterhead and logo. Have a web expert develop your web site. Hire a lawyer to incorporate your business. Select an accountant to do your taxes and filing. If you can't type and you have a large volume of literature to create, hire a student by the hour. Place a premium on your time. You're not saving money by struggling over something you have no flair for or ability to complete. You're wasting money.

4. *Don't dally over low-priority decisions.* The name of your firm is not of cosmic importance. Make a decision and move on. If you want feedback, ask a few potential clients (not friends, since only clients buy your services, not friends) and then make a decision. Don't agonize over the look of a presentation folder or business card. They can always be changed later. Usually your initial sentiment is valid, and weeks of analysis won't change the decision.[4]

5. *Do what feels right at the time.* Don't sit uselessly at your desk and force yourself to make phone calls if the spirit doesn't move you, even though it's 10 o'clock in the morning and you're supposed to be working. That's a construct from an old, bureaucratic system. If you're not ready to do some work, then go to a personal item on your list, and clean out the garage, get the car washed, or buy your spouse's anniversary gift. Conversely, don't mindlessly surf the cable channels if there's nothing interesting on television, even if it is 8 o'clock in the evening. Move to your business items, and write a publicity piece, sketch out a speech, or put a proposal together.

6. *Maintain a sanctum sanctorum.* Never attempt to work in a public area in your home (even if you live alone). Designate a den, a spare bedroom, or a heated part of the garage as your private office. Use what I call a "focused work space" that has all of your equipment and support needs with minimum distractions. When you are working, keep the television off, the door closed, the interruptions few.

7. *Spend money to maximize efficiency.* Have the phone company install a dedicated fax line and a minimum of two lines for your residence/home office—one for personal use, one for business use. There is nothing worse than having your phone line tied to your fax and computer modem lines. Run your computer modem off the fax line, which is used less frequently than your business phone line. Better yet, if you have cable access in your area, run the computer off the cable, which provides Internet and e-mail access at lightning-like speeds. Install call-waiting, voice mail, your own postage meter, a high-speed copier, a plain-paper fax with memory, and a superb computer with a laser printer. This is all investment, not cost.[5]

Career Key I do not know of a single full-time consultant. Even if it were possible, who on earth would want to do it?

8. *Be selfish with your personal time.* Don't allow people to invade your time at their whim. Tell people on the phone that you're busy and can spare only a minute or will have to call them back later. Tell your family that they need to give you another hour to finish what you're doing. Schedule installations, repairs, and maintenance around your convenience, not the vendors'. (You'd be surprised how flexible schedulers and dispatchers get when you say, "Look, either you can schedule this when it's convenient for me or you can cancel our order, and I'll tell the owner of the firm exactly why you've lost our business.")

9. *Plan your long-term time investment.* When you know that you have a major time commitment—preparing a speech, creating a marketing piece, working with web designers, writing a proposal—start with the deadline, work backward, and break it up into manageable chunks. If something is due in four weeks, set your deadline at three weeks out, thereby allowing yourself an entire week for contingencies and problems. Then allocate time each week from the finished product back to the present and the initial steps. Schedule on your calendar (and "to do" lists) three hours every other day, or five hours a week, or one day a week, or whatever will enable you to get the major project completed while also working on a myriad of other things during the same time period. It's all in the planning.

10. Allow for the unexpected. Medical consultants advise doctors never to schedule wall-to-wall appointments during the day, because inevitably there are emergencies, late patients, complications on routine exams, and so forth. These create a domino effect by day's end, and some very unhappy scheduled patients. Instead, they advise some built-in slack time that can absorb the contingencies. If not needed, slack time provides valuable respite. You should do the same. Allow yourself some deliberate slack time during the day and during the week. It will be like money in the bank.

Talking to Consultants

Q. What was your entry into your own practice?

A. When I started my practice in 1989, it was not exactly a planned experience. I was at that time a vice president of marketing at a software start-up in Berkeley, and the new CEO took me to lunch one day and fired me. This was for political not competency reasons. So as I drove home, I was trying to figure out what to do. When my wife got home from work that night, I said, "Guess what. I'm now in the consulting business."

Q. What would you do differently in your start-up if you had to do it again?

A. If I had it to do over again, I would have done a lot more planning and had a lot more money in the bank before starting. It has taken me almost 10 years to overcome starting undercapitalized. In starting my next company, I am making sure this does not happen. If I had it to do over, what I would have done more of is [I would have] planned what I would do, how I would do it, and who I would do it for. I had to learn as I went, and it took me a good three years to craft a service offering that was really meeting the needs of an easily identifiable group of clients.

Q. What has been your biggest surprise?

A. My biggest surprise in all of this is that I really could do it, and be a success at it. I always thought I needed a corporate structure (or some structure) to work within. I found out a lot about myself in the process. I find working for yourself is like constantly being in group therapy, with your clients as the group. They are constantly giving me feedback. The better the relationship with the client the richer the feedback!

—David Coleman, managing director,
Collaborative Strategies LLC

FOCUS: WE'RE ALL WORKING PART-TIME

The pseudo-sage advice in this business is, "You have to be a full-time consultant and work at this profession exclusively if you want to succeed." The only problems with this sagacity are that it's based on a false premise, has never been actually exemplified, and wouldn't work anyway. Other than these drawbacks, it's great.

You have to be serious about your craft, but that doesn't mean you have to engage in it to the exclusion of all else. You have to develop your consulting skills and market your services, but that doesn't mean you have to zealously sacrifice all other interests or even all other sources of income. College professors have moonlighted successfully for years as consultants, as have expert witnesses in a variety of fields, business executives on the lecture circuit, and all sorts of entrepreneurs.

I probably work at the combination of consulting, speaking, and writing about 25 percent of my waking, available time. That's why I'm in this profession—I'm a refugee from the mindless rigors of the nine-to-five corporate world. The key is not how many hours you work. (Nor, for that matter, is it how much you make. The only test of business success is how much you *keep*.)

There isn't much chance to launch a successful consulting career if you're holding down the traditional daily job and want to consult only at night and on weekends; this is mainly because your prospective clients don't want your help at night and on weekends (although there are exceptions here, such as consulting in computers and programming, certain health care and medical consulting, and so forth). You do have to give up the proverbial day job.

However, true consultants aren't constantly on the client's site and, when not there, don't continually work the phones, write, and network. There is a lot of down time in the profession. This isn't unusual or bizarre. Walk around any major organization, and you'll find people chatting in the hallways, spending inordinate time at unnecessary meetings, and playing solitaire on their computers. We all goof off, because no job requires constant attention and no human could endure that demand if the job did.

I'm a part-time speaker, even though that part of my practice generates almost $400,000 annually. Yet I speak only about 30 times a year, for about an hour. That's less than a traditional workweek, one out of 52, for over a third of a million bucks. Ironically, it's the fact that I don't speak more often that makes me so successful, keeps me fresh, creates demand, and makes my fee appropriately high.

Don't judge yourself by your time commitment. Judge yourself by your results. My ideal, I often tell people (and silence a room in doing so) is to work five minutes a year for $10 million. My wife says that if I can work 5 minutes at those rates, I should be able to work 10. We'll see.

However, keep the following separation in mind at all times as you launch your career and plan its growth:

✔ Condition one is that you intend to build a self-sustaining business in consulting, one that is profitable, creates a personal or company identity, and can support your lifestyle and goals, no matter how much or how little you are actively engaged in it.

✔ Condition two is that you intend to consult on the side as opportunity presents itself, and the resultant income is simply gravy on top of the predominant income derived in your other pursuit or pursuits.

Conditions one and two are mutually exclusive. In the first condition you must proactively market, and in condition two you can simply reactively accept business. A business failure in condition two is almost inconsequential, while a failure in condition one is catastrophic.

One of the key determinants here is how you identify yourself. When a stranger at a party asks, "What do you do?" and you reply, "I'm a consultant," you've staked out condition one. But if you were to reply, "I'm in insurance," or "I'm in insurance and do a little consulting," then you're in condition two. Condition two is virtually never an entry point for condition one, because it provides too much security, too many comfortable factors, too much status and ego involvement, and very small risk.

This book is written for those in condition one, although the concepts are mostly applicable to condition two, as well. Both approaches are valid and can be quite successful, but there is a big difference between being a consultant and being someone who consults on the side. None of those college professors alluded to previously refer to themselves as "consultants who teach." They are professors who consult on the side. Their advantage is in their safe academic haven and secure salary and benefits, but their disadvantage is their time obligation to the university and the fact that they are not dedicated, focused consultants. (I can't begin to tell you how many clients have said, "Please, not another academic or theoretician" when offered a professor's help.)

A consulting practice is not a question of volume of time but rather of quality of focus.

WHY COLLABORATION CAN KILL YOU

Everyone in the world wants to collaborate. Unfortunately, this means mostly exchanging business cards and hoping for the best.

Understand that people are not going to give you business. Many new consultants want to "collaborate" with me by getting subcontracting work or participating in one of my projects. There is nothing in those deals for me, no value added, no synergy. Similarly, you'd be crazy to offer hard-won business of your own to someone else just on the promise of some vague, future reciprocity.

> **Career Key** Don't simply assume that your content expertise from your former career will be sufficient to meet client needs as a consultant. Ask what results clients need, determine what interventions will enable you to deliver those results, and then make a plan to acquire and continually hone those skills.

Collaboration, alliances, partners, and other "let's work together" offers are just like bank loans, agents, and speakers bureaus: You can't get them when you need them, but they're all over you when you no longer need them. Don't get lulled into wasting precious time, effort, and money on offers of collaboration that don't have a specific piece of business on the table to discuss. Also, remember that in collaborative efforts, 1 plus 1 must equal 64. That means that if I can create $10,000 of business and you can create $10,000 of business, it's silly to collaborate if the result is $20,000. In fact, we'll lose money, because collaboration soaks up time and energy. Only if the joint application of our respective skills can build a $50,000 or $100,000 piece of business where there was only $10,000 before is collaboration worth considering.

There are only two reasons to bring other people into business you've secured early in your career:

1. You need help with the legwork, since you can't manage all of the interviewing, or training, or writing that's required within the client's time frame. This is actually quite rare and usually the result of poor planning. When you're just starting out, try to get to everything yourself so that you maximize your profit.

2. You don't have the expertise for a certain part of the project, and need help with, say, the financial planning or the technical specifications. This is valid, but not so if you need help with basic consulting techniques that you should have mastered, such as running focus groups, conducting surveys, or creating training materials.

(Later in your career you may use subcontractors if the work is tedious and provides no learning, or you simply want to work less.)

In fact, here are some basic consulting *methodologies* that should be in your tool kit if you are a generalist or deal with the people side of the business:

methodology
the systematic, procedural approaches that a consultant uses to implement a project (e.g., surveys, training programs, competitive analyses, etc.).

✔ Focus groups, interviewing, and similar sampling techniques.

✔ Problem solving, decision making, and planning.

✔ Innovation and creativity.

✔ Communication, feedback, and interpersonal relations.

✔ Strategy formulation and implementation.

✔ Behavior modification and morale.

✔ Performance evaluation and succession planning.

✔ Coaching and counseling.

✔ Conflict resolution and negotiating.

If you are a specialist in technology, finance, or health care, for example, your list should include the comparable needs in your field. If you find yourself constantly looking for help because of lack of competence, then you simply haven't prepared yourself adequately to meet client needs, and you should consider some educational help in the form of books, consulting seminars, mentoring, and/or an apprenticeship.

Career Key Always be cognizant of the difference between *process* and *content*. Content refers to the work of the business (e.g., health care or producing cement). Process refers to techniques to run a business that can be applied to any content (e.g., decision making or conflict resolution, the approaches to which are the same in both health care and cement).

process techniques to run a business that can be applied to any content (e.g., decision making or conflict resolution).

SUMMARY

If you're going to start from square zero, begin with a secure financial base, determine whether you have the requisite behaviors and temperament, carefully manage your time, focus on the quality of your approaches, resolve that this is your profession, develop the proper skill sets, and avoid useless collaborations.

content the work of the business (e.g., health care or producing cement).

The number of people who enter the consulting field and fail is staggeringly high. But even more unfortunate are those who enter the field, eke out a living, and get caught in the "success trap." That is, they hit a wall or plateau because they are working hard but not working smart, and are running too fast to stop and understand their own plight.

You have the advantage of beginning the right way, learning from others' mistakes and not placing yourself in a position of having to unlearn before you can learn. Take the time, the energy, and the moderate risk of creating the right start, so that you can more quickly move from square zero to square one.

Final thought: Do not simply emulate others. Determine why they are successful and then adapt their steps to your personal style.

NOTES

1. See Appendix A for a sample business plan for the purpose of raising funds from investors.

2. One exception: If you are beginning with a contract already in place from a prior employer or business contact, you already have some cash flow to offset the year's expenses. But the caveat here is to ensure that you are marketing to attract other business during the initial term of the contract, or you'll be back at square zero when the contract is done and the fees have been spent. See Chapters 4 and 5 on creating a marketing presence from the outset.

3. See Appendix B for sample "to do" lists.

4. By the way, this is why you should never have extra thousands of copies of anything printed, no matter how often you're told, "It's only an extra $200." Keep inventories low on items that you're likely to change. The savings doesn't justify being stuck with out-of-date or out-of-style materials.

5. See Appendix C for suggested office equipment and recommendations.

2

Physical Space and Environmental Needs

Act Like You Have a Business and You'll Have One

I n 1985 I was fired by the owner of the small company I had been employed by as president for two years. It was an unceremonious, and rather parsimonious, departure. My wife and I decided that my best chance for success was to neither work for someone else nor have others work for me. I would be a solo practitioner.

My immediate focus was to secure an office.

"Why do you want an office?" asked my wife.

"Well, I'll be running my own practice, formally incorporated."

"But why do you want an office?" she persisted.

"I'm going to need my own work space, materials, support, image."

"Are clients going to come to your office? Is consulting a walk-in business, like a manicurist or a flower shop?"

I realized that the real consultant was giving me some invaluable advice. I wanted a formal office because I thought it was an accoutrement of the job. What I really needed was a work space.

I've worked out of my home for 18 years, from the time I launched my solo practice to the time I'm writing these words. I know that will never change. A home-based practice is viable for the beginner and for the successful veteran. So don't feel that if you're starting out working in a spare bedroom that you're inferior, temporary, or cutting corners.

Moreover, I estimate that office rent, equipment, utilities, insurance, and even part-time staff would have cost me at least $30,000 a year, which totals $540,000 to date, and still counting. That's significantly more than the amount of money it cost to put our two kids through 17 years of private schooling, and pay for my daughter's wedding (if and when, please the gods, it finally takes place). Spending money for image is one thing, but spending it for ego is another.

Your clients don't see your physical space. You do. If you can work successfully, productively, and happily there, that's all that matters. This chapter details how to set up an initial office environment using one's residence. It also covers office-sharing techniques and formal, external offices. We begin with the most common configurations.

ALTERNATIVE WORK SPACES

You have several options starting out, depending on your budget, work style, personal preferences, and existing physical assets. All of them can be successful, though I want to stress that a home office is by far the most economical alternative available.

Office at Home

This option is dependent on two factors: the size of your residence and the size of your family. If you live in a three-room apartment but have no family, you have ideal conditions for a home office. If you live in a 10-room house, but have 6 kids and 5 pets, you might be too squeezed to accommodate an office in the house.

You need two primary elements for your office: space and privacy. The space is important because you must have certain equipment with appropriate support (electrical outlets, phone lines, files, etc.). The privacy is important because you must be able to talk to clients uninterrupted by domestic noise. (I always allowed my dogs free run of my office without any problem until one day, while I was using the speakerphone as I took notes, my 100-pound shepherd/husky, Trotsky, wandered over after a meal and belched right into the speaker.

Career Key   Most prospects and clients never, ever ask about your office. They will simply inquire, "Where are you located?" or "Where are you based?" Simply say, "Our office is in East Greenwich" and don't offer anything more, or move the conversation onward by saying, "Our office is in East Greenwich. Have you always been located in this area?"

A home office should minimally have the following characteristics:

- ✔ An enclosed, private area with a door.[1]
- ✔ Sufficient space for at least primary equipment, such as a computer and printer, phone, and desk. (The copy machine, for example, might be in another room if necessary.)
- ✔ At least two phone lines, but preferably three (office number, home number, fax).
- ✔ Heating and air-conditioning as needed in your area.
- ✔ Enough storage for frequently needed files, support materials, and supplies.

Ideally, the office should also provide:

✔ Natural lighting from outdoors.

✔ Space for support equipment: copier, postage meter, fax.

✔ Accommodations for a television, radio, and cassette recorder.

✔ Room for a large, spacious desk.

Your home office should be your work refuge for two important reasons: First, you'll need a quiet, private space in which you can leave things in the exact condition you'll want to find them again the next morning. This isn't a hobby, like model building, stamp collecting, or knitting, where you can clear up your stuff from the kitchen table so that dinner can be served and homework can be done, and return again later. You have to be able to create a sanctum sanctorum, no matter how modest, in which your work materials are unmolested by family, visitors, and anyone else in the house. (Our cleaning crew is prohibited from entering my den. My wife and I clean it. Well, I sort of help.)

Second, the IRS will allow you to deduct an office at home only to the extent that it is a full-time office. A shared family room or bedroom won't count. Even a dedicated room, if also used for other functions and not kept exclusively as your place of work, won't count. *This is a significant income tax deduction.*

Ideally, carve out a spare bedroom, den, library, finished basement, attic, guest room over the garage, or whatever space you can manage to use as your initial office. It will serve you nicely at the outset, and you might just find yourself comfortably ensconced there a decade or so later. But if you find that your only alternative at home is a corner of the living room, the kitchen table, or the workbench in the garage, take a look at other options.

One final advantage of a home office: You'll never have to complain about the commute.

Shared Space

There are a great variety of office suites that allow you to use the facility, usually a cubicle but sometimes an office, for a set monthly fee. You will have a receptionist who will forward calls to you if you happen to be on-site, or to your voice mail if you're not. There is often a shared secretarial/administrative function for correspondence, copying, faxing, and so forth. You can get your mail there and also use the postage meter to send your mail.

These spaces exist in most cities of at least medium size, and many people utilize them, especially as temporary support when getting started. Their advantage is that they provide primary support services in a professional setting, affording you both the help and socialization of other people.[2]

The disadvantage, aside from the investment required, which can range from $200 to over $1,000 a month depending on the level of service, location, and space, is that many people fool themselves that they are working because they've "gone to the office." In fact, you use these places on the fly, meaning that you can't leave personal possessions of any significance, the equipment is shared, and sometimes there are even limits on the amount of time you can occupy the space. Simply reporting in doesn't constitute *marketing* or working.

Another disadvantage of shared space is that you can't drop in at 10 o'clock at night if you have a great urge to accomplish something, because the facility probably isn't open and definitely isn't next door. There is no permanence that allows for a continuity of effort and focus.

A different kind of shared space, however, is offered by many professional service firms that rent out their offices. Your accountant, lawyer, designer, or other professional friends and colleagues may have office space available. You can often work out a deal in which a nice office is permanently yours for an annual fee, and the company receptionist will dedicate one incoming line to you and answer your phone appropriately, even taking messages when you're out. You can make arrangements to pay for use of copier, fax, and so on. Many professional firms take on more space than they immediately need, and renting out the excess for even a modest fee is better than allowing it to lie fallow.

These are good arrangements, because you can

marketing
the creation of
need for your
services among
potential buyers.

personalize your office, interact with others, have use of a receptionist, and enjoy most of the benefits of a small organizational setting while being on your own. The only slight disadvantages would be things like the fax headings, which might indicate a law firm and won't have your company name (these are set in the fax machine—I'm not talking about letterhead or stationery). Also, you might not get your own key, so you might be subject to the owner's office hours, meaning you might not have access to your files and computer on the weekends or in the evenings. This can be solved with a laptop computer and some duplicate files, or by securing your own off-hours office access.

Career Key   Since consultants go to clients and not the other way around, it's usually more important to have an office in proximity to your home rather than in a major business center. This will make your commute easier and also keep costs lower.

Shared space with your own office in a small organization of professionals is a good deal, and preferable, for many, to even an excellent office at home. The increased cost for renting the space is offset by the business environment and formal separation of personal and professional life.

There is one final type of shared space, similar to the last one. You might be able to borrow space if you have a relative or close friend who has an office arrangement with extra space. Almost everything would be the same as in the previous example, but with two important exceptions: First, there would probably be no fee at all, hence the term "borrow." Second, you will have some of the advantages and disadvantages of working with family members or close friends. That dynamic can infringe on your privacy and can be uncomfortable. It's one thing if your paid landlord sees you doing a crossword puzzle at two in the afternoon, but it's a different thing if you're seen by your father-in-law or your spouse's best friend's brother.

Look for such borrowed space if the social dynamic will be comfortable and undemanding. However, make sure that the space is part of a compatible business. You don't want to borrow an office in a meatpacking plant or an auto body repair operation, no matter what the savings.

Formal Office

You can rent, lease, or even buy an office that is part of a larger building or stand-alone. For example, I have a friend who bought a condo to use as her office, also looking at it as an investment to sell or rent out should she decide to move to larger quarters or retire. You can acquire a storefront type of office, such as are usually occupied by real estate offices and insurance agencies. You can rent office suites or single rooms in larger office buildings.

Virtually all of these will come unfurnished and unequipped. This means that your initial investment will have to include:

- ✔ Down payment for mortgage, lease, or rental costs.
- ✔ Insurance, including fire, theft, liability, and so on.
- ✔ Utilities.
- ✔ Phones and phone lines.
- ✔ Basic decorating and design.
- ✔ Equipment purchase and installation.
- ✔ Locks and security measures.
- ✔ Possibly part-time or full-time administrative help.[3]
- ✔ Cleaning services.
- ✔ Office amenities: cooler, coffee machine, and so on.

Some words of caution are offered here, even to those who may easily be able to afford an office from the outset due to severance pay, intelligent savings, or the lottery. A formal office provides as much distraction as it does privacy. There will be mail and parcel deliveries, solicitations, cleaning crews, building maintenance, chamber of commerce requests, and a myriad of other intrusions. If you hire someone, you will have further time demands for managing the help, no matter how pleasant, how professional, and how dedicated that help may be.

If you've been a successful consultant for a while and honestly believe that your productivity and performance will be enhanced by making the move to a formal office of your own—and you're not being sideswiped by your own ego—then, by all means, have a go at it. But if you're new to the profession and trying to establish priorities as you begin your career, put the external office on hold for as long as you can. Use one of the alternatives just described, for at least the first year.

And, above all else, remember that half-million-plus that could have gone into the office but wound up in my pocket. How much business at what average fee would it take to recoup that amount of money?

THE BASICS AROUND YOU

This is what you'll minimally require from the outset. We'll tackle the more esoteric, nonessential stuff a little later. But don't start your practice without the following:

Two-Line Phone

Like most other technological advances, phones are becoming cheaper and more diverse all the time. The two lines I'm talking about are not two business lines, but rather one line for the business and one line for home if you're working at home. If you're working in an office outside of your home, two business lines are fine, but call-waiting works equally well. The phone service should include call-waiting, call forwarding, and caller ID. Ideally, the phone should have both speed dial and memory capability so that you can store and quickly retrieve your most frequently called numbers. A speaker feature is nice but not essential. Many people like to use a headset, which affords very high quality while leaving your hands free for notes and providing mobility to look for files or search on the computer.

Estimated cost: $150 to $300.

Voice Mail

Don't use an answering machine, which has limited flexibility. Acquire voice mail support from your phone company or from a private supplier. The primary features you'll need are message length and capacity. Some people are verbose, and you don't want the system to cut them off before they finally get to their phone number. Nor do you want the dreaded "voice mail box full" announcement to be made to a potential client. Most voice mail will also provide branching, whereby the caller has an option to leave a message for you or someone else. This can be helpful if you want to differentiate between general messages for the firm and private messages for you, or if you sell products and want to use one of the branches for product orders. If you're a trainer, you could provide a branch for seminar registration, as well. No one minds voice mail too much anymore, since it's become a part of our business culture. What they do mind is not being called back promptly, so make sure your system retains messages indefinitely, can be accessed easily from the road, and has security devices built in to protect privacy.

Estimated cost: $50 to $150 per month.

Fax with Dedicated Line

Select a plain-paper fax with a memory. The memory is absolutely mandatory, since faxes will always run out of paper, jam, or lose the ink cartridge precisely when important documents are being sent. The memory feature has saved me grief more times than I can count. Do not have a system wherein there is one line for phone and fax, and the caller has to wait for the prompt to choose phone message or fax. It's unprofessional, annoying, and unreliable. Have a separate line installed just for the fax, which can also be used as a backup phone line in an emergency. Sharp and Canon make good, small faxes for home offices, and they can be purchased through discount office supply stores such as Staples.

Estimated cost: $200 to $400.

Copier

You can't run to Kinko's every time you need copies, and you can't rely on the fax machine, because even the best are good at being fax machines and terrible at being copiers. Minimally, you'll want excellent resolution, the ability to make 100 copies at a time, and small size and footprint (the machines in which the top slides back and forth take up far more room, for example). Don't buy a used copier. These are notoriously temperamental machines to begin with. Buy a new one with a warranty which, in the case of a copier, is well worth the small extra investment. You don't need automated paper feeders or sorters, but the ability to copy photographs and book text, and to enlarge and reduce are important features. Find a model that can make a lot of copies before toner cartridges have to be changed. Have preventive maintenance and cleaning performed at least yearly. Canon, Xerox, and Sharp all make fine home office copiers, and are available at discount office supply stores.

Estimated cost: $300 to $600. One-year warranty is often included.

Computer and Peripherals

Your computer needs are going to overwhelmingly be for word processing (letters, invoices, reports), spreadsheets (tracking revenues, logging mileage, client reporting) and

Talking to Consultants

Q. What one key approach or activity would you do differently today from when you started?

A. Being the first person in my family who didn't have "a real job," I didn't know what I didn't know about marketing my services. I was so concerned about bootstrapping and positive cash flow that I didn't take the long view and invest in getting outside help to advise me on pricing and other issues. As a result, I left a lot of money on the table because I didn't know my worth in the marketplace, or even where the most profitable clients were. Looking back, that unwillingness to invest cost me at least five years of struggle—the only thing that saved me was that I had a good track record and reputation.

Q. What was your biggest surprise—what do you wish you had known that you didn't know?

A. I am surprised at how successful you can be without knowing everything you need to know. In the beginning, I wouldn't implement a new idea until it was analyzed to death. I realize now that I was using perfection to hide my fear of failing. Now I'm willing to have more faith in my abilities and just jump in and learn along the way.

—Vickie Sullivan, president, Sullivan Speaker Services

databases (clients, prospects, newsletter subscribers). You may have some graphics needs (slides, charts, course materials, presentations). That's four primary software needs at the outset. Invest in the best machine you can that will handle all of your basic needs supremely well, but don't worry about additional bells and whistles. I've found that my scanner was used so infrequently that, when I upgraded my system, I removed it.

Career Key Learn supremely well the 20 percent of the computer system that you actually need and ignore the rest. Be expert at all the word processing shortcuts, for example, but don't worry about the more esoteric sound features. You can always look up some rarely used feature in the manual when you need it.

I favor Macs (Apple's Macintosh computers) because the technology is so user-friendly and intuitive. Modern software allows you to open nearly any application on any platform, so compatibility is not an issue. No matter what brand you purchase, however, include the following as a wise investment:

- ✔ A computer with the maximum storage space and speed that your budget can afford.[4] You should buy enough extra capability that the computer can serve you well for a minimum of five years without upgrading. You'll need a backup drive of some kind, such as a zip drive, to protect you in the case of a crash or other data loss.

- ✔ A first-rate monitor with a diagonal screen size of at least 16 inches. ViewSonic is highly rated and is a fine monitor at a reasonable price.

- ✔ A laser printer with the fastest printing you can afford. Hewlett-Packard makes terrific, highly reliable printers. Purchase a model with at least two paper trays. (You can also acquire an HP color printer for less than $200. But this should be a second printer, not the primary one.)

- ✔ A high-speed modem. If you can in your area, create your Internet access through the local cable system, which is hundreds of times faster than the fastest modems. Although this might cost $100 to $200 per month, the cost is more than justified in the time and frustration saved in accessing e-mail and downloading from the

Internet. I save over 100 hours a year—that's more than two workweeks—through the speed of the cable.

Estimated cost for the entire computer system: $3,500 to $6,000.

Postage Meter

This device makes your life easier and also provides a professional image. Clients and prospects aren't accustomed to seeing postage stamps on business correspondence. Meters are generally leased from organizations such as Pitney Bowes, although there is a growing trend toward electronic postage from the Internet, which hasn't yet proved very popular. The latter is still problematic, requires special software, and can't accommodate certain envelopes, so a meter is still required, especially for larger packages. You should obtain an electronic scale with it that will allow you to be economical with postage, determine what class of service makes sense (e.g., Priority Mail versus book rate), and most of all help you avoid the long lines at the post office. Final major advantage: You can insert additional postage in the meter using a code over the phone lines at any time.

Estimated cost: Leases from $800 to $2,000 per year.

The Bottom Line

The basic investment in your office equipment, if you have absolutely nothing and have to purchase it all, ranges from $5,000 to $20,000, depending on quality and capabilities. You can offset this if you have existing equipment, by purchasing from discount houses and catalogs, by purchasing used equipment, or by borrowing or sharing equipment. However, for $5,000 at square zero, you can equip yourself professionally and well with equipment that will last for years. (See the Quick Start chapter that concludes this book for still another view of basic purchases that can be made rapidly to maximize start-up success and speed.)

BEYOND THE BASICS

As you're able to afford them, there are additional items that can significantly improve productivity. Although they may seem like luxuries, after one use you begin to wonder how you could have survived without them.

Laptop Computer

These have become tremendous aids to productivity for those of us who travel a great deal. You can switch files readily with your desktop machine, sometimes as easily as with an infrared connection, but usually through exchanging disks or sending yourself e-mail. Again, Apple Computer makes some wonderful, easy-to-use machines. Whatever you buy, purchase the maximum speed, storage, and screen size that your budget will allow. Make sure it has an internal, high-speed modem, and a keyboard that is comfortable to use. Battery life is steadily improving, and many airlines have introduced on-board power sources at the seats. If you're careful, you can sometimes find excellent used machines that will fit your needs nicely for a fraction of the original price.
   Estimated cost: $2,000 to $4,000.

Scanners, Color Printers, Digital Cameras

If you will be doing a lot of graphics work, materials production, course design, and similar types of production, scanners are a major asset in integrating external sources, color printers provide a more professional touch, and digital cameras can immediately insert contemporary photos.
   Estimated cost: Varies with models and abilities, and is continually declining, but probably from $500 to $1,000 each.

Cell Phone/Pager

These ubiquitous devices have become less and less expensive and more and more reliable, proving that they are

Talking to Consultants

Q. What was an early example of new learning for marketing?

A. I had no idea how deeply interrelated speaking and consulting are. Providing you speak to the right level of audience, you have before you a captive group of high-value prospects. Through careful honing of the communication and leaving the audience knowing that you have much, much more to offer them, you will have them lining up with their business cards after the presentation. I wish I had realized much earlier that speaking was a perfect road to consulting work.

Q. What was your biggest surprise?

A. The biggest surprise for me was that I got the fee I asked for when I had priced the job to the point where I thought the client would turn me down. I wish that I had known that value to the client and your perception of your value can be miles apart. The skill is to bring the two together.

—Michael Hick, president, Global Business Initiatives

legitimate business tools. Contrary to popular opinion, you don't need a cell phone to be a consultant, but it does help. If you acquire one, make sure it handles *both* digital (the rising) and analog (the declining) service. This is a must: Use a service provider that has nationwide affiliations and coverage; otherwise your roaming feature will be limited and the phone will be useless in certain locations. Insist on national coverage. Many services offer "one fee" roaming rates, meaning that unlimited roaming throughout the country can be done at a set fee each month (mine is only $150). That's a huge money saver. Often, the phone will be free or leased for $5 a month if you take the provider's service plan. Some phones also serve as beepers or pagers, or you may choose a separate device. These services vary widely from simply informing you that you're wanted to providing callback numbers and messages.[5] We also now have phones that take pictures, but I fail to see the business need.

Caveat: No executives wear beepers. If you want to look like your buyers, don't walk around with an obvious beeper. If you have a cell phone to call and retrieve messages from your answering service, that's probably sufficient if you discipline yourself to do so a few times a day. None of us is so urgently needed that we have to be located instantly. But do not wear the thing in a holster on your belt unless you have delusions of starring in *Gunsmoke*.

Estimated cost for cellular service: $50 to $250 per month, depending on your usage.

Dictation Device

These small recorders come in handy when you're driving and realize that you forgot something, want to dictate some notes for later, and need to update your "to do" list. A small one fits neatly in a pocket or in the car console. I use it to take notes during a phone call in the car (since I don't want to write) while I listen to the hands-free speaker. You can also record a short opening you've practiced in anticipation of an important meeting or presentation, and play it back as you prepare to enter the room as a reminder. Some of these can be hooked up to your desk phone to capture the details of a phone conversation you may not have been able to write down.

Estimated cost: $50 to $150.

Some Final Considerations

I'm not going to go into detail about the obvious, but you should have in your office a television with video playback so that you can keep abreast of news and watch videos that pertain to your business. A radio is important for everything from local traffic conditions to background music. An audiocassette player will take care of your practicing and replaying speeches or presentations as well as listening to some educational material.

My father-in-law was terrific at fixing nearly anything, no matter what the problem. He told me that the secret was in having the right tools for the job. Don't try to get by with poor equipment or without essentials. You'll wind up spending more time on your busywork than you do marketing, and you'll tarnish your image as well. Get things right from the outset.

> **Career Key**   Confederate General Nathan Bedford Forrest was credited with explaining his success by saying, "I get there firstest with the mostest," although he was an educated man who actually said something like, "I arrive more quickly with the greater force of arms." In either case, he was right.

COMMUNICATING AT THE SPEED OF LIGHT

Your office is your base of operations, no matter how modest or how grand. The only important perspective is that of the caller—prospect or client, *lead* or supplier. The most important process as you enter consulting is *responsiveness*.

lead
a prospective client's name and contact information, from any source.

Before we even talk about marketing or the sales process, you have to embrace this philosophy: You must respond to inquiries, messages, and other contacts rapidly. A rapid response denotes a professional firm, even if the firm is actually in a spare bedroom. A slow (or missing) response denotes an unprofessional firm, even if that firm occupies 10,000 square feet on the 40th floor of a modern office building.

Decide at the outset how you will handle your communications. After all, the object of your marketing will be to generate interest and leads—contacts, people coming to you, interested parties seeking you out. Here are some guidelines to consider to make the best of your investment and to appear highly professional.

Phone Response

If you use voice mail, keep your message short and simple. Don't attempt to use voice mail as an opportunity to advertise, which many misguided consultants do because they are consultant-centered. We ought to be buyer-centered, meaning that we have to use the buyer's perspective when providing service, and the buyer doesn't want to listen to an ad and may be calling from an airplane or car where time is precious.

Here is a poor, but all too common, voice mail greeting:

"Hi, this is Andy Jones of Vista Consulting. I'm not in the office because I'm in Peoria this week providing training for Acme Plumbing. I'm then going to Dubuque to make a speech for the American Society of Software Engineers. I'll be back in the office on the 21st. Be sure to visit our web site, www.vistaconsulting.com. Remember, no one has a day like today tomorrow if they continually improve. Press 1 for a general message, and 2 for a personal message for Andy. Have a great day!"

Here is a professional greeting:

"You've reached Vista Consulting. Please leave a message of any length with your phone number and we'll return your call within two hours. Thank you."

Keep voice mail concise and oriented toward the caller. Even the statement "We're either out of the office or on another line" is silly, since the caller can tell that from the voice mail itself that you're not personally answering!

If you choose to use an answering service, which is a poor alternative due to both cost and the unreliability of the operators to represent you well (how many times has an answering service slapped you onto hold without allowing you to say a thing?), take the time to educate the operators about your services and business. Provide some basic literature and tell them how you want the phone answered and how messages should be taken. Even more important, check up on your own service a few times a month by calling in as someone seeking to speak to you. From the way you're treated you can tell how others are being treated.

General Response Time

My commitment is a response to all phone calls within 90 minutes during business hours. I meet that standard 99 percent of the time, and it distinguishes me from most other firms. You needn't choose that same standard, but you should make a commitment to at least return all calls the same day, unless received after three o'clock. (Fleet Bank, the eighth largest in the nation and one of my clients, has a standard of 24 hours for customer calls to officers, for example.) If you commit to that in your voice mail message, then you create an expectation for the caller and a commitment for yourself. In an age of cell phones in briefcases and phones in cars and on airplanes, there is no excuse for not returning calls promptly. Even if you're in a class or a prolonged meeting, there are breaks.[6]

Letters and faxes requiring a response should be addressed on the same day when you're in the office, and within a day of your return if you're traveling. E-mail should be responded to as read—or at least acknowledged, if further investigation is required on your part—and you should access it three or four times a day.[7] If you don't travel with a laptop, then utilize the ubiquitous computer kiosks in malls, airports, and hotel business centers.

Packaged Responses

We talk more about this in later chapters, but it helps to have preassembled packages ready to use when responding to inquiries about your work. These *press kits* are nothing more than presentation folders with information about you, your firm, client results, *testimonials*, articles, and so forth. By writing a one-page, tailored cover letter, you can personalize each kit for that inquiry, and you can respond quickly with a professional package to any business lead.

I can't begin to count the amount of business I've secured by getting back to the prospect before anyone else, thereby not only gaining an inside track but also demonstrating how responsive I'd be during our project. This is a

press kit
a formalized, professional set of documents assembled in a folder that is used for promotion and credibility. Press kits typically include references, testimonials, a biographical sketch, client lists, articles, interviews, and related materials; also called media kit, publicity kit.

testimonial
a written endorsement on a client's stationery validating your value and contributions to the writer's organization.

no-cost asset you can utilize that is particularly powerful when you begin your career. Get into the response groove early and continually increase the speed of your reactions.

It's the return contact that's important. If you have just a few moments, return the call anyway to acknowledge that it was received, and ask when a mutually convenient time might be to have a lengthier discussion. People greatly appreciate the mere thoughtfulness in getting back to them quickly.

GETTING SOME HELP FROM SOME FRIENDS

There are times when a one-person show needs help. Extended business trips can lead to a huge pileup of mail, overseas travel and time zone changes make return calls impractical, and sometimes skills are simply limited (e.g., you're a poor typist and there is a lot of correspondence demanding reply[8]).

It's always a good idea to have some help. Sometimes a spouse or teenager can be of help, but not all of us have families, and sometimes those families have their own jobs and time commitments. Here are some alternatives if you need help at first to coordinate your work demands with your travels or priorities.

1. *Employ a neighbor.* This sounds bizarre, but I'm speaking factually and from experience in contemporary America. There happen to be a great many people who are permanently or temporarily unemployed outside of the home. They are home for their school-age children for all or a major portion of their schooling. They constitute an educated and reliable untapped workforce, many of whom relish the opportunity to apply their talents while the children are attending school.

I've employed such people to respond to my phone messages when I'm traveling, get the mail, respond to certain types of mail, check for faxes, forward me important material, and, generally, keep things up-to-date. I pay an hourly wage that is mutually agreed upon, and it's a win-

win proposition. When you're able to use the same people over and over, you no longer have to train your assistant, and a nice partnership forms.[9] I once used a neighbor's basement to store my excess books and materials and paid a rental fee each year. (Later, when I had more funds available, I found formal, climate-controlled storage facilities.)

2. *Employ a student.* The local college or community college will have a list of students seeking work. You can usually find a responsible student—preferably a business major—whose schedule coordinates with your needs. Sometimes this can be an intern relationship with college credit, meaning that no pay is required.

3. *Use a temporary help agency.* This is more expensive, but you'll have a choice of competent people to choose from, supported by the agency. You can hire people for an hour, a day, a week, or any time allotment that makes sense for your needs.

4. *Establish a reciprocal arrangement with another professional.* Find someone in your networking who is in approximately the same position (though preferably not a direct competitor) and make a deal that you will cover for each other as needed. This doesn't help with skill deficits (e.g., you need typing help), but it does help when you're out of town or otherwise occupied. This is my least favored approach, since the other person also has a business to run, but I have seen it work when the relationship is solid.

If you're in shared space, some of these ideas will not matter, since there will be some central support present. Nonetheless, no one will be opening your mail or returning phone messages unless you arrange for it. It's a good idea to have those press kits prepared so that your assistant can simply send them out with a cover letter in response to certain inquiries. Also, don't expect your assistant to qualitatively and substantively respond to a call. The assistant should simply state that you're unavailable, but the call has been received, and you'll get back to the caller as quickly as possible.

In your networking, association meetings, and socializing, stay alert for people whom you might want to call upon for assistance. It's always better to have sounded out a few and have a tentative plan in place than to madly scramble for help just before you board an airplane.

You don't need full-time help, and you should not make that expenditure. But situational help can make sense if you use it wisely.

Final thought: The only perception that matters is the prospect's. What image is the prospect seeing when calling or writing to you?

NOTES

1. Exception: If you live alone, you don't need the same degree of privacy protection, but you still need a dedicated area.

2. Not a small issue. Many people find it difficult to leave an organizational setting and its complex social structure for the isolation of working by themselves.

3. With any kind of employee you will also incur payroll costs, benefits, additional insurance, added paperwork, and so on.

4. I'm not listing specific system requirements because they change and improve before I can finish a sentence. The computer this is being written on has 1,024 megabytes and 1 GHz.

5. Virtually all public phones today accept credit cards, so you should always be able to make calls without cash while traveling.

6. This is one of the strongest arguments for buying a cell phone. Public phones, even when available, are usually mobbed during meeting breaks.

7. This is the reason for a laptop computer on the road, especially if your practice relies heavily on e-mail. Otherwise, a week's trip can result in 100–500 e-mails awaiting your return.

8. One of the most productive things I've ever done is to teach myself to touch-type. I can type 60 words a minute, which greatly facilitates my communications. Self-teaching packages in books, on tape, and/or on the computer can increase your speed in just a few hours of practice.

9. Check with your own financial adviser on issues related to taxes and reporting, but generally this is a simple part-time and situational relationship.

Sorting Out the Legal, Financial, and Administrative

First, Let's Kill All the Lawyers

T he information in this chapter is designed to provide you with options as you organize legally and financially. It is not intended to be legal or investment advice, and you should see your personal attorney and financial adviser to determine what is best for you. (But make absolutely certain that they are professionals who understand solo practitioners and small, professional services firms. Not every lawyer and accountant is good at this, though they all claim to be. More on this later.)

Now, having made that disclaimer, let's look at some smart moves. That quote above about killing the lawyers is almost always misconstrued. Shakespeare put the words into the mouth of his character Dick Butcher in *Henry VI*, meaning it satirically: If we blame the lawyers and kill them all, we'll be in even worse shape than we are now.

Here is an unqualified rule: Find the absolute best help you can for your legal and financial matters. Do not use your cousin Louie, or the attorney who closed on your mortgage, or the accountant who does your taxes. You need professionals who are wise in the ways of small business and entrepreneurship and, believe me, those traits do not reside in every lawyer and accountant. *Ideally, you want someone who was once where you are,* beginning a firm, forging a new business, balancing work and private lives, and prone to take prudent risk. That person will empathize with you and appreciate your position.

How to do you find them? Ask other entrepreneurs whom they use for legal and financial advice. (This isn't like the hairdressing or catering business where people want to keep their favorites a secret. Referral business is considered a professional courtesy.) Interview the referrals through a brief visit to their offices at their convenience. Look around. Get to know them. Experience the chemistry.

This is a person whom you're going to have to trust implicitly. Don't be bashful about exploring your position and learning what kind of help you can get. One great advantage: Attorneys and accountants still bill by the hour (though more and more are joining my Mentor Program, finally understanding that hourly billing cannot create wealth), so you'll have a controlled investment, without worrying about *retainers*, although you will have to worry about a meter running during tax season, incorporation, and so on.[1]

These are the criteria to use in selecting an attorney and an accountant:

 retainer
a set fee paid for access to the consultant's expertise and support without regard for specific projects or objectives. Retainers should be paid in one sum or in installments at the beginning of each designated period.

✔ *Professional staff.* You do not want a one-person operation, even though you are one, yourself. You will need backup when they are not there, and you will want a support staff and resources. This is no time for a one-person band, no matter how inexpensive.

✔ *Entrepreneurial experience.* The managing partner should have the experience of building a professional services firm, and the firm should have other entrepreneurs as clients. Ask for references.

✔ *Accessibility of managing partner.* You don't want to be foisted off on the most junior person. Ask to meet the managing partner and establish a relationship with him or her.

✔ *Contacts.* It is quite common for your attorney or financial adviser to refer business to you, to recommend banking relationships, to introduce you to key *pro bono work*, and so forth. Find out if the firm has that kind of history and culture.

✔ *Atmosphere.* Is the office professional and pleasant? Although not a must, is there the potential for a borrowed office on occasion? There may be times when you have to refer people to your lawyer or accountant. Is the office run professionally?

✔ *Support resources.* Does the office reach out with newsletters, advisories, and proactive services about issues affecting your practice? Or will they simply respond when you send in your taxes or a legal question? Ask about such services, or check with references.

✔ *Risk-taking match.* You and your professional advisers should have a common value set about the amount of risk you want to take in financing, taxes, investment, and so on. This is essential to your ultimate comfort level. It's equally bad to have an adviser who is too conservative for your taste as it is to have one who is too aggressive. The younger you are, the more prudent risk you should be willing to assume.

Make your decisions carefully about these two professionals, and your business will be helped immeasurably. Make hasty decisions here, and you will find yourself paying for support that isn't effective.

pro bono work
work undertaken deliberately for no compensation, for the purposes of marketing, charitable contribution, longer-term visibility, networking, and other such purposes.

Career Key Your legal and financial advisers should ask you a lot of questions about your objectives, risk toleration, and professional plans. If they do all the talking and fit you into a pigeonhole, go elsewhere. You have to soar with the eagles, not sit in a coop.

LEGAL REQUIREMENTS AND ORGANIZATIONAL OPTIONS

Always incorporate. There are various ways to incorporate, but choose one of them. You do not want to be Charles Jones d/b/a (doing business as) Jones Consulting. The reasons are unequivocal:

1. A legal entity affords legal protection. Although your company can be sued (and this is an increasingly litigious society), you can purchase errors and omissions (malpractice) insurance to protect it, and your company will not have much in the way of assets, anyway. This protects you from someone coming after your house, car, and personal property.

2. A legal entity can raise money on its own. Your firm can secure its own credit line, borrow money, own property, and so forth.

3. It is always a good idea to separate personal from business affairs in the event of unanticipated trauma. Divorces, deaths, family lawsuits, private lawsuits, and other unpleasantness can be isolated from the business if it is a corporate entity.

4. You should look like your clients. You will have to file certain forms with clients to obtain payment, and a federal corporate identification number looks a lot better than a personal Social Security number. You want to give the impression of a complete professional operation, and that means incorporation.

Incorporation can take several forms, all of which have their own advantages. The most common ones follow. Consult with your financial and legal advisers to determine which is best in your circumstances. The costs for these configurations vary, but the range should be from $300 to $1,000, which will include all government forms, corporate seal, all registrations, and related matters. You will be required to file annual reports with a fee in most cases, which your law firm should handle for you automatically. Annual filings generally cost from $25 to $300.

C corporation
traditional corporate configuration, which I believe offers more advantages than an S corporation, though either is appropriate for a consulting practice.

✔ *C corporation.* The C corporation is the common form of incorporation in the United States, and mirrors what the overwhelming number of your clients use. The corporation here is a completely discrete and separate entity, with separate bank accounts, tax returns, and so forth. There will be shares issued in the company, presumably in your name and in the names of any others you designate.

Important: Only C corporations can make certain deductions. For example, the benefits cited elsewhere in this chapter about deducting uninsured portions of medical expenses, insurance premiums for almost all medical care, and so on, are legitimate expenses only in a C corporation with a written, nondiscriminatory plan in which all full-time employees are treated equally (not just the stockholders). So, when just you and family members are the employees, this is ideal. In the other configurations, such expenses must be reported on Schedule A of a personal return. These rules can change, however, so check with a financial specialist. (*Note:* For details—many attorneys still don't understand the benefits of a C corporation for solo practitioners—see *Inc. Yourself: How to Profit by Setting Up Your Own Corporation, Tenth Edition* (Career Press, 2003), by Judith H. McQuown. This is the longest continually published business book in American trade publishing, 26 years and counting, according to *Bottom Line Personal*.)

As long as you take all profits out of the C corporation at the end of the year as salary or bonus, you will avoid double taxation (corporate tax and personal tax on the same earnings). There's nothing wrong, unethical, or illegal about your company's simply breaking even each year.

✔ *Subchapter S corporation.* In the *S corporation* configuration, the corporate money flows through the

S corporation
form of incorporation designed for small businesses, wherein the profits flow through the owners' personal tax returns.

individual's tax return. Some people feel that this is an advantage for small personal services firms, but I've never seen much of an advantage, especially under current tax and retirement laws. There is less administrative work, though.

Generally speaking, C corporations are much better for solo practitioners showing a profit, and/or who are grossing six figures and better. If you start as an S corporation, you can always change to a C when the profits start rolling in.

limited liability company (LLC) a form of incorporation increasingly popular, and very appropriate for consulting practices.

✔ *Limited liability company.* Unlike the aforementioned two forms, which have traditional stockholders, the *limited liability company (LLC)* has "members," although the principle is the same. This is often a desired configuration for two or more partners, and you'll find many medical, legal, and accounting firms use it. Instead of "Inc." after the corporate name, as in the first two examples, this form uses "LLC."

An LLC is usually best for managing assets, such as property, and can own the building, for example, from which your C corporation operates.

Legal configurations can always be changed. Using your advisers, select the one that best meets your needs for the present and the next couple of years. The key is to get this done quickly. When you incorporate, you will have to do a search to make sure the name of your company does not infringe on someone else's trademark. Your attorney will do this in conjunction with the incorporation. Be prepared, because you may find that your first choice of names is not available.

Using your own name is always an option. It certainly worked for McKinsey and others. Since ultimately your brand should be your name itself, there's nothing wrong with using it from the outset: Donald Walters Corporation, Jamie Johnson Consulting, Inc., or Francis Carrolle and Associates.

ACCOUNTING, FINANCIAL, AND TAX MATTERS—EXPLOITING OPPORTUNITIES

Establish your company so as to exploit the advantages that corporate entities and business dealings permit. Legal and financial regulations are not merely constraints, but really are road maps to help determine where you can, and can't, go. You can go more places than you think.

The key consideration here is this: The more you can pay for with corporate, pretax dollars, the wealthier you will be. Depending on your tax bracket and the success of your business, an after-tax dollar (that is, a dollar taken out of the company and paid to you as payroll, subject to federal tax, state tax, city tax, disability tax, Medicare, and other sundry assessments) will be worth only about 60 to 75 cents. The more you can legitimately pay from pretax, company earnings, the more powerful your money (which is worth 100 cents).

In almost all cases, a personal services C corporation or LLC firm should break even at the end of the fiscal year. Any remaining profits in the company should be paid out as salary or bonus; otherwise the money would be double-taxed: Corporate income taxes would apply to these retained earnings, and then individual taxes would apply eventually when the money is ultimately paid as salary. With very rare exceptions, the corporation should show no profit at the end of its year. A large bonus check to you is a pleasant problem to have to deal with.

For example, here are some advantages that you can establish early by building these into your corporate by-laws and procedures:

✔ Medical bills such as noninsurance-reimbursed health costs (e.g., eyeglasses, dental bills, aspirin, other nonprescription medicines, etc.) can be paid from company funds for the employee and dependents.

✔ Directors' fees can be paid to the members of the board (you and your spouse or significant other, for example) without a tax deduction. Although taxes have to be paid on the director's fee on your personal return, you have use of the entire sum until the next tax return is due.

✔ Directors' meetings can be held and paid for by the firm. While you can't be outrageous—Naples, Italy, is not a possibility—you can certainly be bold—nothing wrong with Naples, Florida. All attendant costs pertaining to business are legitimate company expenses.

✔ You can pay your spouse, children, or significant other a salary for performing office work or any other support activities. Taxes should be withheld according to the applicable formulas, but this is a fine way to use company funds to pay your kids, for example, for typing, running errands, handling mailings, and so on.

✔ Establish a credit line and overdraft protection for the company. The quick way to do this is by using your personal assets as collateral (the business at start-up will have no collateral). However, there are credit card companies that will provide a credit line, which is unsecured, and, when you show some decent income, your bank will also begin to consider a separate credit line for the business.

Hint: When you receive any kind of business credit line, take a loan and pay it back with the same funds later that month. The interest cost will be minimal and you'll be establishing a nice credit rating for your business.

✔ Establish a withholding amount that will pay your taxes but leave you with maximum disposable income. You can determine how much you pay in payroll taxes (see later in the chapter for advice on payroll services). The best formula is one that manages to pay almost all of your federal and state taxes (so that you're not hit with a major payment in April) while maximizing your after-tax salary. Your financial adviser should be able to give you advice on exact amounts, which might change during the year.

Career Key   Keep your attorney, financial adviser, banker, and others on your mailing lists and treat them like prospects. This will apprise them of your activities, and might just prompt them to refer business to you.

✔ An office at home and a myriad of other expenses are payable through company funds. Some things are clearly qualified (computer), some things are clearly not qualified (college tuition for the kids), and some things are qualified but ill-advised (premiums for disability insurance, because if you ever need it, the proceeds will be subject to tax if the premiums were paid by the company and not by you personally).

✔ Memberships and subscriptions are generally deductible if recognized by your incorporation: health clubs, airline clubs, business clubs, professional journals, newspaper subscriptions, business book purchases, and so on.

Do not listen to friends, others in consulting, or family in these matters. Rely on legal and financial professionals who know their business, know your business, and know the law. That's why a common degree of comfort in risk taking is so important, since the law is often more shades of gray than an October sky in Vermont.

FINDING A BANKER AND OBTAINING CREDIT

Your financial adviser should be able to set you up with a banking relationship if you don't already have one. By a "banking relationship" I don't mean a bank where you have a checking account and know where the lines to the tellers are. I mean having a bank officer who is familiar with your business, provides personalized assistance, and can expedite matters for you. I mean someone who takes your calls.

If you're dealing with the bank's headquarters, you should seek out a relationship manager, a small business banker, a vice president of commercial business, or a similar title. If you're dealing with a branch, go to the branch manager. Explain that you're starting your own firm, expect substantial growth, and would like to become an increasingly active partner with the bank for all of your financial needs. Don't show up as a supplicant with your hat in your hand. Meet with the officer as a peer who is exploring a banking relationship. Don't be bashful about explaining that you're looking at several different banks if necessary.

Ideally, a banking relationship should provide the following:

- ✔ A specific professional to handle your questions, not a toll-free number or a generic customer service operation.
- ✔ Expedited banking: special ATM cards, special lines, bank by phone, bank by Internet, bank by mail, and so on.
- ✔ Small business services: loans, payroll help, rapid crediting of out-of-state checks, small business advisories, special investment options, and so on.
- ✔ Overdraft protection on your business checks, and a flagged account, so that checks will never be returned unpaid until you are called and apprised of the overdraft. (Your credit history is one of your most important assets. Never allow a bank to return a check for insufficient funds.)
- ✔ Preferable rates on loans and investments, and low-fee checking options.
- ✔ Proactive notice to you of opportunities, e.g., new Small Business Administration offerings. (I found a far less expensive loan provision when my banker discovered that the SBA would guarantee the bank's loans to my business.)

Cultivate your banker. Share your printed materials, your client expectations, your marketing strategy, and your methodology. Buy your banker coffee or take him or her to lunch. Your banker may be able to send business your way, making a win/win/win proposition for two customers and the bank.

You will be offered credit cards for your company from a variety of sources. Your name will be found in the incorporation listings, or the Internet, or from local publicity. Although the rates may be very high, you should accept a couple of these cards in order to have a credit card

Talking to Consultants

Q. What one key approach or activity would you do differently today from when you started?

A. I undernetworked and overprinted. When I started I had all kinds of brochures designed and printed, and dutifully mailed them out to all kinds of people—and then sat back waiting for the phone to ring, which it rarely did. What I failed to do was capitalize on the vast network I had (as a result of working for Johnson & Johnson for 10 years) and had ignored. As a result, I think it took me much longer to get started.

Q. What was your biggest surprise—what do you wish you had known that you didn't know?

A. I'd actually name two: first, how easy it is to get my name in print once I learned how to approach a writer or editor with a good story idea.

Second, how valuable the maxim "give a little—get a lot" really is. The more I give away (within reason) the more business I get back in return. This was true in the 1980s and is even more true on the Internet.

—Gil Gordon, president, Gil Gordon Associates

for the company and to establish credit not related to you personally. The best cards are those with no annual fee and no interest if paid in full each month, but those are virtually nonexistent in the business market. American Express, MasterCard, and Visa all offer business cards, which are easy to obtain *if* you also have a personal card with their companies. These cards also provide a quarterly report of your business expenditures, although that is of dubious value.

However, try not to mix your personal and business charges on the same credit card account. Maintain separate accounts so that there is no problem at tax time and never a problem if you are audited.[2]

> **Career Key**   When considering a banker, ask yourself if you're being treated as a successful businessperson or as a neophyte. A professional banker should see you as an excellent customer, with all due consideration, not as a risk, with all due trepidation.

The bank where you have your home mortgage, car loan, or other major business may be very amenable to providing you with business services and gaining the rest of your business. However, that bank may be more retail than commercially oriented, and you may want to explore a second banking relationship with an institution more attuned to small business needs. A first-class financial adviser should be able to expedite your meeting with the right people in the right bank. As my adviser informed me when we started working together 16 years ago, "Alan, if your financial guy can't get you a loan, who can?"

OTHER PROFESSIONAL HELP

Design

You will need a designer to help with the following elements at some point in your early business development:

- ✔ Letterhead, business cards, labels.
- ✔ Logo.
- ✔ Brochure and/or other publicity material you create.
- ✔ Presentation folder or media kit.
- ✔ Course materials if you use them.
- ✔ Product catalogs if you mail them.
- ✔ Direct mail pieces if you use them.

Of these, absolutely essential at the outset are the logo, business card, and related stationery. Your image to the world will reflect on your professionalism and what you think about yourself. In the first week I had been thrust into my own business, with no logistical preparation, I received a significant lead from a major bank in New York City. My choice was to wait to respond until I had business stationery in about two weeks, or respond immediately on plain white paper. I chose the latter, and was never able to make any progress. I'm convinced that in this case speed was not an asset but image would have been. Don't kid yourself; people do judge the book by the cover.

Don't use computer-generated stationery, nor material you buy off the shelf. As a stopgap, there are catalogs that offer an attractive and inexpensive array of stationery with various logo options and your particulars printed into their templates. The disadvantage is that many people use them, they've become fairly evident, and a buyer might actually find that your stationery is of the same design as another consultant's.

The ideal approach is to invest in a designer who will create a look that will pervade all of your print materials as they appear. (There is no law that these have to be eternal. I've changed my logo and look as my business has matured, and so can you.)

Find brochures and letterhead you like, from any source, and inquire about the designer. Ask for references in your early networking activity. I called the president of a public relations firm whose materials I liked, and asked for recommendations for designers. She provided two, one of whom I hired.

A good designer should always provide options. I received about two dozen that my wife and I could combine to our hearts' content. Always remember this, however: The designer provides the aesthetic images, but you provide the copy. Never allow the designer to do the writing. If you need help in committing your intent and concepts to paper, then hire a copywriter, but don't use your designer as a writer.[3]

Here are two examples from my own firm. Figure 3.1 is called a type solution because the logo uses the firm's name with some artwork around the type. Figure 3.2 is a

Box 1009 • East Greenwich, Rhode Island 02818
Telephone: 401/884-2778 • FAX: 401/884-5068

FIGURE 3.1   "Type-solution" logo.

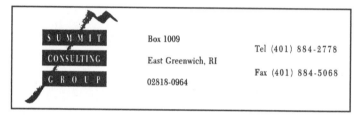

FIGURE 3.2   Graphic logo projecting quality image.

logo incorporating my firm's name that I changed to about five or six years into the business after feedback from clients indicated that the first version didn't adequately represent my quality.

Finally, try to deal with a local designer if you can find one who offers the quality you're seeking in the general area. It's important to meet face-to-face, to look at visual ideas together, and to be able to quickly exchange and critique material that would otherwise have to be sent by courier. Don't settle for just anyone, and don't use the least expensive person available. You're designing your future.

Insurance

You'll need the following types of insurance in your business:

Disability. You are much more likely to be disabled than to die while running your business. Since your independent income is key to your future and your family's future, you must protect it with disability insurance. Normally, disability payments are tax-free if you pay the premiums, but taxed if your company has paid them, so pay them out of after-tax income. Disability insurance will usually pay a maximum of 80 percent of normal income, but since it's tax-free, that's a good deal. Multiple carriers engage in coordination of benefits, meaning that if you have more than one policy, their sum total will match the 80 percent, though there is a movement now that any one policy will pay up to 80 percent despite other coverage.

Disability insurance is cheapest when purchased through groups, and many trade associations offer it. Individual policies are more expensive, but generally have better benefits. (If you've left a prior employer with disability insurance, you are often offered the option of converting that policy to your individual use. That's almost always a wise move.)

Career Key Don't attempt to cut back or ignore insurance needs. By all means look for the best deals, but make sure that you're fully covered from the outset for peace of mind and prudence.

The two keys about disability insurance provisions are these:

1. Obtain a policy that will pay until you're able to fully perform your normal, prior job, not just until you're able to work at any job no matter what the pay.

2. You can adjust premium amounts by the length of the waiting period, which is the amount of time—typically one month to six months—that you're disabled before benefits begin. The longer the wait, the lower the premium, so this will depend on whether you have other resources to draw upon during the waiting period.

Talking to Consultants

Q. What was your biggest surprise?

A. I have to say that my biggest surprise was the amount of work involved (the number of 10 to 12-hour days was astonishing), the amount of fear I felt (which is very humbling), and the amount of growth I experienced from both of the above. Without these, I feel I would have been much less effective with my clients, generally small businesses, who face these realities almost every day. Looking back, I actually give thanks to the workload, the fear, and the growth I have had from facing these and a myriad of other challenges in the 15 years I have been in business.

Q. What is your greatest insight at this point?

A. I'm sure these thoughts are hardly profound, and maybe they are obvious, but I really was not prepared for facing my fears in the beginning. As someone said, what doesn't kill us makes us stronger. I am quite strong now. I still work hard and have fears, but I have learned to understand that these are the times when we start to really grow—as people, as parents, as students, and as teachers—which is what we as consultants really are.

—Idora Silver, CEO, I. Silver Management Group

Keep careful track of your income via tax returns, W-2 statements, pay stubs, and so on, because your income will vary from year to year in this business, and the disability amount should be based on accurate recent averages, not on the lowest-paying year the insurance company can find.

Individual policies can cost several thousand dollars a year, depending on benefits and age, and group policies generally cost a few hundred dollars a year. In many cases, leaving the group will mean forfeiting the insurance.

Errors and Omissions. This is the colloquial "malpractice" insurance, called "E&O" in the industry. You can obtain individual policies or coverage through group plans in some trade associations. This protects you from a suit alleging that your advice, training, interventions, coaching, or other actions caused the client harm. This insurance will normally pay for legal fees as well as any actual judgments against you, up to the limit of the policy. It is relatively inexpensive when you're starting out, since premiums are usually based on revenue volume.

Some organizations—Hewlett-Packard being a large and prime example—currently will not do business with a consultant or consulting firm without evidence of an in-force malpractice policy, so this insurance is often a pragmatic business necessity; but it should be a must in any case. Expect to pay a few hundred dollars annually in your first years in business.

Liability. Liability insurance protects you in the event someone trips over the wire leading to the projector you're using during your presentation. It doesn't matter that the projector isn't yours or the participant was drunk or clumsy. The hotel, client, projector manufacturer, and you will all be sued.

This coverage is inexpensive and also available individually or in groups. You can expect to pay a few hundred dollars annually.

Property. This insurance comes under several names, including the misleading "marine policy." Essentially, it covers your equipment and property in your office and while traveling. Be very careful, because business equipment you own and leased equipment in your home office are often not covered by your homeowners or renters insurance. Consequently, you need either a separate endorsement with an extra premium from your homeowners or renters insurance company, or separate business coverage.

Since we're talking about computers, copiers, fax machines, and the like, the cost of damage or theft is significant. And some leasing companies will want themselves named as first payee on a discrete policy. Under whatever name, make sure all of your expensive equipment is covered, especially since the premium cost is minimal.

Major Medical and Health. Your company should provide for health coverage. (See the discussion earlier in the chapter on C corporations as the best way to do this economically.) You can often access very favorable rates through collaboratives that put small businesses together in order to secure group rates. Sometimes you can continue coverage from a former employer, although that is usually limited in duration. If a spouse works and plans to continue working, and coverage is provided through that employment, then this coverage is probably not needed (and can't be duplicated legally, anyway).

You can secure hospitalization, major medical, dental, eye care, and other coverages, depending on what you need and the size and ages of your family. My bias is that you should incorporate in such a way that all health insurance premiums are paid by the company for your entire family, all noninsured costs are paid directly from company funds, and you pay no health costs whatsoever from after-tax income. This is simply smart money management in an era of rising health care costs.

Life. I'm not going to dwell on this, since it's important regardless of your employment status. Under current laws, the company can pay for only the first $50,000 in coverage as a business expense, and even that will be reflected as compensation, so life insurance is essentially a private matter. My bias: Never use insurance as an investment vehicle, so use term insurance solely.

Umbrella Disability. This is also an individual coverage that can't be paid for through company funds. However, this is very inexpensive insurance (costing only hundreds of dollars for millions in coverage) which kicks in when your auto insurance, liability insurance, or other insurance runs out in the event of a lawsuit or judgment. Consequently, it can protect your company and your family, and should be a part of every professional's insurance portfolio.

Payroll Services

At first, it will seem easy to merely pay yourself a salary out of company funds and make the appropriate tax deductions. However, determining the appropriate tax deductions is never easy, the government has made electronic filings mandatory, and error here can result in serious repercussions. My financial adviser ordered me to get a payroll service and a bookkeeper when I turned in an overflowing shoe box of receipts and salary records.

The two largest services I know of are Paychex and ADT. Both services will issue payroll checks electronically deducted from your business account and deposited into your personal account. The checks can be scheduled, identical amounts, or they can be situational in any amount you desire. If other family members are on the payroll, they will be included per your instructions. They will deduct taxes at all levels, Medicare, Social Security, and other liens automatically. They will provide electronic reporting to all necessary agencies and provide you with a hard copy for your records. They also offer ancillary services, such as 401(k) investing.

The best payroll service at our levels of transactions will generally cost from $75 to $200 per month. You can't afford not to do this.

Bookkeeper

You may not need a bookkeeper at the outset, but you will once you move into six figures. Find a local person who will charge you by the hour only when services are actually needed, usually monthly. The bookkeeper will run a general ledger, furnish a balance sheet plus expense and income statements, and balance your checkbooks, reconciling differences. The bookkeeper will also provide the input for your financial adviser's tax requirements at the end of the year.

Get references from other small businesses. Absolute

must: The bookkeeper must use a computer for all transactions, with no manual posting.

A good bookkeeper and payroll service will actually save you thousands of dollars of your time, and hundreds of hours of stress. You should be able to get a first-rate bookkeeper for $15 to $30 per hour, or about $125 to $225 per month's returns.

Career Key   The more your legal, financial, and administrative/logistical needs are built into your routine and handled by competent professionals, the more you can focus solely on growing your business. If you are not output oriented and are consumed by tasks, you will not succeed as an entrepreneur. Wise professional services investments actually save you money. Aren't you telling your prospects the exact same thing?

Web Designer

You may not have a web site from the beginning, but you'll need one relatively quickly.[4] The Internet is too much of a global marketing asset for individual consultants to ignore for long.

The web site designer will probably be different from the literature designer discussed earlier. This person should be able to create a unique and attractive site, making the best use of technology while not overwhelming your message with too many bells and whistles.

The best web site designers are people whose work you can see on others' sites, who will work with you personally (even if only by phone and e-mail—they're not likely to be down the block), and who create user-friendly sites. As with any other designer, you provide the copy and what you want to communicate, and the designer should take care of the aesthetics and technology.

The hallmarks of an effective web site for consultants are:

- ✔ Ability to download quickly. Most people are still using relatively slow modems, and long downloads will drive people away.

- ✔ Graphics and photos that accentuate the site (but that don't unduly delay downloads).

- ✔ Easy navigability. The visitor can move from one page to another expeditiously, and readily return to the first page.

- ✔ Value offered. On a monthly basis there are free articles to download, techniques for clients to employ, and links to other relevant sites, products, and so on.

- ✔ Clear client results. The site doesn't talk endlessly about what you do, but rather about how the client benefits. Supporting these results statements should be testimonials, references, and client lists.

- ✔ An easy way to contact you. A visitor should be able to e-mail to you with ease while visiting.

- ✔ An ability to capture names of interested visitors by offering them the choice of sending for something for free, buying a product, or otherwise leaving their names with you for follow-up.

If you don't establish a web page from the outset, at least make it a habit to visit others and find out what makes sense for you. Merely being a small part of other sites (trade associations, consultant listings) is not sufficient. These days, a web site is more important than a corporate brochure.

Trade Associations

Finally, we briefly discuss trade association membership. These associations serve the following purposes for a start-up practice:

✔ Networking, not only for business, but for business services to support your practice.

✔ Learning how others have moved from start-up to success.

✔ Education in your field.

✔ Access to further resources and support (e.g., web site inclusion, directories, advertising).

✔ Visibility and marketing (assuming leadership positions, presenting at meetings, attending sponsored events, etc.).

✔ Opportunities to publish in newsletters and magazines.

✔ Group rates for insurance, rentals, and other business needs.

✔ Credibility in being a part of the voice of your profession.

The major trade association for consultants in the United States is the Institute of Management Consultants (IMC).[5] It has chapters around the country, and affiliations internationally with similar organizations. It provides the Certified Management Consultant (CMC) designation when certain criteria are met (successful consulting assignments, testimonials, examination on ethics, etc.) although, alas, the designation is not widely known or respected outside of the organization itself. The local chapter meetings can provide solid networking support, and the two annual conventions (east and west) attract 300 to 400 consultants at all levels. Annual dues are $300. The IMC is headquartered in Washington, D.C.

There are smaller, even less well known consulting organizations that also have chapter meetings, issue publications, and provide networking. Their quality is based almost entirely on the strength and leadership of the local chapters, and can vary widely. The National Bureau of Certified Consultants, for example, is headquartered in San Diego, and provides a certification known as CPCM (Certified Professional Consultant to Management).

The American Society for Training and Development (ASTD) is the longtime trade association for training professionals, although increasingly (almost half) the people at both chapter and annual conventions seem to be consultants. The ASTD provides a resource center and monthly magazine (*T&D Journal*) as well as other products and services, including a buyers guide, and a members directory.[6] If you focus on training and/or human resources issues, membership makes sense.

An allied group is the Society for Human Resource Management (SHRM). This is strongly oriented toward human resources executives and managers. It, too, hosts an annual convention and regional meetings, and it publishes *HRMagazine*. It has a very large and active special interest group for consultants across the country, with local chapters.

The OD Network has chapter and national meetings, and is focused on consultants, internal and external, specializing in organizational development and change management.

All of these groups offer a variety of insurance, travel, and related benefits group plans that may make sense for you to consider.

Take the time to establish your practice with the professional underpinning it needs for success, and you won't have to waste time while you're pursuing that success.

Final thought: There is no one right way, but there are uniquely correct destinations. Ensure that your legal and financial status is in good hands and providing the proper support.

NOTES

1. In Chapter 8 we talk about fees, but suffice it to say here that you should never pattern your billing practices after your lawyer or accountant. They have never learned how to bill for value. See my book *Million Dollar Consulting* (McGraw-Hill, 1992, 1998, 2002) for

a detailed discussion, or more specifically *Value Based Fees* (Jossey-Bass/Pfeiffer, 2002).

2. I've been audited twice in my life, once personally and once professionally, both through random luck of the draw. I've seen firsthand that meticulous, separate accounting with receipts and appropriate details not only speeds the audit (and reduces your accountant's fees) but also satisfies the IRS that nothing is hidden and that the audit is routine.

3. Caveat: There's reason to believe that if you can't write your own marketing copy about what you do, then you don't understand your value proposition or your potential buyer sufficiently.

4. If you're thinking about entering the business but are still employed elsewhere, it makes sense, on your own time, to prepare your literature, set up your web site, and find the key resources that will help you hit the ground running when you do go out on your own.

5. See Appendix D for contact points for all groups mentioned and others.

6. I obtained a $156,000 contract with the American Institute of Architects as a result of a $120 listing in the buyers guide. That ad has literally paid for itself for a lifetime.

Fundamental Marketing
Creating a Gravity for Your Business

C onsulting services are not a cold call sale. Buyers no more would purchase from someone calling them from out of the blue than you would send a check to the smarmy securities salesperson who calls you at home at 8:30 in the evening and says, "Alan, how are you? This is John Smith from XYZ Investments and I was given your name by a mutual friend. . . ."

Buyers must be attracted to you. That might sound counterintuitive, but it makes the difference between your beating the bushes trying to sell a commodity and dealing with a buyer on a peer-level, collaborative basis. The buying psychology is 180° different when you are sought out, rather than attempting to ingratiate yourself with a buyer.

The gravitational pull has many spokes to it, some of which can wait until you're more firmly established, more confident, and/or wealthier. (See Figure 4.1.) But you should begin the marketing gravity as soon as you decide to go into the profession. *Note that this can and should be begun even before you've formally established your firm.* The fundamental components of your gravity can be begun at any time, and the sooner the better.

FIGURE 4.1 Creating marketing gravity.

Marketing is not selling. Marketing is the act of creating and accentuating need among potential buyers of your services. The creation is important, because not all buyers realize that they need your help, and even what they want is not always what they actually need. The difference between what clients want and what they really need is your value-added as a consultant. (More about that later.) The accentuation is vital because even when the need is felt, it may not be of sufficient priority or urgency to merit the buyer's taking action.

In this chapter, we explore the fundamentals of the gravity:

- ✔ Press kit.
- ✔ Stationery and related image products.
- ✔ Networking.

✔ Pro bono work.

✔ Listings, ads, and other passive sources.

These initial aspects of gravitational pull do not require that you be a known entity. In fact, you can begin with them even though you're the only one who realizes you're a consultant at the moment!

CREATING A PRESS KIT

A press kit (or media kit, or client information kit, or presentation kit) is your primary marketing tool because it is flexible, immediately required, and the mark of a professional. It also obviates the immediate need for more expensive alternatives, such as brochures and four-color flyers, though you may choose to include those later.

A solid beginning press kit can be assembled using a presentation folder, which is simply a large folder with two deep pockets inside, and usually a die-cut opening to accommodate a business card. You can purchase these at large office supply houses such as Staples or with catalogs through the mail. They range from plain stock to expensive finishes, and they can be plain, printed with your firm's contact information, or embossed. Begin with the best one you can afford, but remember that you can always upgrade when finances permit. If you have them printed, don't order more than a few hundred to begin with, no matter what the cost savings of printing larger amounts.

The press kit is the single item that will be ubiquitous for your marketing purposes. It will go to prospects, serve as a leave-behind, be used for media inquiries and interviews, house proposals and confirmations, and be employed for a myriad of other purposes as you progress. There is nothing worse than a prospect's receiving from you a mass of loose papers or uncoordinated materials. (DO NOT listen to people who claim you need only have an electronic version. Senior level buyers aren't always technologically savvy, often like to sit back and page through literature, and also often need to pass around material to others at meetings.)

> **Career Key**   Once you know that you're going to launch a consulting practice, immediately begin on your marketing gravity, no matter how modest or early. Don't wait until you're officially independent, or you'll be confined to a standing start.

A good beginning press kit contains the following items.

Results a Client Can Expect

Don't make the mistake of listing everything you do or want to do and leaving it at that. Prospects don't care how good you think you are; *they care about how they might benefit if they hired you.* Consequently, insert a sheet with a heading such as Typical Client Results or Benefits of Our Approaches, or something similar.[1] Practice stating and writing these as client outcomes, not as your inputs. Examples:

Consultant Input	*Client Output or Result*
Conduct focus groups.	Understand employee concerns, and act.
Lead sales training program.	Accelerate sales and build business.
Facilitate strategy retreat.	Create a pragmatic strategy with buy-in.
Teach presentation skills.	Enable managers to listen and act.
Teach delegation skills.	Empower employees as business owners.
Implement Internet solutions.	Enhance business using cyberspace.
Provide for diversity sensitivity.	Create a global mind-set and business.

Orient your results toward organizational improvement, not toward tasks or programs.

Testimonials

Buyers want assurances. When you're just beginning, however, you don't have any clients, let alone testimonials. Here's what you do about that. Provide a free speech or do some pro bono work discussed later in the chapter. When people in the audience or on your committee or task force say, "Nice job!" simply say thanks and ask for their cards if you don't already know them. Then send them a letter explaining that references and testimonials are key to any professional services firm, and ask if they'd be willing to put their brief laudatory remarks in writing on their letterhead. You'll then have a testimonial letter on the letterhead of a vice president of the local bank or utility. You're not claiming them as clients, merely providing support that they believe you do good work. Try to obtain five or six of these for inclusion in the press kit. (When you actually get them from clients, be sure to include them!)

You can also obtain character testimonials about your honesty, work ethic, quality, intellect, and so on at any time.

Biographical Sketch

Your *biographical sketch* should be a brief description of who you are, not a resume. You're not looking for a job; you're looking for a client. No one cares if you love to travel or play golf. Keep this professional. It will also double as an introduction when you speak, and/or can be distributed to people in your meetings and presentations. Keep it simple, honest, and relevant. Don't be afraid to use some humor. Many consultants make the mistake of not updating their biographical sketch. You'll be surprised how much you can add every six months if you're active in the business.[2]

biographical sketch
a brief (one page or less) description of the consultant's accomplishments, credentials, and credible background. Note: This is not a resume.

Position Papers

These are also known as "white papers," and they are one of the most powerful marketing tools for beginners. A position paper is simply your firm's position on an issue in an area about which you consult. They are nonpromotional, and should be filled with pragmatic information and/or provocative opinions. For example, if you consult about employee recruiting and retention, your position papers might be on:[3]

✔ How to find the right person the first time.

✔ How to conduct behavioral interviews.

✔ The fallacy of personality profile tests.

✔ Why money is not a motivator.

✔ Why exit interviews must be mandatory.

Position papers should be from two to six pages. The longer ones may contain graphics and illustrations. They should have your copyright at the bottom of each page, including the cover sheet. You can use nice borders and fonts thanks to modern computer printing, and you can simply whip them off the computer or have your local print shop publish them. In either case, do not use copier paper. Use higher-quality bond, either matte or glossy, for a quality image. (Position papers will also serve as the basis for articles, pamphlets, web site postings, and, perhaps, even a book.)

Position papers enable you to quickly establish credibility and value for the reader/prospect. You should plan to create at least one a month until you have a couple of dozen. They will also force you to think through your positions and justify the nature of your work. If you use others' ideas or words, give full and complete attribution. Keep such excerpts minimal.

As long as your work is original, you can copyright it. Place this copyright line at the bottom of every page:

© (or) Copyright John Smith 2000. All rights reserved. (You do not need both © and "copyright." Either one suffices.)

References

Since you don't want to make the prospect work, provide *references* automatically, rather than force the prospect to

reference
a source, usually a client, serving as a contact for prospective clients to ascertain the quality of your work, veracity of your claims, and so on.

request them. When you're new to the profession, use character references: your attorney, accountant, former employer if you left under good circumstances, customers of your former employer, civic and charitable contacts, friends and acquaintances who hold professional or managerial positions. Always ask permission and alert the references that they are on your reference list. Do not assume a positive response or take chances. I've personally contacted references who gave poor feedback on individuals on no less than three occasions.

Hint: If and when you can, fill up one piece of stationery with references, including for each title, organization, address, phone, fax, and e-mail. The more references you provide, the less likely the prospect is to call any of them. The psychology is not surprising: The more references provided, the more the prospect assumes that none need be called. When you provide only two or three, the prospect may be uncomfortable and not only call all of them, but ask the references for further references (a very common technique these days). Provide as many as possible, up to a complete page (about 15 will do it, in three columns of five).

Career Key When you put things in writing, they will be passed around if they are any good. It's better to be brief with powerful points than lengthy and boring. Write from the outside, in: Think about what will create the most reaction on the part of the reader, not about recording everything that you know.

Your press kit will grow with articles, interviews, advertising reprints, and so forth, but for now this is a solid beginning.

STATIONERY AND RELATED IMAGE PRODUCTS

The initial image your prospects will actually see is usually your print materials. This is why a good designer is a wise investment at the outset. In any case, following are the must items when you open the doors.

Letterhead

Your stationery should have your company name and logo printed on it, as well as a minimum of phone number and address. You may wish to include fax, web site (if available), and e-mail address. Don't overdo it. The letterhead design and layout should allow you to write a standard business letter cleanly and should be unobtrusive. If you choose a colored paper, make sure it's professional looking and dignified. Earth tones usually work well; pastels never do.

Second Sheets

An inexpensive way to add a great deal of class is to purchase matching second sheets. A great deal of your correspondence—as well as nearly all your reports, proposals, and evaluations—will require multiple sheets. Use your letterhead for the opening page (except for reports) and the matching second sheets for all other pages. The second sheets can be completely plain, simply matching the color and texture of the letterhead. However, some consultants like to have their firm's name printed on the second sheet as well, aesthetically as a design element, and pragmatically in case the sheets are inadvertently separated by the reader. In this case, use small print and a small portion of the page, and never include contact information on second sheets.

Envelopes

Envelopes should be the same color and texture as the letterhead, with your company name, address, and logo in the upper left-hand corner. (They can be on the reverse, but your company will be recognized faster when they're on the front, which is also more professional.) Buy number 10 envelopes for this purpose, so that you're able to put quite a bit of material into them.

Labels

Create a matching address label to use with shipments requiring boxes and larger envelopes that won't go through
your printer for addressing. These should also have your
name, address, and logo, and should be self-adhesive. *Hint:*
I have labels that are the same size as number 10 envelopes
so that I can simply feed them through the envelope feeder
of my printer. This way I don't have to reconfigure anything to put sheets of labels through, and can either print
them one at a time or feed them automatically for large
mailings. These large labels also display my name and logo
to greater advantage.

Business Cards

Contrary to contemporary trends and advice from marketing coaches, business cards should be elegant in their
simplicity. These are not advertising posters; they are re-
minders for people who may want to call you. (And remember that automatic scanning devices that import
business card information into people's computers have
trouble identifying a myriad of data and graphics.)

 Your business card should have your name, title, organization, phone, and fax. You may also include your e-
mail address and web site. However, that's it. Information
such as cell phone, pager, home phone, alternative addresses, and a variety of association memberships and
honorifics simply cheapen the card. Printing information
about yourself or your offerings on the reverse side of the
card is a waste of money, and amateurish. Your photo
should not be on your card, although this is a beloved
technique of professional speakers and realtors. (When
was the last time you read an executive's business card
and it had promotional material about the business on the
back? Never?)

 The card should be of the same color and design as
your letterhead and envelopes. However, make sure you use
a quality, sturdy stock, so that corners won't tend to bend
and it can stand up to life in a pocket or briefcase. The only
thing worse than having no business card for a prospect is

whipping out one that looks like it had been serving as a beer coaster at a rowdy bar. Keep your card to the standard size, since many people store them in holders that assume a common size. You don't want to be cast out as a misfit.

Your initial purchase of letterhead, second sheets, envelopes, labels, and business cards will take care of the immediate future. If you can afford it, carry the same design and logo over to the presentation folder itself. When you're ready, you can add more sophisticated image literature, such as a *brochure* and *one-sheet*, which we discuss later. For now, keep your initial order volume relatively low—a thousand of each item should be more than sufficient. If you have so many prospects and inquiries that you're running out of materials, simply order more and thank your lucky stars for such a wonderful problem.

Ask your designer to provide you with a graphics file of your logo and other art work to keep on your computer. This is very useful for inclusion on your web site, on certain mailings, and for others who want to run graphics with your articles, reports, and so on.

Career Key   Keep your business card simple, but personalize it for the other party. It's a nice gesture to write your home phone on the reverse if appropriate, or to write down a book title that you're recommending or a business referral. The person will have that useful information and immediately know whom to thank.

NETWORKING

Now that you have a press kit and appropriate business image literature, you can begin the interactive aspects of marketing. The least expensive yet still potentially powerful marketing device for a new consultant is networking.

Networking is not merely talking to people and handing out business cards. In fact, most people who think they're networking really aren't, and they waste their time

brochure
a bound booklet that describes your firm's services, client results, and approaches; provides testimonials; and contains other relevant information for a prospective buyer. You are better off with no brochure than a cheap foldout version. Wait until you can afford a decent one of four to a dozen pages.

one-sheet
a single sheet in black and white (for faxing) and color that succinctly describes the consultant's accomplishments, clients, results, and credibility. The one-sheet is particularly important for speaking engagements.

Talking to Consultants

Q. What has been your greatest challenge setting up your practice?

A. I have found my greatest challenge to be that of honing my message about what I do and the results I can provide to the client. This has been especially daunting in my case, as my expertise is in *process*, rather than *content*. I can work with a client team on almost any problem they are attempting to tackle, and by getting them to work more creatively—both individually and as a team—help them accomplish their goal with fresh, new solutions and action plans. I can also teach the principles of innovative teamwork to project teams, as well as impart an internal capability by training facilitators. However, translating all of this into a clear message of tangible benefits has been a real test.

Q. How did you overcome that challenge?

A. The challenge goes beyond merely finding the right words. Those consultants whose expertise falls into a fairly circumscribed area of content (say, information technology or finance) not only know *what* to say about their services, but *where* and *to whom* to say it. While few would argue that innovation and creative problem-solving are extremely important in any organization, it is difficult to identify the person within the organization who may be interested enough to buy. This, in turn, has implications for where you might place an article, offer to do a speech, advertise, and so on. In addition, in today's business environment, many decision makers want the answers, not the ability to come up with answers themselves (although I feel that from a strategic standpoint, the latter is far more important). At this point I feel I am faced with some decisions. I can focus on one or two industries where I've had some success and craft a message specifically for them (thereby limiting possibilities in other kinds of business), or attempt to do a better job at communicating the benefits of my process expertise to a variety of industries. I could use continuing help with this.

—Jeff Govendo, president, Appellation Trails

and resources while wondering, "Why is this highly touted tactic so frustrating?" So, let's define what we mean.

✔ *What:* Networking is interactive pursuit of others and development of reciprocally beneficial relationships through interpersonal, telephonic, electronic, and correspondence activities.

✔ *Why:* One networks in order to reach new buyers and to close business.

✔ *How:* Effective networking involves a combination of providing value to others so that they will be moved to reciprocate and becoming an object of interest to others so that they will direct third parties to you. Direct networking means that you are interacting with potential buyers of your products and services, and indirect networking means that you are interacting with people who can direct you to those buyers or can direct such buyers to you.

> **Career Key** Build some kind of networking into your weekly schedule every week, not only at the outset of your career but also throughout your career. You will build a momentum for gathering leads and contacts that will keep your business pipeline filled on a permanent basis.

Is this more formalistic and complex than you thought? I've deliberately tried to interpret it that way, so that you can appreciate that networking is a methodical, systematic, disciplined approach to selected people, and not merely casual chat and haphazard meetings.

Among those who constitute networking potential for you are:

Buyers.	Bankers.
Media people.	Key advisers.
Key vendors.	High-profile individuals in
Mentors.	your business.
Recommenders to buyers.	

| Endorsers. | Trade association executives. |
| Meeting planners. | Community leaders. |

Networking is far easier than ever with the advent of e-mail, voice mail, and other communication alternatives, but nothing is as effective as the face-to-face interaction that allows for personal chemistry to develop. If possible, networking should be done in person, and followed up on or reinforced through other communications avenues.

Here is a sequence for networking, whether at a trade association meeting, civic event, business conference, recreational outing, or nearly any other activity that you know in advance you'll be attending.

1. Learn who will likely attend the event. Obtain a participant list, a brochure, the names of the committee members, or make an educated guess. Prepare yourself for whom you're likely to encounter, and create a target list of the best prospects. For example, if you know the local newspaper's business page editor is attending a charity fund-raiser, you may want to make his or her acquaintance so that you can eventually suggest an article. If the general manager for the local utility (and a potential buyer) is at the dance recital, you may want to try to identify him or her and begin a casual conversation during intermission.

2. Begin casual conversations during the gathering to both identify those targets you've chosen and to learn who else might be there who could be of help. For example, you might want to introduce yourself to another consultant whose web pages you think are excellent to explore whether he might make his web designer's number available to you, or approach a local designer because you'd like to understand how she might work with you even as a novice.

3. Introduce yourself to people without describing anything about your work and simply listen to them. If in a group, which is likely, don't attempt your personal networking. Wait until you can find the person alone later, and approach him or her one-on-one, preferably where you will have a few minutes in private. That's all you need. Don't talk to someone while your eyes work the rest of the room, and talk only as much as required to get others talking. You want to hear about them, their views, and their preferences.

4. When you're able to spend a few minutes one-on-one, offer something of value, based on what you've heard. For example, if the person is a potential buyer who has mentioned the problem she's having with attracting and retaining good people, suggest a book that you would be happy to pass along or a web site that you'll send by e-mail which has articles on the subject. If the person is a graphic artist, ask permission to give his name to some people you know need literature designed. The key here is to provide value to the other person.

5. In the event you're asked what you do, practice providing very succinct responses. Here's a dreadful response:

> I'm a consultant who focuses on the interactions of teams, especially cross-functionally, raises sensitivity to synergies possible in greater collaboration, and implements processes to enhance team connectedness. I use instruments such as . . .

Here's a terrific response:

> I assist clients in improving individual and organizational performance.

If the other person says, "That's a bit vague. How do you do that?" then you reply,

> Well, if you tell me something about your organization and the issues you're facing, I'll show you how the approaches may apply specifically to you.

Talking to Consultants

Q. What one key approach or activity would you do differently today from when you started?

A. I would offer a specific service to a predetermined-sized market (i.e., based on revenues). I tried to offer everything to everyone and eventually burned myself out. Today, I offer two areas of specialization: strategic counseling and interim management to high-growth, technology-based companies.

Q. What was your biggest surprise—what do you wish you had known that you didn't know?

A. I consistently undercharged for my (many) services to the wrong market, thus reaping little or no profit. I didn't realize how much value I was giving away for free! Although flexible (depending on the size of company and/or overall effort), my fees are now more well-defined and structured.

—Judith W. Isaacson, founder and president,
Effective Corporate Communications

6. Exchange a card or somehow gather the other person's contact information so that you can send the promised material or information. At a minimum get a phone number and e-mail address. Do not provide brochures, materials, or any other gimmicks. No one wants to lug around material at any kind of event, and this stuff usually winds up in the nearest discreet garbage can.

7. Immediately—the next morning at the latest—deliver what you promised. If you're providing the other party as a resource to someone else, send a copy of your correspondence to the person you're recommending, or let them know that you've given their name to the individuals you had mentioned.

8. In a week or so, follow up to see if the material was helpful, the reference worked out, the prospects called, and so forth. Ask if there is anything further along those lines that might be helpful. Then, summarize or reaffirm your offer of further help with a letter accompanied by your promotional material and literature. Suggest to the other person that you thought he or she might want to learn a little more about you and what you do.

9. In a few weeks, send still more value in the form of a contact, potential customer, article of interest, and so on.

10. If the other party replies with a thank-you for your latest offer of value, then get back to them and suggest a brief meeting, breakfast, lunch, or other opportunity to get together at their convenience. Simply say that you'd like to learn more about what they do and also get their advice about what you do. If they have not responded with a thank-you of any kind, then wait one more week, call to see if they received the additional value you sent, and then suggest the meeting as described. (Their active response simply enables you to shorten the waiting time.)

You've just been through 10 steps of successful networking. This is not a numbers game. Obviously, if you leave an event with a fistful of unqualified and undifferentiated business cards, you'll spend your entire existence on the steps as laid out. The power of networking is not in the quantity of the contacts, but in the quality of the contacts in terms of what they are able to do for you: buy your services, recommend you to buyers, provide publicity, offer important advice, serve as a vendor or resource, and so forth.

Networking is not about how to work a room, but rather about how to establish your value with others. Working a room is a task and an activity; establishing your value is a marketing strategy. Your success or failure in utilizing networking will reside in your own philosophy and discipline in approaching the opportunity strategically.

If you provide disciplined and dedicated marketing time and energy to this virtually free opportunity every week, you will always have prospects in your pipeline and always have a surfeit of resources to call upon no matter what your particular needs.

Special Second Edition Focus on Networking

In putting the preceding rules to the test repeatedly with mentorees over the past two years, I've found five important tenets to high-powered networking:

1. *Distance Power.* You're better off networking with those who don't know you, and therefore have no preconceptions, than you are with people who do know you and have assumptions that color their thinking.

2. *Nexus Contact.* There is often a person who may not be one of the key people just noted, but who can provide a direct introduction. This may be a subordinate, friend, adviser, or peer. Nexus people are very valuable.

3. *Unique Multiplier.* On occasion you will meet someone who knows everyone. This may be a community leader, a long-time employee, a newspaper person, and so on. No one is more valuable long term than the unique multiplier.

4. *Adhesion Principle.* What will make you memorable to the other person? How will you adhere in their memory? This is where "give to get" comes in, so try to provide powerful value to the other individual.

5. *Contextual Connection.* Don't forget that you and the other person are both there in support of a common interest, be it civic, sports, awards, political, charitable, and so on. Use this to achieve rapid commonality and collegiality.

PRO BONO WORK

Pro bono work is work you deliberately decide to do for free, not work you wish you were getting paid for but aren't! As a general rule, I suggest that you confine pro bono work to nonprofits, and never provide your services for free to profit-making organizations. The latter involvement will stereotype you as a desperate consultant who will work for nothing for exposure only, and will present all kinds of difficulties if you ever want to bid on a project on a normal basis within that organization.

Career Key   Try to have at least one pro bono activity going on at all times. Fortunately, when you're new to the consulting world, you'll have more time to engage in this work, when you can use the marketing help the most!

The great value of pro bono work is threefold:

1. You are legitimately contributing to a worthy cause.
2. You are honing your skills in a nonthreatening, appreciative environment.
3. Potential buyers and recommenders are seeing you in the best possible light—they are watching you perform as a colleague, not as a potential consultant or business partner.

Try to find pro bono opportunities that will involve you with potential customers. Fortunately, no organization soliciting free help is going to question your experience, credentials, or motives. These are ideal opportunities for new consultants.[4] Typically, local associations, civic entities, and community help groups have people on their boards, committees, task forces, and fund-raisers who are also senior managers and executives. This could include groups as disparate as the soccer association, United Way campaign, Girl Scouts, shelter for battered women, chamber of commerce, planning commission, or Audubon Society.

Assume a position of trust, visibility, and impact. I suggest you volunteer to take on the dirtiest jobs, those that no one else readily accepts. These usually include fund-raising chair, volunteer head, corporate sponsor chair, and so on.

Also, the more your pro bono position lends itself to meeting other potential customers outside the volunteer organization, the more powerful. So tough jobs such as fund-raising and seeking corporate sponsorships do enable you to meet still more potential buyers. (As a rule, pro bono work that involves contact only with individuals within the organizations will be least effective for your networking and marketing, though these may be organizations that you still help because you believe in their causes. I'm simply suggesting that some of your pro bono work be with the former, as well.)

While doing pro bono work, throw yourself into it and get to know your colleagues who represent your potential customers or recommenders. Make their jobs easier. Take on more than your share. Give them credit.

Then, when the time feels right and you've developed a cordial, trusting relationship, suggest that you meet outside the organization for breakfast or lunch simply to get to know each other a little better. Don't make a sales pitch, but merely seek to build on the relationship and find out still more about their issues and priorities so that, eventually, you can suggest how you might be of help.

Two keys: First, patience is essential. Second, don't wait, however, until your pro bono work is done or the event is completed. It's much harder to link up after the fact. So, suggest your meeting and relationship building while you're together and have the opportunity to see each other on some regular basis. This makes stalling almost impossible because the individual is seeing you regularly.

Obviously, networking and pro bono work are closely allied, and the skills of the former should be employed in the latter. Any publicity you gather from the work (newspaper articles, photos, event literature) can play an important role in your press kit to demonstrate your community involvement and the results you help achieve in an organizational setting.

LISTINGS, ADS, AND PASSIVE SOURCES

There is a wide variety of places where you, your firm, and your services can appear. For information about how to find them, see Appendix G. But as part of your fundamental marketing approach, some bear discussion before we move on.

One place to arrange for your presence is in so-called buyers' guides. These are listings of resources in certain fields offered by a variety of publications. Some listings are free, some require payment (depending on listing size, inclusion of logo, placement, etc.) of about $200 to $1,000.

Career Key Invest in some permanent (annually renewable) listings, with fewer that require more investment and have a powerful appearance, and more that are simple in order to stretch your budget. These can also be sources to which you can refer inquiries ("See our listing in . . .").

Never make the mistake of trying to calculate how many hits you receive from a listing source. One hit that results in a $25,000 piece of business is far superior to 5,000 hits that produce nothing. (The same will hold true, by the way, for your web site.) Since none of us is smart enough to know when a particular buyer or recommender will be looking in a particular source for a particular service, simply maintaining a presence in these directories annually makes a lot of sense.

Directories also are useful when circulated to editors, reporters, talk show hosts, radio producers, television producers, assignment editors, and other media people, because they afford the opportunity to be interviewed, thereby reaching potential buyers in even more credible ways.

Some of the best directories and buyers' guides for attracting business and/or media attention for consultants are published by:

- ✔ American Society for Training and Development.
- ✔ *Training* magazine.
- ✔ Society for Human Resource Management.
- ✔ Kennedy Publications *Consultant Guide*.
- ✔ Institute of Management *Consultants Directory* (membership required).
- ✔ National Press Club *Directory*.
- ✔ *Yearbook of Experts, Authorities and Spokespersons*.

A modest budget of $1,000 annually would probably secure a decent-sized listing in a combination of three or four of these sources, so the investment is very reasonable, and you can add more listings as your business grows.

You should also appear in your local telephone book's yellow pages under headings such as Business Consulting, Management Consulting, Training, Facilitation, and/or whatever listings best describe your work. Many local organizations do use the telephone book to locate service providers. Spend the few extra dollars to have a bold listing and a small display ad. Statistics show that such ads draw far more phone calls than do simple one-line listings.

When you create these listings and ads, give some thought to their appearance. Look through the book or magazine to see which ad formats strike you as the most effective. Frequently, the publication will offer free advice on layout, and sometimes even provide complimentary camera-ready production work. It's wise to spend a small amount of money with a designer on your own to maximize the visual appeal of the listing. Your logo, for example, will add eye appeal to it. Usually, bullet points are highly effective and lengthy narrative is not. Don't talk about how good you are, demonstrate how clients will benefit (e.g., do not say, "We provide superb presentation skill coaching," but rather, "Our clients are able to deliver their message crisply and powerfully to potential customers and the media."

SUMMARY

You should begin thinking about marketing prior to starting your business if possible, but strenuously engage in it as soon as you can. The press kit is your cornerstone, and the look of your literature and stationery will provide your early image for prospects and media sources. Fewer items of high quality are always superior to many items of mediocre quality.

Networking and pro bono work are inexpensive, excellent investments of your time, which can be begun immediately and which should be continued no matter how successful you may be at gaining initial work. The key is to keep the pipeline filled, and too many consultants mistakenly abandon this when they secure their first business. This shortsightedness means that the marketing cycle has to be started from scratch every time an assignment is completed, and that is a guaranteed way to destroy cash flow and to flounder.

Passive listings are excellent devices to maintain visibility before certain readers and inquirers. They are valuable for the quality of the business they can generate, not the number of inquiries. Sometimes excessive inquiries can simply mean that an ineffectual or ambiguous listing is providing mixed messages to readers.

When you've mastered the fundamentals, you can embark on advanced marketing techniques, which we now turn to in Chapter 5.

Final thought: Revisit your fundamental marketing techniques at least semiannually. You may well find that you've outgrown them, and should either upgrade your contacts or spend more time on more sophisticated techniques.

NOTES

1. I realize that there may be no results to date, which is why we're simply stating what can be expected.

2. See Appendix E for a sample biographical sketch for a beginning consultant.

3. See Appendix F for a sample position paper.

4. You may well already be involved in pro bono work from current or prior employment. If your colleagues do represent potential customers, then you are fortunate to have already begun this process! However, bear in mind that you'll be adopting a somewhat different strategy in the future.

Advanced Marketing
Creating a Brand

A fter discussing the fundamental spokes of the marketing gravity chart in the prior chapter, we now examine those aspects of marketing gravity that will tend to create a "brand" about you and your work. (See Figure 5.1.) By this I mean quite simply that a certain repute and distinction is attached to you by dint of what people read, hear, and experience about you. "Branding" can be done quite elegantly with minimal investment if you are clearly focused, disciplined, and relentless about it.

ESTABLISHING A WEB SITE

You will need a web site sooner or later, and my rule is to establish one as soon as you can afford to do a quality job. Bear in mind that good web sites are organic—they grow and evolve. So your initial effort will never represent your final look or, for that matter, your look even next year.

The Internet has presented a huge opportunity for professional services providers to gain visibility, to network, and even to sell products. However, there are two problems that have blunted most of the opportunity:

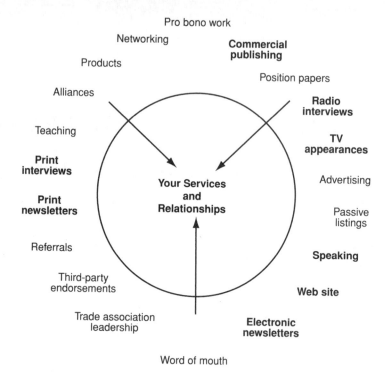

FIGURE 5.1 Aspects of marketing gravity that tend to create a "brand" about you and your work.

1. Professionals using the web for marketing do not do so from the standpoint of the potential customer, but rather as an advertiser.

2. The influence of the technical experts, from web page designers to systems administrators, has been far too profound, creating an emphasis on the technology rather than on the message.

No one gets into the car to drive down the road to look at billboards. No one surfs the cable television channels looking for commercials. No one advertises their phone numbers to direct marketing people lest they have a burning desire to be called in the middle of a favorite program in the evening with an offer to buy securities for a start-up biotech firm in Lithuania.

Similarly, no one in their right mind decides to

spend several hours a day combing the Internet for ads. Yet, most web sites read exactly like advertisements.

You should use a web site to allow people to find you, provide value so that they become interested in you, and enable them to contact you to initiate a relationship. The objectives of excellent, beginning web sites should include:

✔ *Clarity of your image.* Do you help with team building, or mergers and acquisitions, or executive coaching? Is it crystal clear what your image (brand) is to the visitor? One of the best is that of a consultant who helps people communicate and sell over the phone. She calls herself The Telephone Doctor.

✔ *An allure to prompt people to return.* The key is to have not a single hit but an enduring connection with you, so that the visitor returns periodically until such time as a personal contact can be established.

✔ *Credibility of yourself and your firm.* The visitor should be able to learn enough so that further investigation of you (or any doubts about you) are overwhelmingly put to rest by the evidence on your site.

✔ *A personal contact.* The visitor should reach you by phone or you should be able to reach the visitor by phone, with the intent of closing on the next phase—a personal meeting.

✔ *The results your typical clients can expect of you.* (You may not have any actual clients yet, but what would typically be the case?)

Career Key Visit as many other consultants' web sites as you can. Figure out what elements account for the most compelling sites and make sure you include them, without copying any words or proprietary material.

The first step for you is to find a superb web site designer. Fortunately, there are tons of such people around, all charging reasonable rates in a highly competitive industry. Don't use your son or daughter or a moonlighting college student. Get the names of the people who have designed the web sites you most admire (the designer will usually have his or her own web site listed in small print on the opening page, and you can establish contact merely by clicking on the address). Use these criteria in your selection process:

1. Get references about the designer's reliability.

2. Establish costs clearly, both for initial setup, ongoing changes, and yearly fees.

3. Make sure the chemistry is right. If the designer starts telling you how to write your copy or describe your business, head for the hills.

4. Agree to a test site before going live, to work out the inevitable bugs.

5. Test for responsiveness. Some designers seem to disappear into cyberspace for weeks at a time, while others simply pay attention to the squeakiest wheel.

 domain name
your firm's address on the Internet (e.g., summitconsulting.com).

 search engine
those functions on the Internet that provide information about web sites by keywords, topics, subjects, and so on. Your web site and firm should be listed with the major search engines and updated periodically.

Use your technical expert the way you do your auto expert. You want preventive maintenance, quick fixes to problems, fast response, and modern equipment. But you don't need advice of what your transportation needs are, how much money you have to spend, or why you should continue to upgrade to faster and larger vehicles when all you need is reliability, consistency, and effectiveness.

Expect to pay anywhere from $2,500 to $5,000 for an initial design and launch, depending on your complexity and bells and whistles, and from $1,000 to $2,500 for annual maintenance. Make it clear whether your designer will take care of registering your *domain name*, listing you with *search engines*, and so forth. If not, make sure you do that yourself right at the outset.

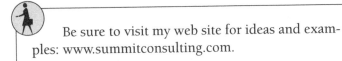

Be sure to visit my web site for ideas and examples: www.summitconsulting.com.

PUBLISHING

There are two ways in which to publish:

1. *Commercial publishing*, in which an independent book or magazine publisher publishes your material, usually paying you a fee or royalty.
2. *Self-publishing*, in which you publish your own material by contracting for all technological and logistical assistance.

commercial publishing
producing print or recorded material through a third party, which pays you a royalty for the intellectual property but controls all production and distribution (as opposed to self-publishing).

Commercial publishing is the strongest way to gain credibility. A book or article published by an independent source creates tremendous credibility, and a body of work (e.g., a dozen articles, two books, a newspaper column, etc.) provides enduring support for the validity of your work and the integrity of your business. (I knew that many clients had never read my strategy book, but they saw a major publisher's name on the spine next to mine, and that was good enough!)

Self-publishing can be useful, however, in providing less expensive books, booklets, and related printed material that you can give away as marketing material, sell on your web site, use in client presentations, and so forth. I both commercially and self-publish, and I advise all consultants to do both through their careers. These are not mutually exclusive endeavors.[1]

Here's how to publish an article:

First, find out what your intended audience tends to read. Ask clients and prospects what they use as valuable sources. Visit any large bookstore and take a look at the periodical racks. Study the *Readers' Guide to Periodical Literature* that is in any library's reference section and online. You can also access sources like *Writer's Digest* for titles, subjects, contact data, and so on (www.writersdigest.com).

self-publishing
producing your own printed or recorded material by contracting for all technological and logistical assistance (as opposed to commercial publishing).

Some Internet Tips from an Expert

✔ The ethic of the Internet is "free." Give away some of your expertise—don't just sell it—using articles, tips, excerpts, links, and so on.

✔ A site needs frequent attention, since changes are what create interest, repeat visitors, and appeals to new visitors.

✔ Always design from the viewer's point of view.

✔ Use search engines intelligently, but understand that there is no magic solution in their use. You will probably get more visitors by promoting your site in other ways, such as articles, ads in trade journals, and targeted mailings.

✔ Don't cut corners. Invest in a topflight professional to get topflight results. Just because your son or daughter can do it for you doesn't mean it's a good idea.

—Ken Braly, president, Info Mastery (Ken@Kenb.com)

Read the publications you want to approach. Read at least three or four issues with the following intent:

✔ Ascertain that the publication accepts outside submissions. Some use only in-house articles. The editorial policy stated in the beginning of the magazine will indicate this.

✔ Find the tone or voice of the publication. For example, does it favor contrarian opinions or mainstream views? Do the articles usually include interviews, graphs, or statistics?

✔ Determine the sources of the articles. Are you a likely source, or can you position yourself to be one?

✔ Get the name of the editor from the masthead. Sometimes you'll also find instructions for submissions listed, as well.

Send a letter of inquiry to the editor, by name. The letter should fit on a single page, if possible, and should include the following concisely, and to the point:

- ✔ The article you would like to submit, and why it would be of interest to the readers, including skills, insights, techniques, warnings, and so on.
- ✔ Your credentials, and why you are the right person to write the article.
- ✔ A brief summary of content (e.g., who would be interviewed or three points on employee retention).

Enclose a self-addressed, stamped envelope (known as an SASE in the trade) and wait, do not call. If the editor is interested, you will receive his or her permission to submit "on spec" ("on speculation," meaning there's no guarantee the piece will be published), the publication's specifications (length, style, deadline, rights being obtained), and payment criteria (which range from no payment to considerable payment—but you're doing this for marketing, not as a revenue stream).

Career Key Think of the customer's customers, in this case, the editor's readers, and make a case for how they will benefit, not a case about how good you are.

Some periodicals have theme issues—for example, international business or recruiting—and actively solicit articles for the themes. Typically, these must be provided six months or so in advance.

See Appendix H for a sample inquiry letter.

Some people submit entire articles and avoid a letter of inquiry. This technique can work, but I don't think it's as effective in the long run. Usually, the article will not be exactly what the editor wants, and even good ones need rewriting. But, more importantly, an editor has the time to quickly scan a letter of inquiry and scribble a response if interested, but unsolicited manuscripts often get thrown into a corner or onto an intern's desk.

If you find that the same publication is publishing several of your articles or, better yet, actively requesting more from you, suggest a column. I once wrote a monthly column for six years, providing me with 72 reprints for circulation, a regular publicity window, and an opportunity to experiment with varied topics. The paper publishing them paid $50 per column, which was just icing on the cake.

Finally, for magazines or newspapers, here are some techniques to significantly improve your chances of being published:

✔ Meet the editor. If the publication is local, stop by, arrange to be at a meeting the editor is attending, or call on the phone. A personal contact is always an advantage. Don't sell yourself; just meet the editor and establish name recognition. If you know a mutual acquaintance, use that edge.

✔ For newspapers in particular, with much shorter deadline dates, attach your story to a current event or controversial event. If a local firm is downsizing, use that to support your article on how to avoid being downsized.

✔ Use facts, examples, and supporting evidence. Opinion pieces are usually harder to sell, unless you are a recognizable name or expert. And research your sources. Editors will throw out hackneyed statistics and questionable premises. Editors love specific names, examples, quotes, and experiences.

✔ Use some humor. There are few subjects that don't lend themselves to some lightheartedness.

✔ Use a "hook." For example, be contrarian. No editor wants to print the seven millionth story on employees resisting change. But quite a few would consider a story that focuses on how we actually all change every day, and on how "fear of change" is an empty rubric tossed around by academics who never set foot in the business world (which is true).

✔ There are agents who will help you place articles. Some charge on a monthly retainer basis, and some charge on a placement basis (e.g., you pay only for performance). These resources range from quite professional to abjectly awful. If you have the cash to spend, check references carefully. But you might want to try placing articles yourself at the outset in any case, to avoid the expense and, more importantly, to get direct experience in what the process actually entails.

Book publishing is beyond our scope here for someone entering the profession, but if you'd like to read more about how to get a book commercially published, read the words of a top agent, Jeff Herman, in his book, *Writer's Guide to Book Editors, Publishers, and Literary Agents, 2000–2001: Who They Are! What They Want! and How to Win Them Over!* (Prima Publications).

For self-publishing, don't get involved with *vanity publishing* or with anyone who wants substantial money to print your work. Start with simple but content-heavy booklets about your topics, create them on your computer, have your graphics artist create a nice cover, and have the local print shop run a thousand at a time. These are inexpensive and easy to change and evolve, yet still serve you well as marketing materials, handouts, and salable products.

Put an *ISBN* number on all of your self-published work, which allows your publications to be distributed by bookstores, Amazon.com, and other sources. ISBN stands for "International Standard Book Number," and is required by distributors in order to access a universal location system to find publishers (in this case, you). You can acquire them by writing to R. R. Bowker, 121 Chanlon Road, New Providence, NJ 07974 (908-665-6770), or by going to Bowker.com.

OBTAINING MEDIA INTERVIEWS

You can add to your brand by actively pursuing interviews by third parties in independent sources. There are several alternatives available:

vanity publishing
the paying of a third party to publish your material, sometimes including design, distribution, order fulfillment, and so on. It is more expensive than self-publishing, in which you are paying only for actual printing, and is not credible in the marketplace. Eschew vanity publishing.

ISBN
"International Standard Book Number," which should be applied to all your printed and recorded products that you wish to sell. This is how all bookstores and online sources order your material. ISBNs are available from R.R. Bowker.

✔ Print.

✔ Cyberspace.

✔ Radio.

✔ Television.

Print

Suggest to your local newspaper, business publication, and trade association newsletters that you have an interesting story to tell. Again, think of *their* readers. Provide an angle or slant that the editors will look on as novel. "Local entrepreneur successfully converts from organizational life" is a possibility for the local newspaper, and "Starting your new firm with a contract from your former employer" is a good bet for a trade association newsletter.

Cyberspace

There are wonderful opportunities to be interviewed on the Web and establish your brand. Send e-mails to the editors of sites that feature interviews and explain why you're a good choice, in the same vein that you would for print sources. But remember that your audience will be far more diverse than with particular periodicals. (I've published an editorial piece monthly for years at HR.com, for example.)

Career Key Practice creating sound bites, which are catchy phrases and memorable viewpoints. These will stand you in good stead in interviews of all types, and solidify your brand with readers and listeners.

Radio and Television

The broadcast media sources are surprisingly easy to access if you know the tricks of the trade. There has been such a proliferation of talk shows that they are thirsty for topics and personalities.

Locally, find the talk shows that are on the major radio stations, call the switchboards, and get the names of the producers of the talk shows you're interested in. Listen to the talk shows daily so that you can judge what kind of guests and topics are best received. Send your media kit with a cover letter to the producer, not to the on-air personality. Make your unique case: why you, why now, why this topic is important to the listeners. Remember that radio and television are about ratings, not your message. Follow up in a week with a phone call to see if the material was received. If you're told that "It's not something we can use right now," ask what topics are of interest, so that you can adjust your approach.

Nationally, you can reach talk show producers, on-air talent, assignment editors, and reporters in several ways. Here are three sources that produce pretty good results, although they require an investment:

1. *The Yearbook of Experts, Authorities and Spokespersons* (Broadcast Interview Source, 2233 Wisconsin Avenue, NW, Washington, DC 20007, 202-333-4904, www.yearbook.com or Expertclick.com). This book and online listing provides the opportunity to place an advertisement in front of a wide variety of media types, including talk show hosts, producers, assignment editors, and reporters. It also provides other services, such as automated press releases. A half-page ad will probably run from $500 to $750. You can include photos of yourself, book jackets, and so on, and be listed in a number of categories for cross-reference (e.g., change management, strategy, expert witness, etc.).

2. *The Directory of Memberships and News Sources* (National Press Club of Washington, 529 14th Street, NW, Washington, DC 20045, 202-662-7500, www.npc.press.org). Published and distributed by the National Press Club, this is a similar listing to the

Yearbook of Experts and costs roughly the same, although ancillary services are far less.

Both of these directories are distributed for free to professionals having need to interview experts in various fields to support stories, appear in support of (or opposition to) certain theme shows, respond to breaking developments, and so forth. It's not unusual to be called on a very short deadline due to contemporary news developments. Nor is it unusual for otherwise remote sources to ask for interviews (I've been interviewed about both sports and acting from the perspective of a business consultant).

3. *Radio and TV Interview Reporter* (Bradley Communications, 135 East Plumstead Avenue, Lansdowne, PA 19050, 610-259-1070). This is a tabloid that circulates widely in the industry. You can buy ads, which the publication will help you format for receptivity and punch with its audience of producers and talk show hosts. I've had good results here when I present something topical (a new book, a new approach) and when I appear consistently—you need to have a presence at least once a month for several months. You'll be alongside weight-reduction specialists and UFO trackers, but don't despair. This publication does produce bookings if you are consistent and patient. Rates are determined by the size of the ad and the frequency. The publisher will send you a free copy with suggestions for effective ads if you inquire.

Most radio shows are done from your home over the phone. The interview time may range from five minutes to an hour. Some will be call-in, and some will be simply a dialogue with the host. Some hosts will have read your descriptive material and have intelligent questions; some will barely glance at it and will be mostly interested in hearing their own voice.

Since you know this going in (because I've just told you), you can prepare yourself for a maximally effective interview, no matter what the length, by following these guidelines:

Talking to Consultants

Q. What were you least prepared for and why?

A. The absence of the traditional office environment I had been accustomed to. Suddenly, there were no people to bounce ideas off. While I knew it would be that way, experiencing it was a bit of a shock.

Q. What was the single most important aspect for your early success?

A. Creating a network of contacts to call on as I built the business. It's extremely difficult to open a business and be completely unknown, especially if you're changing geographically.

Q. What single strength was most important as you began?

A. Confidence in myself. Self-doubt would have killed me during the start-up and during some slow times.

Q. What single piece of advice do you have for a new solo practitioner?

A. Find a quick piece of work, even as a subcontractor, to validate your belief that you can get out there and get things done on your own.

—Stub Estey, Triple E & Associates, LLC

Ten Steps to Powerful Broadcast Interviews

1. Listen to the show several times to understand the host's biases, tone, and approach.

2. Ask the producer in advance about the demographics: Who listens and at what times?

3. Prepare one to five points that you will include in your responses *no matter what you are asked.* This is an old political device. In a five-minute interview, one point is all you can manage, but in an hour five points are achievable. (Example: If you're asked about a current company that is

in the news for downsizing, your response might include: "Actually, Joan, that's one of the topics that my workshops constantly address . . . ," thereby getting in a plug for your courses.)

4. Ensure that you get a tape. If the station doesn't do it as a matter of course, offer to pr ovide the tape and a mailer. If that is unacceptable, have someone tape the show from the radio on a good piece of equipment (you can't do it yourself unless it's done far from your phone interview or the feedback will bring the roof down).

5. Use notes. When you know the topic in advance, as is usually the case, make some notes about times, dates, examples, and so on to appear proficient and knowledgeable. Don't ever try to wing it.

6. Be prepared for change. The host will sometimes come up with a bright idea at the last minute and ask you to address another topic. Don't get testy. Go with the flow.

7. Use the host's name and speak favorably—for example, "Randy, you just asked a question that I wish I could get corporate America to answer." The more host-friendly you are, the better chance of a return engagement.

 Talking to Consultants

Q. What approach or activity would you do differently today from when you started?

A. I would have set my playing field a little larger and expanded my marketing (and marketing methods) to cover the whole field. Because of market conditions, I overemphasized one consulting niche in which I specialize. In retrospect, I should have done some marketing for my other areas of expertise. I would have started speaking and writing earlier and more often.

Talking to Consultants (*Continued*)

It's a real key to get your name out around town. Many times a prospect will tell me that multiple people mentioned my name as the person to see. On the other hand, one of the things I did right from day one was cultivate a referral network. I started from scratch. When I met a new source of referral I mailed them something every week for four weeks and then once a month. I currently send my network some type of mailing 8 to 10 times per year. This is a variety of articles I wrote, postcards, or, most importantly, a copy of an article relating to my expertise from a known publication along with a cover letter giving my interpretation or critique of the article. I convened a focus group of some of my best sources of referral recently, and their opinion was that the individualized letters offering commentary on an article were valuable, insightful, and very personal (it made them feel good to get an addressed letter, not just a generic mailing). This caused me to shift from a newsletter format back to the letter giving an overview of an article.

Q. What was one of your biggest surprises—what do you wish you had known that you didn't know?

A. I came out of the financial services field. It is very competitive and you need to treat people with kid gloves because there are plenty of people out there who have the same products and are more than willing to take over your client or prospect. Consultants have power and need to display the attitude of "You need me more than I need you," because it's true. My largest obstacle was overcoming the nice guy approach and displaying an attitude of confidence and power. One of the things I learned in the financial services industry was to walk away from bad business. This has helped me as a consultant. I get stronger every month about telling prospects "no."

—John Martinka, president, Business Resource Group

8. Tell everyone you know that you'll be on the show, and send out a press release if you have time (e-mail is a good alternative here).

9. If it's a call-in show, stack the deck and have some supporters call in to ask questions you want to answer and that will promote your services.

10. Duplicate the tapes with the collected interviews (for about a dollar apiece), and include them in your press kit, to create tremendous credibility.

11. Bonus! Propose the host or producer a return interview if it went really well, and offer a compelling follow-up set of topics.

If you pursue local broadcast media opportunities, advertise judiciously in national sources, and put in the work to be a fine interviewee (media producers are constantly talking to each other and even have a private-access web site to exchange suggestions on good guests), you should be able to generate media appearances very early in your career, which helps the branding process enormously.

SPEAKING

Many of us pursue professional speaking as a separate, lucrative professional endeavor. That is not my purpose in this chapter.[2] I'm focusing here on speaking as a marketing tactic (part of your "gravity") for your consulting business.

At an early stage, you can speak in front of local groups without problems. Groups such as the Rotary, Kiwanis, Elks, Lions, chamber of commerce, and other service and civic clubs are always interested in luncheon and/or dinner speakers. They don't pay, but the appearances do serve as effective, early ways to accomplish these objectives:

✔ You will get practice speaking about your approaches and techniques.

✔ You will be in front of local buyers and recommenders (bank, utility, retail store managers).

✔ You will be listed in programs and brochures, which you can place in your press kit.

✔ You may have the opportunity to write an article or be interviewed in the organization's newsletter or magazine.

✔ You can gather testimonials. (If the general manager of the electric company says that you did a good job, ask if he or she would care to send you that accolade on company letterhead.)

✔ You can gather references.

✔ You'll learn what the local hot topics and issues really are.

As you can see, speaking for free locally, which is time-efficient and nonthreatening, offers the new consultant a wonderful set of marketing possibilities.

Once you feel proficient as a speaker (at least insofar as imparting knowledge and helping the audience to understand helpful techniques), you can reach out to organizations further afield. The most important organizations to approach in terms of marketing are trade and professional organizations, since these groups specialize in educating their membership, and the conference participants generally constitute recommenders and/or buyers of your services.

Career Key If you're at a loss for what to write, begin with bullet points or numbered lists of quickly applicable techniques for your readers. People enjoy items that they can apply immediately in their lives and professions.

In other words, it's not bad work to speak to 100 people at a trade association conference concurrent session, when many of them will be potential buyers and you're being paid (at least your expenses, and maybe a fee) to be there.

The key source here is a book called *National Trade*

and Professional Associations of the United States (published annually by Columbia Books, 1212 New York Avenue, Suite 330, Washington, DC 20005, 202-898-0662). This amazing source (also available at most libraries and online) provides every trade association in the country, its membership, scheduled meetings (nationally and regionally), meeting themes, annual budget, and the name of the executive director. There's really not much more you can hope for in one source.

Start with a manageable number of associations (I'd recommend no more than a dozen) whose membership and meeting themes are relevant to your work. For each, write a cover letter to the executive director by name, and enclose your press kit. Suggest to the executive director why your topic and techniques would be of immense help to the association's membership. Provide references and testimonials (ergo, the prior local speaking engagements). If you're told that the next year's agenda is full, then inquire about when to be in contact again for the following year, and ask about local chapter meetings and whom you might contact to be considered for them (and then let the local chapter person know that the executive director provided the name).

In speaking for trade associations and other groups that represent potential consulting business, you can stack the deck in your favor.

Ten Steps to Powerful Trade Show Presentations

1. A speech has a beginning, a middle, and an end. At the beginning, use a hook to draw people in, since an audience will decide in the first two minutes whether they want to listen to what you have to say.

2. The hook should be a story, statistic, illustration, humor, or some fact that captivates the audience and generates interest in you. Using something from the audience's own industry and frame of reference is a good idea.

3. The middle of the speech should have clear points you want the audience to remember or practice. It's a good idea to list them: "I have six

points about employee retention that I want to share with you today."

4. The end should be a brief summary and call to action. Emphasize your key points and ask the audience to apply what you've discussed.

5. Use a professional introduction and ask the introducer to read it verbatim. Bring an extra one with you, because the one you sent will inevitably be lost.

6. Practice in the room, with the microphone and any visual aids, before your speech. Have the audio/visual technician with you.

7. Use visuals that can be seen, and make the best use of the medium. For example, don't use overhead slides that simply duplicate pages of text already in people's hands.

8. Make sure you use handouts with your contact information liberally distributed throughout, and copyright all of your proprietary materials.

9. *Never* use other people's materials, or generic stories. It's all been done before. Be original and use personal examples. Ignoring this is not only bad practice, it's a crime.

10. Tape your presentations. You can use these both for practice and as potential marketing aids (and even products). Hire a sound engineer or videotape expert. The relatively small investment is far better than your own amateurish efforts, and you don't want to be distracted in your delivery in any case.

Almost every consultant is going to have to become comfortable making presentations to buyers and evaluators. You might as well turn this trait into a positive and aggressive marketing tactic. If you speak in front of one trade association each quarter and follow the advice just given, I can promise that your business pipeline will get a considerable boost.[3]

The best organization for perfecting your speaking skills is Toastmasters, which has chapters in virtually every major city (Toastmasters International, Box 9052, Mission Viejo, CA 92690, 949-858-8255, www.toast masters.org). The meetings provide a safe, nonthreatening place to practice public speaking and receive feedback. If you're interested in a professional speaking career, then consider the National Speakers Association, which holds annual and regional conventions and has over 30 active chapters (1500 South Priest Drive, Tempe, AZ 85281, 480-968-2552, www.nsaspeaker.org). The latter organization will also have lists of professional speaking coaches if you desire to have your technique evaluated and improved by experts.

NEWSLETTERS

Newsletters are an ideal way to gain credibility early. The key to any newsletter, which even most veterans lose sight of, is that *it should not be blatantly promotional*. No one is interested in taking their precious time to read about how good you are, what clients you've worked with, where you're speaking, or your latest merit badge. What people want to read about is how they can improve, personally and professionally. Simply by providing that help you'll be engaging in powerful "soft" promotion, because readers will come to depend on your advice and respect your expertise.

Ten Steps to a Powerful Newsletter

1. Keep it brief. In print, four pages or even one two-sided sheet is sufficient. Electronically, one to two screens will be maximum for most people's attention span.

2. Be absolutely consistent. Publish your newsletter on the same day and at the same interval religiously.

3. Monthly is best, quarterly barely adequate, more than monthly too much.

4. Write three or four newsletters in advance so as to avoid being under deadline pressure.

5. Make the format professional. In hard copy, use at least two-color printing from a local print shop, and don't try to print it off your computer. Electronically, don't use "curly quotes" or other symbols that might cause strange characters to appear on some software, and keep the line width to 76 characters or fewer since not everyone has a word wrap feature.

6. You are better off with short pieces and bullet lists of techniques than with long narratives.

7. Cite other books, articles, web sites, and useful resources, always providing clear attribution.

8. Ask others who have distribution lists and newsletters whether they'd be agreeable to mentioning yours in return for a mention of theirs. You can easily gain 100 or more subscribers at a shot through one such credible mention in a widely distributed list.

9. Encourage readers to write with letters, questions, and comments, and include the pertinent ones in future issues.

10. Have your contact information at the end of each newsletter, and include modestly any important future information (a public appearance, a new article, a radio interview). This can be in a box or smaller print somewhere in the newsletter.

11. Bonus!! Archive past newsletters on your web site to add value and leverage your past work.

Newsletters should be free for your marketing purposes. You can include the latest issue in your press kit, and hand them out at meetings or speeches. They can also be used in your approaches to interview sources and trade associations.

These have been some advanced marketing techniques to help you establish a brand and image in the public eye, and to more effectively create a gravity so that buyers are willing to seek you out. As you can see, even the advanced practices are easily within your grasp and probably your budget.

Assuming you've been successful in creating your gravity, let's turn to the sales process so that you can begin to get some money in the bank.

———————

Final thought: You have to invest money to make money. Marketing activity is about return on investment. If a $500 ad creates $150,000 in business, you've done better than the stock market or a casino trip.

NOTES

1. In fact, when a commercially published book goes out of print, the author usually has a reversion of rights clause, meaning the book can at that point be self-published by the author, changing nothing but the name of the publisher.

2. If professional speaking interests you as an additional career option, then read the author's book *Money Talks: How to Make a Million as a Speaker* (McGraw-Hill, 1998).

3. And you never know which associations may turn out to be the most promising. I've spoken in front of the National Fisheries Association and generated consulting business, and spoken for the American Council of Life Insurance and generated nothing. You never know.

Initiating the Sales Process and Acquiring Business

Building Relationships

relationship
the interaction created between consultant and buyer based on mutual trust, candor, respect, and a perception of peer-level credibility.

Selling consulting services is about creating *relationships*. No one sells to GE or IBM or Ford, but rather we sell to *people* within those organizations. Those potential buyers have titles such as director of development, vice president of sales, training manager, chief financial officer, and so on. Within education, the buyers are people in positions such as school superintendent, principal, director of curriculum development, and supervisor of counseling. Even in small businesses, the buyers are readily identifiable: owner, principal, managing partner, executive director.

Secondly, consultants must build relationships, not make sales calls. Think about it: Do you really enjoy listening to those people reading scripts over the phone to attempt to convince you to change your long distance provider? Well, no one buys consulting services through those techniques, either. (A woman recently berated me because she did make a cold call telephone appointment and sale. You can also find $1,000 on the sidewalk, I imagine, or hit the number 24 in roulette with a $100 bet. But do you really want to base your living and future on those odds?)

Here are the five key principles for acquiring business right from the outset in the consulting profession. If you ignore them, you will have to be extraordinarily lucky to be successful in this business. If you heed them, you will accelerate your ability to obtain new clients.

Principle #1: Acquiring consulting clients is totally dependent on building solid relationships, not making sales.

Principle #2: Relationships are always built with specific people, not with organizations or legal entities.

Principle #3: The best way to build relationships is by placing yourself in the buyer's shoes and thinking from the outside in.

Principle #4: The buyer doesn't care how good you are; the buyer only cares what's in it for the buyer, so you must focus on business outcomes, not methodology.

Principle #5: Trust is the key to strong and healthy relationships, and trust is the honest-to-goodness belief that the other person has your best interests in mind.

These five principles are discussed in detail throughout the business acquisition process described in this chapter. But trust me—put these principles up on the wall over your desk, write them in your daily calendar, ask your spouse to test you on them daily. If you adhere to them, you will be head and shoulders above most people who attempt to enter the consulting business. Kennedy Information, publisher of *Consultant's News* and *What's Working in Consulting*, estimates that there are in excess of 500,000 consultants working in the United States at the moment. And I estimate that most of them are not making even $100,000 a year from consulting work, and will not be in the profession for longer than two years at a time.

Career Key   Ironically and counterintuitively, if you are patient and methodical about building relationships—taking whatever time is required—you will actually increase the velocity of new business acquisition.

FINDING THE RIGHT BUYER

There is only one potential buyer who matters. I often call this individual the "true buyer" or the "economic buyer." This buyer is the person who can write a check for your services.

Earlier in the book I present three questions to determine marketing scope:

1. What is the value-added that you bring to clients?
2. Who is likely to write a check for that value?
3. How do you reach that person?

The economic buyer is the person identified in the second question. He or she has a budget, does not need approval from anyone else to spend it, can obtain additional funding if necessary, and can sign a check (or cause the computer to disgorge a check). Here are the criteria to determine if you are interacting with an economic buyer. Note the following critical considerations:

1. The economic buyer is not always identifiable by dint of hierarchical title. Although the CEO of DuPont is an economic buyer, the chances are remote that you will interact with that person. Major organizations may have hundreds of economic buyers for consulting services.
2. *It is self-defeating and futile to attempt to develop long-term relationships with noneconomic buyers, no matter how friendly, promising, or likable they may be.* This is one of the toughest lessons for new consultants to learn.

Questions to Ask to Identify a True Economic Buyer
✔ Whose budget will support this initiative?
✔ Whose operation is most affected by the outcomes?

✔ Who should set the specific objectives for this project?

✔ Who will be evaluated for the results of this work?

✔ Who is the most important sponsor?

✔ Who has the most at stake in terms of credibility?

✔ Who determined that you should be moving in this direction?

✔ Whose support is most vital to success?

✔ Whom will people look to in order to determine if this project is real, and not just an empty gesture to achieve a short-term goal?

✔ Whom do you turn to for approval on options?

✔ Who, at the end of the day, will make the final decision?

✔ If you and I reach agreement today, can we shake hands and begin tomorrow?

This last question I call "the handshake test." If someone says, "Yes, we can shake hands and begin, and the paperwork can all follow in due course," then you probably have a buyer. But if the individual says, "Well, there are others who must be involved and approvals to get," then you're dealing with an intermediary or *gatekeeper*. (Don't forget that an oral approval is a contract.)

gatekeeper
that person who is not a buyer but advertently or inadvertently stands between the consultant and buyer.

You don't have to ask all of these questions, and a police interrogation under a bare light bulb is usually not necessary. Just a few of these questions and the handshake test will tell you if you're talking to a true buyer or not. Bear in mind that titles are deceptive. My main buyer within Merck & Co. was a man with the title "manager of international management development," and within Hewlett-Packard was a woman with the title "director of knowledge management." Some vice presidents are not economic buyers (particularly in banks, where *everyone* is a vice president), and some managers are economic buyers (particularly in flat organizations where titles aren't important).

There are other people we meet in attempting to acquire new business, but they are only gatekeepers or *feasibility buyers* if they do not meet the criteria just given. *Note that committees are always gatekeepers.* Committees virtually never have the characteristics we're seeking in our questions. A committee serves as a screening and recommending body to someone who really does have a budget and really can sign a check. Committees don't sign checks (though someone *within* the committee might be a hidden economic buyer).

feasibility buyer
that person who is responsible for determining whether a consultant may fit certain criteria or otherwise be acceptable, but who cannot buy the services and can only recommend alternatives to the real economic buyer.

Career Key   Sometimes you will find a gatekeeper who can be a key recommender to help you to meet a true buyer. Develop those relationships but only to the extent that you actually meet the buyer. Otherwise, you'll be meeting with the gatekeeper forever.

WHAT TO DO ABOUT GATEKEEPERS

Gatekeepers can be wonderful people. However, they see their jobs as shielding the buyer, and your job is to get to the buyer. No gatekeeper, no matter how sincere and reliable, will ever promote you, represent you, or advance your cause as sincerely, passionately, and skillfully as you can. It's a mistake to expect it, a blunder to allow it, and a waste of time to think anything will come of it.

There are three tactics to employ when you find yourself dealing with gatekeepers. These people may be anyone from an administrative assistant, to a training director, to a vice president of human resources. Again, titles don't matter; buying ability does. (In general, human resources and training functions are almost always gatekeepers, virtually never real buyers.)[1]

Tactic #1: Use rational self-interest to gain access to the economic buyer. Convince the gatekeeper that it's unfair of you to allow the gatekeeper to serve as your marketer, and that the two of you should devise a plan to approach the true buyer. You may do this in tandem, or the gatekeeper may simply set up a meeting for you. Assure the gatekeeper that you'll look forward to collaborating with him or her on the project itself, and that you'll continue to work closely with him or her. However, you should be the one taking the risks and making the case for the project at the moment.

This approach, using a partnership but insisting on contact with the real buyer, is accepted about 40 percent of the time.

Tactic #2: Use guile, or artistry, to reach the buyer. Tell the gatekeeper that, as much as you enjoy the relationship with him or her, you must, ethically, meet with the true buyer. You have to be certain that the buyer is not expecting things that you can't deliver, and that the buyer is clear on the degree of support, sponsorship, and resource commitment required internally. While you trust the gatekeeper, no one can actually speak for what's on the buyer's mind, and it's imperative to have a face-to-face conversation and relationship.

This approach, resorting to your policy on the matter, is accepted about 40 percent of the time when the first tactic doesn't work.

Tactic #3: Sometimes you have to apply brute force. That means that the gatekeeper is intransigent and does not respond to either of the first two tactics, and you will be wasting your time if you continue to pursue things at the gatekeeper's level. In this case, simply write to the buyer by mail or e-mail or fax, inform the buyer that you'd love to send a proposal on this project for which you are ideally suited, but you've been unable to make contact with him or her. Invite the buyer to contact you if a meeting is at all possible. This will undoubtedly ruin your relationship with the gatekeeper, but that doesn't matter, since you're not going to get the business anyway at this rate, and the gatekeeper can't sign a check in any case.

This approach, a last resort, usually works about 10 percent of the time when the first two fail.

Talking to Consultants

Q. What's the most important thing you've learned?

A. The first is the simplicity of value-based marketing. Value-based marketing consists of things such as presentation folders with position papers included that add value to prospects even if we don't work together, a web site with articles and ideas that provide value to other people, e-mail, newsletters, articles in magazines, and pro bono presentations. Even at the beginning, I could have taken the basic 45-minute speech that I had and spun it into magazine articles, position papers for the presentation folder and web site, and newsletters. This would have created a more diverse client base much faster.

Q. What do you wish you had known earlier in your start-up?

A. I wish I had known the variety of ways to provide value to clients such as executive coaching for individuals and groups, facilitating, focus groups, keynotes, workshops, seminars, executive summaries, and so on. I stumbled onto executive coaching and it has become a significant revenue source for me. Also, each of these inputs can lead to other types of work. For example, a training session can lead to a coaching assignment that can lead to a keynote that can lead to. . . . Of course, the biggest thing I wish I had known from day one was the power of outcome-based selling and the ensuing fee structure. Finally, providing prospects with options of how we could work together has multiplied my business several times.

—Dan Coughlin, president, The Coughlin Company

You should always apply the tactics in the order suggested. If Tactic #3 doesn't work, then move on. *A chronic mistake that new consultants make is that they tend to hang on to low-level relationships in the hope of somehow getting a recommendation or even actual business.* This just compounds the loss of time and money. If you can't forge a relationship with an economic buyer, you are not going to acquire new business. Move on.

> **Career Key** Although consulting is a relationship business, don't mistake that fact with the need to make friends. If you need love and affection, get a dog.

Here's something of a case study in finding the economic buyer. I was asked by an event planner at Fleet Bank if I'd consider submitting materials to be considered for a presentation at the meeting of the relationship managers of the Private Clients Group. I said I would, but then the conversation went this way:

> ME: May I ask a question? Whose meeting is this?
>
> HER: The executive vice president of the Private Clients Group holds this meeting every year for all her management team.
>
> ME: How might I meet her?
>
> HER: Why would you want to do that? No one else has made that request. Her schedule is incredibly tight.
>
> ME: I understand, but it's important to determine whether or not she and I will view this presentation in the same way, how I can tie my talk into her general theme, and what she would like to accomplish. I think you can see that I can do a much better job of meeting her objectives if I can talk to her, even briefly.
>
> HER: I can probably get you 20 minutes on her schedule if you come to Boston.
>
> ME: Deal! I can guarantee it will be worth it.

I met with the buyer for that 20 minutes (while her three subordinates in the room said absolutely nothing and stared straight ahead). We hit it off, I found out what she wanted to accomplish, I gave her some choices, *and she hired me on the spot, without asking about fees.* She said to her people in the room, "Work out the details with Alan." I eventually obtained $125,000 in consulting work and $40,000 in speaking assignments within the organization. The buyer eventually left to become CEO of another firm, and I've already done work for her in that company.

Most of the people whom you'll initially meet will be gatekeepers. They are paid to do a certain job, and that's fine. But your job is to get to the decision maker and check writer, and that's more than fine, that's mandatory if you want to succeed, let alone thrive, in the consulting profession.

Before moving on, let's be absolutely clear on what a relationship with an economic buyer actually constitutes. By "relationship" I don't mean playing golf, going to lunch, sharing secrets, or exchanging pictures of children. The relationship is usually better, in fact, if it's not social at all. In my terms, the relationship has these attributes:

- ✔ *Honesty and candor.* You and the buyer feel comfortable disagreeing.
- ✔ *Peer-level perception.* You are seen as an equal and colleague of the buyer, not as a salesperson, vendor, or supplier. You are not in attendance with your hat in your hand, a sycophant begging for business. You are a peer who is jointly evaluating, with the buyer, whether a business relationship will be mutually beneficial.
- ✔ *Patience to develop.* Sometimes you can hit it off immediately; sometimes you need months before the relationship is solid.
- ✔ *Respect.* Although you may not be best buddies and may even agree to disagree, you respect what the buyer's value and intent are, and the buyer respects your approach to business and your professionalism.
- ✔ *The aforementioned trust.* If I trust you, I'll accept even adverse feedback, because it's in my

perceived best interest to do so. If I don't trust you, I won't even accept praise and accolade, because I perceive that you have your own agenda.

The ability to develop relationships with economic buyers is the single most important factor in launching and perpetuating a consulting practice.

GAINING CONCEPTUAL AGREEMENT

values
those fundamental beliefs that guide our behaviors, and which should be congruent between the consultant and buyer in terms of the project and the relationship.

conceptual agreement
the oral agreement with the buyer that the objectives, measures of success, and value to the organization are accurate and acknowledged.

In Figure 6.1 we can see that finding the right buyer, establishing shared *values* (e.g., you can't do a downsizing project if you don't believe in downsizing, and you shouldn't take on a project to "increase morale while we reduce benefits" unless you really believe in the premise), and developing relationships are the starting points for business success.

We're now ready to move to the heart of the process, which is what I call *conceptual agreement*. Conceptual agreement means that you and the buyer agree on three basic issues:

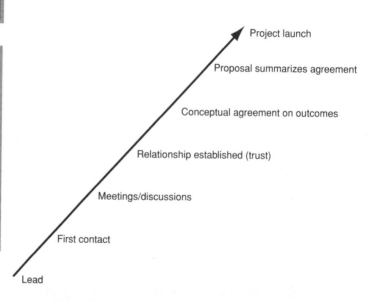

FIGURE 6.1 The business success sequence.

1. What are the objectives to be achieved through this project?
2. How will we measure progress and success?
3. What is the value or impact to the organization?

What Are the Objectives to Be Achieved?

Consultants often talk of "scope creep," which means that they began a project with the rough understanding that they would improve the performance evaluation process, and suddenly find themselves on a scaffold painting the outside of the building. The client kept asking for more and more, and the consultant didn't know how to say no.

objectives
those end results whose achievement will indicate project success. Objectives should always be stated as business outcomes.

The *objectives* constitute the framework within which the project proceeds. They should always be stated in terms of business outcomes, not methodology or interventions. In other words, a training program, focus group, survey, and coaching are only techniques, not ends in themselves. Moreover, focus groups, as an example, are simply a commodity that can be purchased, meaning the buyer will tend to be very price conscious. However, the results of the focus groups—improved cross-functional collaboration and faster customer response time—are significant business outcomes that can justify substantial investment in light of that return.

Career Key No matter what the client says or how far down the road to alternatives the client has traveled, insist on starting with the objectives for the project, and make absolutely certain that the client identifies and specifies the outcomes to be achieved.

inputs
tasks and activities required to generate outputs.

outputs
results that have a demonstrable impact in improving the client's condition. These are always business-related.

Some examples of interventions or *inputs* turned into business results or *outputs*:

Input	Output
Conduct surveys.	Improve employee morale.
Conduct focus groups.	Design product around customer needs.

Create sales training program.	Improve rate of business acquisition.
Observe the interviewing process.	Reduce attrition among new hires.
Facilitate executive retreat.	Create strategy to guide business.
Redesign performance evaluation.	Reward performance fairly, accurately.

Establishing objectives is the starting point of any consulting project. It's impossible to do anything else until and unless you know the desired ending point. Here are some questions to elicit outcome-based business objectives. You can carry these around in your notebook and readily refer to them in order to prompt your buyer in the right direction. You don't need to ask them all, but different variations might work in differing circumstances.

Questions to Develop Outcome-Based Business Objectives

✔ How would conditions ideally improve as a result of this project?

✔ Ideally, what would you like to accomplish?

✔ What would be the difference in the organization if we were successful?

✔ How would your customer (the buyer's customer) be better served?

✔ What is the impact you seek on return on investment/equity/sales/assets?

✔ What is the impact you seek on shareholder value?

✔ What is the market share/profitability/productivity improvement expected?

✔ How will you (the buyer) be evaluated in terms of the results of this project?

✔ How would your boss recognize the improvement?

✔ How would employees notice the difference?

✔ What precise aspects are most troubling to you? (What keeps you up at night?)

✔ What are the three top priorities to be accomplished?

In establishing conceptual agreement about objectives you are ensuring the following:

1. The client is not expecting anything that you cannot deliver.

2. The client is not expecting anything that is unreasonable under the circumstances and within that culture and environment.

3. There will be no misunderstandings later about why additional work wasn't performed.

4. The client is maximizing your contribution and talents, so that the project is maximally effective for the client and maximally lucrative for you.

If you begin with carefully constructed objectives, you create a playing field or a framework within which the project can be launched, can progress, and eventually will end. The time to do that is right at the outset, prior to any proposals or agreements.

How Will We Measure Progress and Success?

Some objectives are readily quantifiable, for example: percentages of sales increase, number of new employees, reduction in expenses, faster response time. However, some are qualitative, not quantitative, for example: improved teamwork, increased aesthetics, greater comfort, reduced stress. In either case, we need measures in place that assure us—and can be used to resolve client unease—that the intervention is, in fact, making progress toward the objectives (and inform us when the objectives have, in fact, been achieved and it's time to go home).

Thus, the second step in conceptual agreement is establishing *measures of success*. Here are some questions to assist you.

 measures of success those indicators of progress (metrics) that tell the consultant and the buyer whether the project is meeting the agreed-upon objectives.

Questions to Develop Measures of Success

✔ How will you (the buyer) know we've accomplished the objective?

✔ Who will be accountable for determining progress, and how will they do it?

✔ What information would we need from customers, and in what form?

✔ What information would we need from vendors, and in what form?

✔ What information would we need from employees, and in what form?

✔ How would your boss be convinced that we've met this objective?

✔ How will the environment and/or culture be improved?

✔ What will be the impact on return on investment/equity/sales/assets?

✔ How will we determine attrition/morale/safety/retention?

✔ How frequently do we need to assess progress, and how?

✔ What is acceptable improvement, and what is ideal improvement?

✔ How will you be able to prove to others that the objective has been met?

Once again, asking all the questions might be overkill, but being prepared to ask several is simply prudent and professional. Sometimes, the prospect will not have any measures in mind, in which case you can suggest what they ought to be (thereby providing both value to the client and the measures of your own eventual success). Sometimes the prospect will have measures in place already (e.g., sales reports, response time indexes) and you'll want to be sure that they are functioning well and apply to your project.

What Is the Value or Impact to the Organization?

Most consultants fail ever to gain agreement on the value of the project. Yet this is a keystone of the sequence. Only by obtaining the buyer's assessment of the value to the organization of the objectives being met can you generate:

1. Leverage to guarantee the buyer's continuing sponsorship.
2. The commitment of organizational resources.
3. The proper priority among other client activities.
4. Justification for your fee.

> **Career Key** If you don't work with the prospect to determine the worth of the project, you have no basis upon which to establish value-based fees. If you charge by the hour or time unit as a consultant, you're an amateur who will never be very successful in this profession.

You've already established the outcomes desired and how progress toward them will be measured. Now it's time to discuss what the impact will be, while you have the proper momentum created with the buyer. These three questions, comprising conceptual agreement, are in this order for that purpose.

Once again, this is a process through which the buyer can be guided.

Questions to Establish Value

✔ What would be the impact or result if you (the buyer) did nothing at all?

✔ What would happen if this project failed?

✔ What does this mean to you, personally?

✔ What is the difference for the organization/customers/employees?

✔ How will this affect performance and productivity?

✔ How will this affect profitability/market share/competitive advantage?

✔ What is this currently costing you annually, and what might you save or gain?

✔ What is the impact on return on investment/equity/sales/assets?

See Figure 6.2. We've now gained conceptual agreement, the heart of our process, by gaining agreement on objectives, measures of success, and value to the organization.

CREATING A SUCCESSION OF "YESES"

We continue with our business process in the next chapter. Let's conclude this one by focusing on the subtle ways

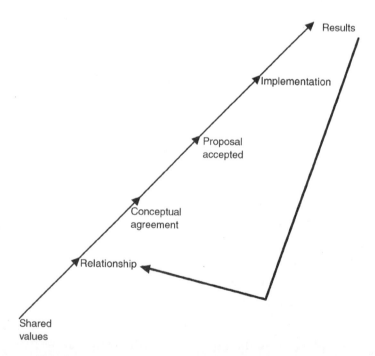

FIGURE 6.2 The key role of conceptual agreement.

to make progress with a prospect, from initial contact, through first meeting, through relationship building, through conceptual agreement.

One of the most important things I ever learned when managing sales forces was that life is about a series of small closes. I call them small "yeses." By that I mean that virtually no one is going to buy a car, purchase a home, or undertake a consulting project on first contact. While there is the one-in-a-million rash and impulsive buyer at these levels, we need to deal with the other 999,999. Thus, the need for small yeses.

Never attempt to sell a project, service, product, or approach over the phone. What is reasonable for the small yes? An initial meeting is the reasonable and modest yes that we need. What's reasonable at that meeting? Some agreements on basic values, the beginnings of a relationship, and the willingness to meet again on more substantive issues. At that meeting, the conceptual agreement might be appropriate, followed by agreement to entertain a *proposal*.

proposal
the document that summarizes conceptual agreement, and also details timing, accountabilities, terms, and conditions of the engagement.

Consultants who talk to someone on the phone and offer to send a proposal are wasting their time. Not only is the potential for business a long shot, but even worse is the fact that if they got lucky and received the business, it would not be optimal for the client or for the consultant.

Bear in mind that life is a series of small yeses, occasionally punctuated by a roaring, yelling acceptance. But it's the small, constant, consistent yeses that put business into the pipeline and provide for a strong stream of business year after year.

The progression usually looks like this:

referral
a prospective client's name provided by another source. The best referrals include an introduction of some kind. The barest are those that simply provide a name of someone who may be interested.

1. Initial contact through lead, *referral*, or serendipity. "Yes" desired: Hear some background, read some material, agree to second contact.

2. Second contact, after material/information exchanged. "Yes" desired: Agree to a brief meeting.

3. Brief meeting. "Yes" desired: Form a relationship, agree on second, substantive meeting.

4. Second meeting.
   "Yes" desired: Conceptual agreement, willingness to entertain a proposal.

5. Proposal.
   "Yes" desired: Acceptance and project initiation.

> **Career Key** With each prospect and lead, determine where you are in the process described in this chapter, and move to create a small "yes" leading to the next step. That is the methodical, organized way to create and maintain a pipeline of potential business.

You may be able to shortcut my five steps, or you might find that you become involved in steps 2a, 2b, and so on. I've completed this process at times within a week and at other times over a year. The key is that you realize that you have a template to utilize, a methodical, systematic sequence to follow, and a "royal road," if you will, toward a comprehensive proposal with a high chance of acceptance.

I submit far fewer proposals than most consultants, but I connect on 80 percent of them, because I already have conceptual agreement with the client. That's what I mean by a more patient, systematic approach actually being more efficient and productive than trying to accomplish too much too soon with too little agreement.

One of the ways to accelerate your way through the process—to increase the velocity of the small yeses—is to provide value to the prospect early and often. In other words, you want the buyer to think, "If I'm getting this much value from this consultant already, what would I get if I hired him and had the benefit of this relationship on a regular basis?"

Some consultants feel that they should share virtually nothing unless they are paid for it. I don't agree at all. I think we should provide value immediately, for free, so that the prospect comes to value our relationship and is readily disposed to formalize it.

Techniques to Utilize to Provide Value Early in the Relationship

✔ Provide experiences similar to the buyer's from elsewhere.

✔ Offer suggestions (not solutions) from experience, reading, research.

✔ Refer books, articles, Internet sites of relevance.

✔ Provide a contact or reference who has experienced similar issues.

✔ Provide a concise description of what you've heard, with analysis.[2]

✔ Ask questions to help clarify the issues and problems.

✔ Provide reactions to what the buyer is already doing well.

A British visitor to the court of the sultan, at the height of the Ottoman Empire, was amazed to see a line of petitioners waiting patiently to have their cases heard personally by the sultan himself. When the visitor asked why the sultan bothered spending his time this way, an aide explained, "Most men are satisfied merely by having their stories heard."

Allow your prospect to tell his or her story. It will help both of you immeasurably.

In the next chapters we discuss fees and proposals. But remember that *prior to establishing any fee, you must:*

1. Determine who the economic buyer is and how to reach that person.

2. Develop a trusting relationship with the economic buyer.

3. Establish outcome-based business objectives.

4. Establish measures of success.

5. Establish the value or impact for the organization of the project.

Final thought: Be patient with prospects and follow a methodical sequence that will lead to a client relationship. No one pays you for speed, and once you've lost prospects, they're usually gone for good.[3]

NOTES

1. An interesting aspect of dealing with economic buyers is that they are decisive and professional, return their phone calls, and will candidly tell you "yes" or "no." A commentary on gatekeepers, and this is especially true of the human resources function, is that they will not return phone calls, will play political games, and don't always tell you the truth. This is still another reason to seek out real buyers and not waste valuable time on gatekeepers.

2. I once listened to a buyer for 45 minutes while occasionally offering a summary or paraphrase, after which he told me, "You're the first consultant to sit in my office who really understands my business."

3. See Appendix I for 101 Questions to ask throughout all aspects of the sales sequence.

Chapter 7

Closing the Sale

How to Write Proposals and Cash Checks

Proposals are summations, not explorations. Ironically, consultants aren't more successful in getting their proposals accepted when they send out too many, rather then too few. This isn't a numbers game; it's a quality game.[1]

The key to an effective proposal is gaining the conceptual agreement beforehand (described in the prior chapter). Consequently, a proposal isn't a document or an event, or a one-time crucible in which the business is gained or lost. It's simply a normal (though highly important) part of the sales acquisition process. (See Figure 7.1.)

There is a methodical sequence you can use to write proposals. A good proposal needn't be much longer than two or three pages, no matter how large the contract or how elaborate the methodology, because the proposal should not be serving as a negotiating document, a sales brochure, a credibility piece, or any other purpose. It should simply be placing the conceptual agreement in context with other required elements of a good proposal (e.g., accountabilities, terms, etc.).

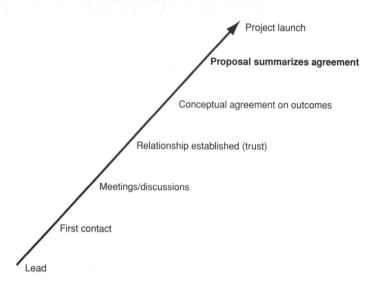

FIGURE 7.1 The proposal's place in the project life cycle.

Finally, proposals shouldn't attempt to be legal contracts, with boilerplate language, "parties of the third part," "agree to hold harmless," and other such legalese. There are several critical reasons to keep proposals conversational and not legal:

✔ This is a relationship business. You should be willing to begin a project on a handshake with a true buyer with whom you've developed a trusting relationship.

✔ Legalese will immediately be sent to two places you never want to go: the legal department and the purchasing department. Either place will delay, crush, attempt to abbreviate, and/or try to change the project for their own interests.

✔ The notion of protection through a legal contract is silly, since you're dealing with clients who will have the resources to contest anything written on paper in any case, and you don't have the resources to contest a contract for too long before you'll lose money even if you win.

✔ In the best of cases, a legal contract will cause delay while it is being routed to the right people for approval, and delay is never good. Only bad things happen during delays. No one ever comes back and says, "Make it bigger."

✔ Lawyers are paid to be conservative and avoid all risk. They'd prefer that the building not even be opened in the morning. Hence, the potential dangers of an interventionist consulting project creates shock waves that reverberate throughout the legal department. (I'm being hypothetical. In reality, it's much worse than this.)

THE NATURE OF EXCELLENT PROPOSALS

Let's begin with the parameters of what proposals can legitimately and pragmatically do and not do:

Proposals Can and Should Do the Following
✔ Stipulate the outcomes of the project.
✔ Describe how progress will be measured.
✔ Establish accountabilities.
✔ Set the intended start and stop dates.
✔ Provide methodologies to be employed.
✔ Explain options available to the client.
✔ Convey the value of the project.
✔ Detail the terms and conditions of payment of fees and reimbursements.
✔ Serve as an ongoing template for the project.
✔ Establish boundaries to avoid scope creep.
✔ Protect both consultant and client.
✔ Offer reasonable guarantees and assurances.

Career Key The ability to write a clear, concise proposal after gaining conceptual agreement and getting it to the true buyer as rapidly as possible is actually the most important factor in closing business.

*Proposals Cannot and/or Should Not Do
the Following*

✔ Sell the interventions being recommended.

✔ Create the relationship.

✔ Serve as a commodity against which other proposals are compared.

✔ Provide the legitimacy and/or credentials of your
firm and approaches.

✔ Validate the proposed intervention.

✔ Make a sale to a buyer you have not met.

✔ Serve as a negotiating position.

✔ Allow for unilateral changes during the project.

✔ Protect one party at the expense of the other.

✔ Position approaches so vaguely as to be unmea-
surable and unenforceable.

The climate or perception that a good proposal
creates with the buyer is shown at the bottom of Figure
7.2, as opposed to the top perception, which is too
often the default position unless we educate the buyer
differently.

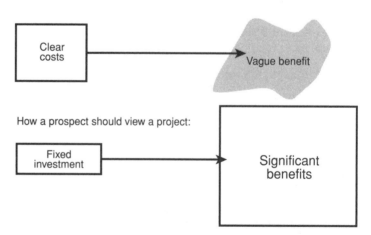

FIGURE 7.2 Creating the right perception of return on
investment.

THE NINE STEPS OF GREAT PROPOSALS

Here is the sequence that I have perfected over the years. It isn't sacrosanct, meaning that you may choose to add two more steps, delete one, or otherwise modify it to your best interests. However, if you follow my general sequence, and you've gained conceptual agreement beforehand, I can guarantee that you'll take less time writing proposals and gain a higher degree of acceptance the very first time. You can't beat those benefits.

1. Situation appraisal.
2. Objectives.
3. Measures of success.
4. Expression of value.
5. Methodologies and options.
6. Timing.
7. Joint accountabilities.
8. Terms and conditions.
9. Acceptance.

Situation Appraisal

What: The *situation appraisal* consists of one or two paragraphs that reiterate the nature of the issues that brought you and the prospect together.

Why: This allows you to start the proposal on a basis of prior understanding and enables the prospect to figuratively (and sometimes literally) nod his or her head in agreement at your opening paragraphs. Psychologically, you're starting on a series of small "yeses."

How: Simply define the current issue with as much brevity and impact as possible. Don't state the obvious, but focus on the real burning issues.

Example: Here's a poor situation appraisal:[2]

Fleet/Boston Financial Corporation is the eighth largest bank holding company in the United States, headquartered in Boston, and

 situation appraisal a summary of the conditions facing a prospective client that need to be improved as a result of the consulting engagement. This brief description should be the first part of a proposal.

continually seeking growth through mergers and acquisitions of institutions providing synergy to the bank's strategic goals.

Your buyer is aware of this. It sounds like something from the annual report. Here's a far better example for the purposes of your proposal:

Fleet has recently merged with BankBoston, which has created both expected and unexpected cultural problems among the Private Clients Group and within the human resources function. The new organization is seeking to create a new culture in these two units that represents the best of the strengths of each former organization, and to do so without disruption to client management and retention. In addition, superfluous positions must be eliminated while providing ethical and legal protection to employees in the form of transfer, reassignment, and/or outplacement.

The second example demonstrates why you were contacted, what issue must be resolved, and why it's of significant import.

Summary: The situation appraisal leads off the proposal by reminding the buyer of the nature and urgency of the issue to be addressed, and gaining a connection with your prior conversations and conceptual agreement.

Objectives

This is the first of three elements in conceptual agreement.

What: The objectives naturally follow the situation appraisal in order to move from the general to the specific. The objectives are the business outcomes to be achieved as a result of your intervention with the client.

Why: The specific business outcomes are the basis for the value that the client will derive, and constitute the raison d'être for the project. Unless business outcomes are achieved or enhanced, there is no real reason to invest in any change. Also, clear objectives prevent scope creep later, enabling you to explain to the client that certain additional (and inevitable) requests are outside of the objectives established.

How: List the objectives, preferably with bullet points, so that they are clear and strongly worded. Objectives should be fairly limited, since you can accomplish only so much with any given intervention, or else they are simply pie-in-the-sky wishes and not practical business objectives.

Career Key Never be bashful about suggesting to the buyer just how important the resolution of the issues is. The more value the buyer sees in the rapid and effective solution, the more your fee is seen as an investment and not a cost.

Example: We discuss outputs versus inputs in Chapter 6, so the list of business-based outcomes might look like this:

The objectives for the project will be:

✔ Determine leanest management team required to speed decision making and reduce overhead.
✔ Determine best candidates for those positions and recommend them based on objective criteria to ensure finest possible leadership.
✔ Improve new business acquisition by creating and separating a new business development team.
✔ Improve current response levels by investigating customer needs, anticipating future needs, and educating service staff accordingly.

Measures of Success

This is the second of three elements in conceptual agreement.

What: These are the indicators of what progress is being made toward the objectives, and of when the objectives are actually accomplished.

Why: Without measures or metrics, there is no objective way to determine whether your intervention is working—or worse, if there is huge success, whether you've had anything to do with it! The metrics enable you and the buyer to jointly determine both progress and your role in achieving it.

How: Measures can be both quantitative and qualitative, the latter being acceptable so long as there is agreement on whose judgment or values are being used to assess results.[3] They should be assigned so that every objective has effective progress indicators to evaluate success.

Example: Measures are also best written in bullet-point form, with precise reference back to prior discussions with the buyer.

As discussed, the measures for this project will be:

- ✔ Current client base is maintained for at least three months with less than 5 percent (industry average) attrition.

- ✔ Client base begins to grow at a greater rate than historical rate beginning six months from now.

- ✔ New management team and structure are in place within 30 days.

- ✔ Any managers or employees without a position after restructuring are reassigned or outplaced within 30 days, with no grievances or lawsuits filed.

- ✔ Staff survey on morale shows improvement from current levels in six months.

✔ Customer surveys reveal increased happiness with response levels and ability of service team to handle concerns within six months.

Expression of Value

This is the third of three elements of conceptual agreement.

What: This is the description of improvement, enhancement, and success that the organization will derive as a result of a successful project.

Why: It's vital for fee acceptance that the buyer be intimately and emotionally connected with the benefits to the organization (and to the buyer) so that the fees that appear later in the proposal are seen as appropriate and even a modest investment for the perceived value return. Otherwise, the fees will be seen as costs and will be attacked to try to reduce them. *Note:* Costs are always subject to attempts at reduction, but investments are almost always justified if the return is perceived to be significant and proportional.

Career Key The simpler, clearer, and briefer a proposal is, the more likely it is that a buyer can simply approve it rapidly without conferring with others or even responding to you with additional questions. Less is more.

How: You may wish to enumerate the value in a narrative or in bullet points. I prefer bullet points because they keep things unambiguously simple and direct.

Example: The value should be expressed in business-related, bold terms, per your prior discussions.

The value that the organization will derive from the successful completion of this project will include but not be limited to:

✔ Overhead costs and administrative expenses will decline by approximately $600,000 annually through the reduction of direct salaries, benefits, and certain support activities.

✔ A growth in the customer base of average private client assets will equal additional assets of about $1 million for each 1 percent gain.

✔ Reduction in the attrition rate to the industry average will result in assets not lost of about $1 million for each 1 percent retained.

✔ The ability to anticipate customer needs and suggest applicable additional products should result in additional revenues of $400,000 annually, growing at a rate of at least 5 percent.

✔ Reduction in unwanted turnover of top performers will improve morale, create better succession planning, and improve client relationships since customers will not be losing their familiar faces.

Methodologies and Options

options
alternative approaches to reach the client's objectives, which provide the client with the ability to determine *how* to use the consultant, rather than *whether* to use the consultant; also called a "choice of yeses."

What: This is the section where you provide the buyer with an overview of the varying ways you may address the issues. *Note:* These are not "deliverables," which many consultants confuse with outcome-based objectives. A deliverable is usually a report, training class, or manual, and has very little intrinsic value.

Why: In presenting the buyer with *options*, you are creating a choice of yeses so that the buyer moves from "Should I use Alan?" to "How should I use Alan?" This is an extremely important nuance, and one that you control. Proposals with options have a much higher rate of acceptance than those that are simply take-it-or-leave-it binary (accept or reject) formats.

How: Explain to the buyer that there are several ways to achieve the objectives, that all of them will work, but that some options provide more value than others. Therefore, the buyer should have the flexibility to decide on what kind of return is most attractive in relation to the various investments.[4]

About Scope Creep

With clear objectives you'll avoid the dreaded *scope creep*, which occurs when buyers approach you during the project to "just add one more element" or "take this over to that department, as well." You're afraid to endanger the business, so you gracefully keep accepting these additional requests until you completely destroy your profit margin!

Objectives create the parameters within which you and the client agree to operate, thereby allowing you to say, "I'll be happy to add that department, but since it's not within our current scope, I'll get a new proposal to you tomorrow which will cover that." The buyer has already expressed need, so you've turned scope creep into revenue enhancement.

Example: Here is an example of three options provided for the project we've been examining thus far.

> Option #1: We will interview all management and supervisory members of staff of the combined organizations, conduct 360° assessments for senior management, monitor customer calls and response times, recommend a new, leaner management staff with specific personnel staffing alternatives, develop methods to speed response time, and identify both people and organizational structure for a new business acquisition team, including goals and performance measures.
>
> Option #2: We will implement option #1, and also interview a select num-

(Continued)

About Scope Creep (*Continued*)

ber of randomly chosen clients to determine their service experiences and preferences, create an evolving organizational structure that will safeguard the status quo while preparing for anticipated client demands, and implement a mail survey for all employees of the department, which we will design, distribute, and administer to obtain inclusion of all employees.

Option #3: We will implement options #1 and #2, and also examine industry standards and other institutions to formulate a "best practices" standard to beat in the marketplace, run focus groups to validate the data gathered in interviews and mail surveys, and interview clients who have left the bank to determine what might be done to prevent such occurrences in the future and/or attract them back to the bank through the new business acquisitions unit.

Note that the options are separate and stand alone, and that any of the three will meet the objectives as stated. However, options #2 and #3 provide more and more value in the form of more valid data, more inclusion, more focus on business retention and acquisition, and so forth. These are not phases or steps that run sequentially. Nor are they needs analyses, which unduly delay any project.

By offering the buyer a choice of "yeses" in the form of increasing value, you tend to migrate up the value chain toward more expensive fees. I call this the "Mercedes-Benz syndrome": Buyers expect to get what they pay for. (If it's a Mercedes, one assumes that the engineering is top-notch and the reliability is superb.)

Always provide stand-alone options for your buyer to consider, and you will increase the rate of proposal acceptance exponentially. It is not necessary to detail how many focus groups, how many interviews, how many people trained, and so on, because with value-based billing numbers of days and numbers of people are irrelevant. The client might ask you to include another 10 people or you may decide you need 4 less focus groups, but it has no bearing on fees. The value of the results are all that counts.[5]

Timing

What: The *timing* section gives an estimate of when the project should probably begin and end.

    Why: Both the buyer and you need to know when services will be performed, when results are likely, and when disengagement is probable.

    How: Provide a range of time, since nothing is completely within your control, and always use calendar dates, not relative dates such as "30 days after commencement," because you and the client might have different perceptions of starting dates and other milestones. But the calendar is in concrete terms.

    Example: Provide timing for each option.

> For all options, we estimate a March 1 starting date. Option #1 should be completed in 30 to 45 days, or between April 1 and 15; option #2 should be completed within 45 to 60 days, or between April 15 and May 1; option #3 should be completed within 60 to 90 days, or between May 1 and June 1.

timing
that part of the proposal that deals with start and end dates, and when certain events are scheduled to occur. Timing should always revolve around calendar dates, not relative dates (e.g., "June 1," not "30 days after our agreement").

Joint Accountabilities

What: These are the responsibilities of the client and you to ensure that the project is successfully undertaken and completed.

    Why: One of the most frequent causes of a consultant's being accused of not doing a good job is that the client actually didn't support the project as agreed or didn't supply resources in a timely manner. This is the part of the proposal that prevents that potential disaster.

How: State simply what is the client's responsibility, your responsibility, and joint responsibilities. These will depend on the nature of the project, and should be specific to each one. For example, an executive coaching project, an information technology (IT) project, and a recruiting project will have very different accountabilities.

Example: Given the ongoing scenario:

✔ Fleet/BankBoston will be responsible for making employees available for confidential interviews, informing them of the project, and providing a private area to conduct the interviews; for providing information about the business and past performance indexes to evaluate competencies; for adhering to the payment schedules established for this project; for client names and contact information for interviews; for reasonable access to senior management for ongoing progress reports, discussions, and problems; and for coordinating work flow and priorities to allow for the project to meet its time frames.

✔ We are responsible for all interviews, focus groups, surveys, and other interventions called for in this proposal; we will sign all appropriate nondisclosure documents; we carry comprehensive errors and omissions insurance;[6] we will ensure minimal disruption in work procedures and adhere to all schedules; we will provide updates and progress reports at your request; we will immediately inform you of any peripheral issues that emerge that we think merit management's attention.

✔ We will both inform each other immediately of any unforeseen changes, new developments, or other issues that impact and influence this project so that we can both adjust accordingly; we will accommodate each other's unexpected scheduling conflicts; we agree to err on the side of overcommunication to keep each other abreast of all aspects of the project.

Career Key In any project, you are likely to find tangential and seemingly unrelated issues that will still be of concern to management (e.g., employee theft, a hostile work environment, turf battles disrupting work flow). Report these to your buyer immediately with suggestions as to how to correct them, irrespective of whether you are involved. This will minimally enhance the relationship, and maximally result in still more business.

Terms and Conditions

What: The *terms and conditions* component specifies fees, expenses, and other financial arrangements.

terms and conditions
that part of the consulting proposal that deals with fees, payment schedules, expense reimbursement, and related matters.

Why: This must be established in writing in case the buyer changes, company circumstances change, and so forth. But most important, this is the first time the buyer actually sees the investment options after basically being in agreement with your entire proposal thus far. Stated simply: You want to prolong the head nodding in agreement right through the fees section.

How: Cite the fees clearly and in an unqualified manner. Cite expense reimbursement policy in the same way, also stressing what is not going to be billed. Provide in this area any discount you offer for advance payment (see the fees chapter, which follows this one). This section needs to be short, crisp, and professional.

Example: Using our current three options:

✔ *Fees:* The fees for this project are as follows:[7]

> Option #1: $58,000
> Option #2: $72,000
> Option #3: $86,000[8]

> One-half of the fee is due upon acceptance of this proposal, and the balance is due 45 days following that payment. As a professional courtesy, we offer a 10 percent discount if the full fee is paid on commencement.[9]

✔ *Expenses:* Expenses will be billed as actually accrued on a monthly basis and are due on receipt of our statement. Reasonable travel expenses include full coach airfare, train, taxi, hotel, meals, and tips. We do not bill for fax, courier, administrative work, telephone, duplication, or related office expenses.

✔ *Conditions:* The quality of our work is guaranteed. Once accepted, this offer is noncancelable for any reason, and payments are to be made at the times specified. However, you may reschedule, postpone, or delay this project as your business needs may unexpectedly dictate without penalty and without time limit, subject only to mutually agreeable time frames in the future.[10]

> **Career Key** All you need is a two-to-three-page proposal on excellent paper in your presentation folder, with two copies, one to keep, one to return. It's that simple if you do the preparatory work well.

acceptance
that part of the proposal that the buyer signs indicating agreement with all details, terms, and provisions included. An acceptance can also be oral, or can be in the form of a payment when you've indicated that a payment will indicate acceptance of the terms.

Acceptance

What: The *acceptance* is the buyer's sign-off indicating approval to begin work.

Why: No matter how trusted a handshake or an oral approval, conditions in client companies change frequently, and you have to have a signed agreement to enforce your rights.

How: Include this as the last item in the proposal, with room to sign off, and return one of two copies. Execute your signature ahead of time in order to speed up the process (in other words, don't wait for the buyer to sign, then sign yours, then return the buyer's copy). This circumvents the need for a separate contract, involvement of legal, involvement of purchasing, and all the other land mines that lurk beneath the ground. Also, by specifying that "a check is as good as a signature" in the verbiage, you're saying that paying you the deposit deems that all terms have been agreed upon.[11]

Example: These are fairly standard, and can be inserted into any proposal.

> The signatures below indicate acceptance of the details, terms, and conditions in this proposal, and provide approval to begin work as specified. Alternatively, your deposit indicates full acceptance, and also will signify approval to begin.
>
> For Summit Consulting Group, Inc.:
>
> _____
> Alan Weiss, Ph.D.
> President
> Date: _____
>
> For Fleet/BankBoston:
>
> _____
> Name
>
> _____
> Title
> Date: _____

WHEN TO FOLLOW UP

Plan your follow-up in advance with the buyer. There are three ways to do this:[12]

1. In the discussions leading up to the actual creation of the proposal, mention that your habit is to give the buyer a day or two to review the details and options, and then to call to respond to any questions and/or to actually begin the project. You merely want to set the stage for your proposal management. (Don't provide the initial proposal in person if you can avoid it, since you want to give the buyer time to read it and think about it.)

When you are actually ready to prepare the proposal, mention to the buyer the exact time he or she will be receiving it, and check for a good follow-up date. "I'll be sending this via courier so that it arrives on your desk Thursday morning. I'd like to call you between 10 and 12 on Monday to discuss your reaction. Does that fit your schedule?" If the buyer says no, that there's a field trip scheduled next week, then ask what a good time would be. Two key criteria:

✔ You want a phone call (or personal visit), not e-mail or voice mail.

✔ You want to initiate it, not the buyer, to ensure positive contact.

2. Mention your intent in your cover letter, which should be a brief note saying, "Here's the proposal you and I discussed." Let the buyer know that you'll be following up at a specified time and date. Leave nothing to chance. Invite the buyer to let you know if that arrangement is not agreeable, but stipulate that, unless you hear otherwise, you'll be contacting the buyer at that time.[13] This technique also enables you to say, "I'm calling as agreed."

3. Do both 1 and 2. If you constantly reinforce the fact that your normal policy is to submit a proposal rapidly after the conceptual agreement, then follow up promptly for reaction, and then are prepared to launch the actual project quickly, you will create the proper expectations—and, one hopes, behaviors—on the part of the buyer.

SIX RULES FOR A COMMAND APPEARANCE

Sometimes the buyer will say, "We need to discuss this in person, and I'd like to get some other people in on it."

> **Career Key**   Sometimes proposals are perfect and buyers are imperfect. Be prepared for other contingencies and don't let go of the relationship. However, never reduce fees without reducing value.

This is good news/bad news. The good news is that the buyer is willing to spend more personal time on the proposal, and wants to give you a chance to close the deal. The bad news is that the proposal itself wasn't sufficient, and that conceptual agreement might not have been as solid as you thought.

Some rules for a personal appearance follow-up:

1. Always accept. Don't try to close on the business by phone.

2. Arrange it as quickly as possible. Remember, the longer the process takes, the more that can go haywire.

3. Ensure that the buyer will be there personally. If he or she will not be, then arrange to see the buyer privately before and after the meeting with subordinates and/or colleagues.

4. Find out who else will be there. Ask the buyer whether the proposal can be made available to them so that everyone is at the same level of understanding.

5. Ask quite candidly if there are any objections, drawbacks, unexpected developments, or anything else that you should know about and prepare for in order to make the best use of everyone's time. Don't wait for an ambush, and then go in unarmed, and then refuse to fight. Determine who will be shooting, from where, and with what, and arm yourself accordingly.

6. Test the status. Ask, "If we can reach agreement at that meeting, are you prepared to proceed?" Try to get the buyer to commit to a proposed course of action (e.g., amend a part of the methodology and we can go on, or shorten the time frame for data gathering and we can probably agree on a start date). If you're particularly assertive, ask this great question: "What will you and I (or you, your colleagues, and I) have to accomplish at that meeting in order to begin the project?"

As a rule, the more specific the buyer is in response to point 6, the better your chances. The more vague the buyer sounds, the more trouble awaiting you.

Let's take one item off the table right now: fees. If the buyer says that your fees are too high—for all of your options—do not offer to lower fees. That tactic will either lose the business immediately ("Hmmm, how low can he go?") or will gain you business that you hate ("I'm actually losing money on this deal").[14]

Instead, offer to reduce value. That's right. All buyers want to reduce fees, but they seldom want to reduce value.

There are other objections, unrelated to fees, that you might hear, either from the buyer in advance or from the buyer and/or colleagues at the actual meeting. They typically include:[15]

- ✔ The timing is too aggressive or too tame.
- ✔ Subordinates are threatened by the outside intervention.
- ✔ Sensitive political/cultural issues are involved (e.g., compensation).
- ✔ A union is presenting problems.
- ✔ Other projects, planned or ongoing, are threatened.

No matter what the objection, you should use the same tactic: Make the resistance a part of the solution. Don't attempt to smash through it, overcome it heroically, or throw yourself onto your sword ("You'll have to trust me on this, I've seen it before, and I'm confident we can overcome it").

Remember: There is NO objection we haven't heard! You may not be able to overcome every one, but to not be prepared for them is negligent. Practice your response to these objections above until you're comfortable, compelling, and virtually irresistible.

Tell the buyer and others that the objection makes sense, and ask what *they would recommend* to overcome it. Tell them that you have some ideas and experience from other clients, but that they know their culture best and you'd be happy to work in their resolutions. At the same time, assure them that there are always objections, that the timing is never perfect, and that there will probably be some more stumbling blocks before this is over. "Nevertheless, successful projects are launched every day in far worse scenarios than this one and we're all intelligent people here, so let's work out the best resolution we can while we're together."

A personal appearance is still a fine opportunity. But take it very seriously and prepare assiduously: It's probably a make-or-break point.

> **Career Key**   Don't always assume the worst, but always expect courtesy and civility. A refusal to return a series of calls over a prolonged period means that you had a relationship with an amateur. Don't throw good money after bad.

TEN STEPS TO FOLLOW IF THE BUYER IS UNRESPONSIVE

A chronic complaint I hear from colleagues is, "We had such a good relationship, but the buyer won't return my calls!" Here are some safeguards:

1. Make your phone call as planned (agreed-upon day).
2. Make a second phone call, with a courteous message (next day).
3. Make a third and final phone call indicating your confusion and saying that you'll send something in writing (three days later).

4. Simultaneously send an e-mail and letter marked personal and confidential, politely asking for a response so that you can plan your time accordingly and offering to see the buyer personally if desired (one week later).

5. Send a certified letter to the buyer indicating professionally that the proposal terms will be honored only for another 30 days, at which time all terms would have to be reviewed and renegotiated. Indicate that this will be your final letter (two weeks later).

I usually don't go beyond this, because I don't want to throw good money after bad, and I never take it personally. After all, just because your buyer has a personality disorder or is neurotic (one of which is probably the case with these "disappearances") doesn't mean that you're a bad person. Further, psychologically, it's depressing to deal with this passive-aggressive rejection, so it's best to remove ourselves from it, which we're quite capable of doing.

If you want to escalate beyond my steps, however, here is the nuclear arsenal:

6. Ask the secretary if the buyer is sick or anything unexpected has happened, then find out what his or her schedule is. If the buyer is visiting the Philadelphia field office on Friday, for example, you can place a call there and almost assuredly ambush the buyer through an unsuspecting local switchboard operator.

7. Send an invoice to the buyer for your expenses to date (which you should actually absorb as marketing expenses) given the fact that the meetings and interaction were apparently to gain information from you but not to consider a project seriously.

8. Send an invoice for your fee in terms of the value you've provided, per step 7.

9. Send a letter with a copy of the proposal to the buyer's boss. Explain the steps you've taken to

try to obtain a response, and that you're worried that your proprietary information, models, material, and so on might be used without your consent or appropriate payment. Ask if there is some way to resolve the impasse.

10. Send a certified letter to the buyer explaining that the buyer's failure to conform to your agreement for response and your consequent inability to determine the status of the project (and the material you've provided) mean that all agreements are null and void. Therefore, you do not feel constrained to conform to any real or implied nondisclosure about what you've learned, nor will you return any of the proprietary materials the company has provided to you.

I do not advocate steps 6 through 10, but you may occasionally be unable to exorcise the demon of the disappearing buyer without resorting to stronger actions. I have met a couple of these people. If you think you're unfortunate for having had to deal with them, think of the great misfortune of their companies, which pay them significant amounts of money in support of unprofessional, aberrant behavior.

Career Key Never take rejection personally, which leads to the desire to get even. View rejection as a flaw in the buyer, and work to reeducate the buyer so that he or she can eventually take advantage of your talents.

HORRORS, WHAT IF THE BUYER SAYS "NO!": SIX STEPS TO REDEMPTION

Even with this methodical approach of relationship building, conceptual agreement, proposal as summation, "choice of yeses," and planned follow-up, sometimes you don't get the business. As someone once said, that's not a failure, only the start of a new opportunity.

First, find out the only important piece of information for the moment: Why? You can't do anything effectively until you learn the reason for your nonacceptance. The causes usually range among these:

1. A legitimate, competing proposal was accepted.
2. Your proposal was flawed in some way.
3. Despite value, you were deemed too expensive.
4. The project was canceled or postponed.
5. The prospect has decided to proceed using internal resources.
6. You weren't dealing with the true buyer.
7. There was an internal upheaval or reorganization.
8. Someone talked the buyer out of using you (you were a threat).
9. Poor profitability has put a freeze on all expenditures.
10. The situation unexpectedly improved or the problem disappeared.
11. Unexpected profits have diminished the problem's priority.
12. A scandal has occurred in the company (harassment, embezzlement, etc.).
13. The organization is being sold, merged, or divested.
14. New technology is eliminating the problem or opportunity.
15. Some combination of these.

Believe it or not, I've heard every one of these reasons and excuses after submitting proposals over 27 years as a consultant. The main reason to find out the cause of your rejection is that you want to be able to correct anything that was in your power to do so. Reasons 2, 3, and 6 are the ones to learn from. You can correct your mistakes or omissions in future proposals (it's too late for this one). The others are simply part of the fates and futures that await all consultants, and there's no use getting upset about them.

Rejection needn't be the final bell. All that it signifies is that at that particular point, for that particular buyer, under those particular conditions, there wasn't sufficient perceived value. You've lost the battle, but the war is far from over. The good news is that you've met the buyer, you've established enough of a relationship to have been able to submit a proposal, and you know where the buyer lives. This is all the ammunition you'll need to begin mounting your counteroffensive.

Here are the six steps to take to turn short-term rejection into long-term business:

First, never walk away angry. The failure to consummate a business deal isn't the buyer's fault or your fault. It's not about fault, it's about *cause*. Take your setback gracefully, thank the buyer for all of the support and interest he or she has demonstrated along the way, and, if another resource was chosen, say something nice about them and assure the buyer that you believe they'll do a fine job. Now, this is *very important*: Ask permission to stay in touch. This vague and simple request is rarely denied, but its acceptance by the buyer creates a legitimacy to the next steps. It's the difference between structured follow-up and incessant hounding.

Second, ask for the cause of your not being chosen. Tell the buyer that we all learn best with honest feedback, and in the spirit of improving your approaches and helping other clients better in the future, ask what you could have done better, included, omitted, or changed. Don't settle for generic pap. ("It was close—it could have just as easily been you who was selected." Yeah, but it wasn't.) Ask for specific areas to work on and, no matter what you think of the advice, demonstrably take notes. (If you're on the phone, say something like, "Just a second, I want to make a note of that.") Use the 15-point list of causes if you want to stimulate the conversation. Remember that there can be multiple causes.

Third, make an open offer to be of informal assistance if the buyer needs anything during the project (e.g., another opinion, a sounding board, etc.). At that juncture, provide your card and brochure or media kit again, for future reference (these are often discarded after a consultant hasn't made the cut).

Fourth, mail something—virtually anything of some value—to the buyer a month later, and bimonthly thereafter. Let the buyer know that there are no hard feelings, and that you have his or her interests in mind on a regular basis. Don't attempt to resurface the project you lost out on; simply send articles and materials that are relevant for the buyer's position, company, and/or industry.

Fifth, call the buyer three to four months after your rejection, and ask any one of, or all of, the following questions: Has the material you've been sending been appropriate? Should you alter the content in any fashion? How has the project progressed? (If it's gone very well, indicate that you're delighted; if it's gone poorly, provide genuine empathy.) Tell the buyer that you'll be in the neighborhood on three different dates, and ask if you might have lunch or briefly meet on any of the three dates that might be convenient.

Sixth, If you can meet with the buyer while you're in the neighborhood, do so. During that meeting, develop a conversation about the current concerns and needs of the organization. Bring the buyer up-to-date on anything you've been doing that's relevant to the buyer's needs. If you're unable to arrange such a meeting, then go back to the fifth step over the phone.

If you're disciplined and unselfishly helpful, eventually the buyer will either agree to see you again or request that you submit a proposal on some issue that has arisen. I've been called continually through the years by people who originally did not click with me, or who did a small amount of business in an unrelated area, merely because I've kept in touch. Consistency is everything. Don't contact people only when you want something, or when it's convenient for you. Establish regular helping patterns. You've already done the hard part in establishing the relationship to begin with.

The legendary coach Vince Lombardi said once that his teams had never lost a football game, although occasionally they had run out of time before they could win it. You have all the time in the world if you're consistent, professional, low-key, and oriented toward a helping relationship.

Final thought: If you can send out just two proposals a month that average, among their options, $50,000 in fees, and you hit 75 percent of them, you have a practice that is generating $450,000 annually. That's just two a month, using this system! Do you think you can live on that, at least at the outset of your career in this profession?

NOTES

1. Although we're dealing with proposals in a full chapter here, if you want an in-depth approach, including templates in hard copy and on CD, see my book *How to Write a Proposal That's Accepted Every Time* (Peterborough, NH: Kennedy Publications, 1999, 2003) or find it on my web site: www.summitconsulting.com.

2. I'm using an actual merger and real organizations, but the specifics of the project are fabricated and bear no resemblance to actual issues within Fleet.

3. For example, if several people all agree that the office aesthetics should be improved, it's far better to also agree that one of them will determine that, rather than trying to gain agreement among several people on what is, basically, a subjective matter.

4. And I want to emphasize that you still haven't discussed fees in any manner yet. Patience.

5. I've long held that I'd be completely happy working 10 minutes a year for a single client for $5 million. My wife tells me that if I can work 10 minutes, I can work 20 minutes.

6. This is the colloquial malpractice insurance cited in Chapter 3.

7. These fees are entirely fictitious. Ignore the amounts and focus on the process.

8. For non-U.S. business, you would specify in this section that all funds quoted are in U.S. dollars, and are to be paid in U.S. dollars drawn on accounts in U.S. banks. In that way, you will not be subject to exchange fluctuations or to severe bank fees applicable to exchanging foreign checks.

9. Many organizations have a purchasing policy that states that all discounts must be accepted, meaning that you will always get the full fee less 10 percent in advance. That is 10 percent well invested on your part, since the money is in your pocket and the project cannot now be canceled (or at least the money can't be returned).

10. This is my quid pro quo for a noncancelable project agreement.

11. I actually had a client make two payments of $125,000 each over 45 days and completed a highly successful six-month project without ever receiving my signed proposal back. The reason was that it was far easier for the executive vice president I was dealing with to approve six-figure checks than it was to get an agreement through his legal department! So, "a check IS as good as a signature!"

12. *Note:* Since there are only so many ways to express simple concepts, much of what follows also appears in similar context in my book *How to Write a Proposal That's Accepted Every Time*, previously cited, and used with permission of the publisher.

13. This is as good a place as any to mention that it's always a good idea to get the buyer's private line, private e-mail, and private fax numbers. Early in the relationship, you might provide your home phone number or private line on a card for the buyer, and ask if there is an expeditious way to reach him or her. This usually avoids gatekeepers entirely.

14. For a detailed discussion of fees, see the next chapter.

15. Don't forget, all of the foregoing assumes that you've been dealing with the real economic buyer. If subsequent events indicate that the resistance is caused by the fact that your presumed buyer really doesn't have that authority, then you must begin the courtship again by finding out who the real buyer is. You cannot sell anything to gatekeepers or recommenders.

Chapter 8

Establishing Fees

How to Make Them Beg to Pay You More

Those of you who have immediately turned to this chapter are welcome to my book. May I suggest that the prior chapters have some important information, and you should go back and read them before going on to Chapter 9. For those of you who have had the discipline to tackle this in sequence, let's continue along!

A *fee* is compensation that is paid to you in return for the value you are delivering to the client. That compensation may be in the form of equity, bartered services, chicken dinners, or future consideration, but 99 percent of the time it is (and had better be) in the form of hard currency. That value may be in the form of your talent, expertise, background, experience, contacts, or other attributes.

Consequently, value delivered that improves the client's condition should be rewarded with a fee. If we can agree on that, we can start down the road to preventing you from doing a lot of business for a little money.

 fees
those payments, usually in cash but sometimes in equity, bartered services, or other forms, which compensate the consultant for the value delivered to the client.

THE FALLACY AND LUNACY
OF TIME-BASED FEES AND PER DIEMS

Most consultants in this country are using time as the basis for their fees, and most consultants in this country are not making much of a living. Attorneys are the prototypical hourly billers, and the average attorney in the United States in 2002 made less than $100,000, according to the American Bar Association. (And the average doctor makes less than $200,000 if you want to really understand how lucrative consulting can be.) Accountants fall into the same dreadful dead end. The reason is that there are only so many hours in a week and so much you can charge per hour (and limits to how much you can fudge the figures). These are two immutable caps on income if time is your determinant of your value.

In the best New York law firms, the most senior partners may be at $500 or $600 per hour and, even if they magically bill 80 hours a week, that's still a weekly cap. Yes, you're saying, but that's a $40,000 weekly cap, which is a cool $2 million a year. But that 80-hour grind, with no personal life (if indeed the 80 hours are real), also requires a substantial staff and office support to deliver the $2 million. Yet I've consistently made about $1 million every year working about 20 to 30 hours a week. I began my practice from scratch in 1985, after I had been fired as CEO of a consulting firm, and reached the seven-figure mark by 1991. Do I have your attention yet?

This hourly cap is insidious. Of course, most attorneys are lucky to get $150 an hour, and be billable for 20 hours a week, and that's only $150,000 a year, and $100,000 ain't what is used to be. That's why the really big legal earners are those who accept *contingency fees*—fees based on a sharing of the value gained by the client, often as much as 30 to 40 percent—and lawmakers are starting to consider limits on that huge share.

Aside from the concrete caps on amounts of hourly charges and hours in a day, there is a more pragmatic reason not to charge by the time unit—namely, that it doesn't represent true value. When I stand on a stage and deliver a keynote speech for 45 minutes for a fee of $10,000, I'm

contingency fees

fees paid only upon achievement of some predetermined goal. As a rule, this is not an attractive fee arrangement.

under no illusion that 45 minutes of my time is worth $10,000 (or that the same amount of Colin Powell's time is worth his rate of $75,000 when he's not in a government job). However, my experiences, talents, background, and intellectual property, combined with my communications abilities and talents to convey a synthesis of that totality, plus the lingering impact, influence, and change within the client organization that follows my presentation, are worth far more than $10,000. The client feels as if it were a bargain, and I feel well paid.

The same dynamic holds true in our consulting work. It's not the day on-site, the training program, the survey, the new IT program, or the new director of sales recruited,[1] it's the improved morale, the better teamwork, the faster customer responsiveness, and the higher departmental productivity that constitutes the real bang for the buck.

The reason that the chapters are in this order in this book is that, if you recall our discussion on input versus output, a sales training program is often sold by a trainer for $2,500 a day, or $250 per participant. Suppose there are 60 salespeople nationally, who are trained in three groups of 20. Our daily per diem would generate $7,500 for three days of work, and our per head charge would generate $15,000.

Now, suppose that this sales training was able to increase sales by just 5 percent on an annualized basis (if not, why even do it?). If each salesperson were generating $300,000 in new business on average ($18 million in business), and you succeeded in raising the total to $18,900,000—a $900,000 increase—would the organization be prepared to pay, say, 10 percent for that return? In other words, is a $900,000 first year (*and continuing*) increase worth an investment of $90,000?

Career Key You must educate the prospect from the outset that you never charge by the day or by the person, because it is unfair to the client. Position value-based billing as the best method for your client's investment and return.

It certainly is. And even if you took only 5 percent, *you still have three times higher a fee than you did under the per head charges, and six times higher a fee than the per diem rate.* In fact, even a 1 percent return on the increased profit is larger than the per diem rate in my example, and that per diem rate of $2,500 per day is higher than many consultants and trainers are currently charging.

Imagine: Many consultants are not working for even a penny on the dollar of client improvement, savings, and bettered circumstances.

If you're going to invest the hard work, discipline, talent, and dedication that this profession requires, let alone tolerate the travel, client demands, and tough environments, you might as well earn money commensurate with your talents and results. Otherwise, you're accepting all the risks and detriments without exploiting the rewards and benefits. You'd never advise a client to do that, so why do it yourself?

Two ironclad rules:

1. *Always* work on a project fee or value-based fee, period.
2. Always demonstrate to the client that this arrangement is in the client's best interest.

Oh, and one third point: Charging by the hour is ethically questionable and a direct conflict of interest, because the more you work, the more you get paid, *and there really is no impetus or benefit to resolving the client issue rapidly.* On the other hand, if you're paid a set fee, then you and the client will both be delighted if you resolve the issue as quickly as possible.

PREPARING AND EDUCATING THE CLIENT

As we've established earlier, the basic conversations with a new prospect should be around relationship building, followed by conceptual agreement over objectives, measures, and value to the organization. This is a deliberate and pragmatic sequence. In focusing on objectives—outcomes—you enable the buyer to visualize and appreciate the end result of the project. The measures deliver a sense of security in understanding progress and recognizing when the objectives have been met. And agreeing on the value establishes early on, before the proposal, what is the worth to the buyer and to the organization of the new state created at the conclusion of the project.

The proposal, in its sequence, does not mention fees until after these points have been summarized and enumerated in writing, options of varying value have been provided for the buyer's selection, and a succession of small "yeses" has been created throughout the proposal. Then, when the buyer is ready to select an option of ultimate value, the proper investment amount can be chosen.

Career Key If you find yourself discussing fees and not value at any time, you have lost control of the discussion with the buyer. Refocus the conversation on outcomes and results immediately.

Here are some reasoning points to use to convince the buyer that a value-based fee is always in the buyer's best interest.

Ten Ways to Convince a Buyer That Value-Based Fees Are Best

1. There is a cap on your investment. You know exactly what is to be spent and there are no surprises.

2. There is never a meter running. You do not have to worry each time my help is requested that I might be here for an hour, a day, or a week.

3. It would be unfair to you to place you in the position of making an investment decision every time you may need my help. Otherwise, you're trying to determine the impossible: Is this an issue that justifies a $2,000 visit or a $500 phone call? No client should ever be in that position.

4. Your people should feel free to use my assistance and to ask for my help without feeling they have to go to someone for budgetary approval. This only makes them more resistant to sharing their views, and at best delays the flow of important information.

5. If I find additional, relevant work that was unanticipated but must be performed, I can do it without having to come to you for additional funds. In those instances, legitimate, additional work would otherwise be viewed as self-aggrandizing and an attempt to generate additional hours or days.

6. If you find additional, related work that must be done, you can freely request it without worrying about increased costs.

7. The overall, set fee, in relation to the project outcomes to be delivered, is inevitably less of a perceived investment than hourly billing.

8. If conditions change in your organization, you won't be in the difficult situation of having to request that the project be completed in less time. The quality approach is assured, since the fee is set and paid. (And your project probably can't be cancelled if it's already paid for!)

9. If I decide that additional resources are necessary, there is no cost to you and I can employ additional help as I see fit.

10. This is the most uncomplicated way to work together. There will never be a debate about what is billable time (e.g., travel, report writing) or what should be done on-site or off-site.

Feel free to add others to my list as you come across them for your practice. The important thing is that I introduce this concept early, using as many of these arguments as I have to in order to convince the prospect, and I do so in the relationship-building part of the sequence. In other words, although the prospect sees my fees for the first time in the proposal itself, the buyer is educated to the point that he or she expects to see a single quoted fee per option, and not a per diem or per head fee assigned.

The key to achieving any kind of interpersonal change is to convince the other person that the change is in his or her best interest. That's why you have to marshal your arguments around the prospect's improved condition, and the sagacity of using a project fee approach. Any and all work required in the early stages is more than justified by the outcome in the acceptance of the fee structure in the proposal. That's why preparatory work is so important in gaining business.

One more hint in buyer education. If the buyer says, "You're the first consultant to propose a single fee," or "We're accustomed to evaluating hourly fees for these projects," respond, "Exactly! That's what makes me different and so popular with clients. I've removed the uncertainty and questionable investments entirely. Here are some reasons that my approach works in your favor. . . ." Then go back to the reasons I've listed.

Career Key   Unless you're convinced that a set project fee is better for the client, you'll never be able to convey the concept effectively. Don't worry about yourself; worry about your client's best interests.

Whenever someone says that everyone else is doing it the other way, use that as a means to stand out in the crowd, and don't flee because you appear to be different.

FORTY WAYS TO INCREASE YOUR FEES

If you buy into the concept strategically, then here are the tactics to help you continually raise fees. You might want to start applying Post-it Notes to the following pages.

1. Establish the fee collaboratively with the client. This means that you work through the objectives/measures/value sequence of conceptual agreement, so that the buyer is continually apprised of the results and the fee is simply the investment that will generate them.

2. Base fees on value, not tasks. Don't specify how many focus groups, how many classes, how much observation, and so forth there will be. Focus on improved sales, not sales training; focus on better communication of corporate values, not executive coaching; focus on highly productive and lean organizations, not reengineering.

3. Never, ever use time as the basis of your value.

4. Don't stop with what the client wants, but pursue what the client needs. Every client will know exactly what's wanted ("better delegation skills") but few will understand what they really need (an environment that rewards risk taking and innovation). The difference between "want" and "need" is your value-added. No one knew they needed a Walkman until Akio Morita and Sony produced them. I've received some of my largest assignments by probing beneath the simplistic want ("training") to find out the true need (a culture of less authoritarianism and more personal empowerment).

5. Think of the fourth sale first. Fees are cumulative, not situational. Don't get overly greedy. Get a decent fee and do great work, and you'll probably have significant additional projects far into the future. Plan for at least 70 percent of your business to be repeat business in this manner, because new business acquisition is always harder and more expensive. You're far better off receiving $100,000 from one company over two years than $10,000 from 10 companies over two years, because your costs will be far less, the time demands will be significantly lower, and you'll keep much more of the revenues from a single source.

6. Engage the client in the diagnosis—don't be prescriptive. An internist makes a lot more than a druggist. The former diagnoses, while the latter simply dispenses pills. Don't confront the client with set solutions, pigeonholed responses, and off-the-shelf products. Listen and converse. Provide the client with the opportunity to be your partner right from the early relationship-building process. If the client feels an ownership in the joint diagnosis of the issues, two things immediately occur: First, your value is perceived as much greater in the collaboration and, second, the resultant fee structure will be far more the result of your joint efforts. The best internists engage the patient ("Does it hurt here? How long has this been occurring? When did this first come to your attention?") and involve the patient's behaviors and lifestyle in the course of the treatment. When the patient buys into the regimen, the healing proceeds much more quickly.[2]

Career Key   Look into the mirror and say, "The fee is $50,000." I'm not kidding. You have to be able to state a fee confidently without losing eye contact, laughing, or hemming and hawing. Most consultants can't do it.

7. Never voluntarily offer options to decrease fees. I once had a member of my private mentoring program who was not happy with the fees she was able to generate. When I role-played a meeting as one of her buyers, we got to the stage when I said, "Joan, you're exactly what we need around here. How much would it be for that customer service program you outlined?" She replied, "Well, it's $7,500, but I could do it for less if that's a problem." (Who could make this up??) Whenever you offer a deal, you express two adverse conditions: The first is that deals are available, and there could be still more. The second is that you're unconfident enough in your own worth to suggest that the buyer should probably get a better deal. If you offer reductions unilaterally, you are undermining not only your fee, but your credibility.

8. Add a premium if you, personally, do it all. Most consultants operate in the reverse. In their options, they tell the client that if they have to bring in more people there will be additional charges. I tell the client the opposite: The fees assume that I'll use whatever resources I need to without additional costs. However, if the client wishes that I do all of the work personally to reduce the number of outsiders, maintain a single filter, keep the same level of quality for all officers, and so on, then there will be a 10 percent premium for my total, personal involvement. In other words, I cost more, not the hired help. I've gained 10 percent on six-figure contracts through this offer. And it's not surprising, since I'm the one who has established that all-important relationship with the buyer early on.

9. If you are forced to consider fee reduction, reduce the value commensurately. Sometimes a buyer will say, "Alan, we just love option one, but we don't have the discretionary money right now. Can we do it for $20,000 less?" And I reply, "Of course we can. What value shall we take out? Should we remove the international surveys?" ("No, international always feels left out.") "Should we remove the one-on-one interviews?" ("No, we need that measure of personal feedback.") "Or should we remove the communications with former customers?" ("No, how else will we know why they left?") Prospects love to reduce fees, but they hate to reduce value, and given this dynamic will probably find the extra money somewhere. But if you reduce fees without a commensurate reduction in value, then the question is simply, "Well, how low can he go? There was certainly enough padding to get a quick reduction with no problem." Don't do anything for a sale. Build a relationship.

> **Career Key** Never allow yourself to be cornered. When you're asked a tough question (e.g., "How long?", "How much?", "Why you?"), turn it around by appealing to the buyer's self-interest. "I'll be able to explain that better once I've heard just a few things from you. Can I begin with a couple of questions, and then we'll return to your concerns?"

Talking to Consultants

Q. What one key approach or activity would you do differently today from when you started?

A. Looking back I would make myself get marketing help sooner. Even though I knew I should do something, I did not pay attention until I almost had no work. I would also build into my schedule marketing time each week and make a marketing plan (not an easy thing to do when starting out and business is good).

Q. What was your biggest surprise—what do you wish you had known that you didn't know?

A. Believe it or not, my biggest surprise when I started consulting was how to write a proposal. I had thought about how to work my sales pitch and who to influence to make a decision, but—*wham*—now I had to write a proposal! I had not been exposed to many proposals, so I called a few colleagues, got some ideas, and used the Proposal Guide on the MicrosoftWorks software to draft my first proposal. And it was accepted!

—Barbara Callan-Bogia, president, Callan Consulting

10. Provide options every time—the choice of "yeses." Do this for a couple of reasons:

✔ Clients believe they get what they pay for.
✔ The choice becomes "*how* to use Alan" not "*whether* to use Alan."
✔ Buyers tend to migrate up the ladder of choices (which is why you should lead with the least expensive and proceed to the most expensive).

Never allow a prospect to have a "go/no go" decision.

11. Always provide an option that is comprehensive and over any stated budget. In many instances, a prospect will share a budget amount, candidly stating that the proposal should stay within the bounds of the available funds. One of the advantages of providing options is that you can provide one that is deliberately over the budgetary limit. By providing two or more within the limit, you give the prospect the opportunity to make a choice of how to use you within current parameters. But seeing one that is packed with value over the budget, the buyer might just say, "You know, option #4 is so attractive that we're going to invest more money in order to have you implement that one." You never know until you ask, and no prospect will ever say, "Make sure one of your options is over our budget limit." Yet we all control more aspects of the sales process than we suspect, and this is a wonderful device that will result in much larger fees every once in a while. If you position it correctly—"I just wanted you to see what we've done for another client at a higher level"—you can do this quite gracefully.

12. Ensure that, as early as possible, you've asked the Question Guaranteed to Result in Higher Fees: "What are your objectives?" Always begin with end results that can be equated with a value and demonstrable return to the client. When a prospect asks early on, "How much will this be?" or "What are your rates?", gently turn the question back and reply, "I can answer that specifically when I understand what's to be accomplished, so perhaps you can start by explaining what results will represent an ideal outcome?" Never discuss fees before value, period.

13. Broaden the objectives as appropriate to increase value. When a buyer says, "We need better sales training," ask, "Why?" The buyer is likely to say, "We have to accelerate the time it takes to close new business, because we're losing ground in compensating for attrition." Your response can then be, "Well, would it also make sense to take a look at the attrition you've accepted, to see if it's reasonable, can be reduced, or is being reported incorrectly?" Every buyer who states early that he or she has an alternative approach in mind, rather than objectives to be met, is usually taking much too narrow a view of the issues. The time to broaden these is prior to the proposal and the fees, not after the narrow project has begun.

14. Ensure that the client is aware of the full range of your services. Many times you will be inadvertently typecast as a trainer, or a survey specialist, or a coach, simply because that was an early role for the organization, or because a source who referred you knew you only in that capacity. Early in the conversation acquaint the buyer with the gamut of your abilities, not by citing a laundry list of options, but rather by providing examples of how you have worked (or are capable of working) with other clients. For example: "I can certainly prepare an approach to coach your sales directors, and I've done that in the past in conjunction with helping clients recruit new sales directors when there are no incumbents capable of doing the job."

15. If a minor part of the proposed project is not within your competence, talents, or interests, don't abandon it—subcontract it. There's a key distinction here. If the entire project is financial in nature, and you know little about financial analysis or balance sheets, you're best off by referring the buyer to someone who can better handle the project. However, if that financial analysis is a minor part of a larger project—say, analyzing customer buying habits—then you should pursue the project with the knowledge that you'll find a competent subcontractor to handle the aspects that you can't. My rule of thumb: If your competence can accommodate the majority of the project, then attempt to own it; if your competence can accommodate a sizable minority of the project, then attempt a collaboration; if your competence isn't relevant for the project, then attempt to refer it to someone else as a professional courtesy to the client and the other consultant. Even this last effort will return dividends from two grateful parties at a later date.

16. Always ask yourself, "Why me, why now, why in this manner?" If you are virtually alone in your ability to provide a service—due to unique talents, experiences, timing, or whatever—you are much more valuable than if any number of readily available people can accomplish the same ends. If timing is key, or the use of an external resource is mandated, or the client has continually failed in the past trying to resolve the same issue, your services are more valuable than otherwise. This is neither mercenary nor greedy. If your particular talent and assistance at a specific time are extremely valuable to the client, you are entitled to charge commensurately for that value. Hotels charge more for the exact same rooms around the holidays. It's more expensive to have someone meet you on the road and tow your car than it is to have preventive maintenance done at set intervals. Timing and need are important indicators of value.

17. Determine how many options the buyer perceives, other than you. If you are the sole source being considered, you're quite valuable. If you have to take a ticket in the waiting room that says "#212," you're not very special. Don't forget, you may find that you're also competing against internal resources. Understand the nature of the competition to better understand your own potential value.

18. Use proposals as confirmations and summations, not explorations. As described in Chapter 7, the proposal is not a negotiating document. The fees established in it should be based on prior areas of conceptual agreement. In the worst case, if options are desired but fees are considered too high, offer to reduce value, not unilaterally reduce fees.

Career Key If you don't know what the competition is charging for similar services, I can guarantee that you're undercharging. Keep your eyes and ears open about market intelligence.

19. When the buyer insists on nailing down rates, use the magic response: "I don't know." The buyer says, "You must have a daily rate. All consultants do." You reply, "Well, I'm different, and in your best interest, I don't have one." Then the buyer says, "Okay, but you can at least give me an estimate of the costs here." And you reply, "I will once I learn more, but I just don't know at the moment. I haven't enough information about outcomes to know what methodology might be most effective, and I'm not sure about scope. It would be irresponsible to quote you any fees without knowing more, but I can get them to you as early as tomorrow in my proposal if you can provide me with some basic information (objectives, measures, value) while we're together." There's nothing wrong with a good old "I don't know." At this point, you're supposed to have questions, not all the answers.

20. If you must lower fees, gain a quid pro quo from the buyer. Sometimes you will feel it makes sense to accept a lower fee: You want to gain entry into an important and potentially long-term client; you know for a fact that money is temporarily tight but will flow again in the new fiscal year; you want to do a favor for someone in need. In those cases, seek a nonfinancial reciprocity. This might be in the form of bartered merchandise, company stock, complimentary services, access to company functions, printing of your materials, an endorsement or testimonial, recording or videotaping of your presentation, and so on. Some of this value might be even higher than the partial fee you're sacrificing. Think in terms of value to you and your career, not just money.

21. Do not accept troublesome, unpleasant, or suspicious business. Annoying prospects inevitably make for worse clients. The chances are that you're going to have trouble collecting your money, or that there will be demands that far exceed the original objectives, or that you'll be blamed for problems that the client should have been accountable for preventing. The only thing worse than lost business is bad business. Every consultant who has succeeded in the profession agrees with me on that one. Stay away from the quicksand and land mines. You'll lose money, no matter what fee you cited.

Career Key You will be pegged within an organization according to the way you enter it. If you take an early project for a cheap fee to get in the door, it is unlikely that the client will accept later projects at significantly higher fees. Early impressions will last, so don't sacrifice too much, too early.

22. When collaborating or subcontracting, use an objective apportionment. This will keep all parties confident that they're treated fairly, and will allow fees to flow unhindered. Here's my rough rule of thumb: The business acquisition itself is one-third, the methodology or technology is one-third, and the delivery is one-third. That means that if you acquire the business and provide the methodology, and subcontract for someone else to deliver it, you keep two-thirds of the fee and pay the subcontractor one-third. If you were to share the delivery equally, then you'd each receive one-sixth. Use whatever categories and breakdowns you like (some people believe that the business acquisition aspect deserves more than one-third in my breakdown, for example), but make them manifest to others and gain their full agreement before proceeding with any collaboration.

23. Any highly compensated employee must bring in new business. Many of you will be prone to take on partners or employees quickly because you prefer to work with others. If you are paying anyone a salary or any fixed income at all of substantial amount, that person must be accountable for new business acquisition. If people are merely responsible for delivery that you can't personally handle, pay them market rates, which are relatively low, because delivery people are in abundant supply. One of the biggest errors of new consultants who quickly generate business is that they build staffs that do not add to business growth but only represent overhead. Do not pay highly for a commodity, but only for unique talent.

24. Seek out new economic buyers laterally during your projects. The time to build new projects and additional fees is while you're visibly on-site and providing results, not after you've packed up and gone. That doesn't mean blatant promotion. It does mean mentioning to the vice president of European operations that you're going to be traveling to Europe for other reasons, but while you're there you'd be happy to provide some feedback on market conditions if desirable. Or you can share with the director of human resources some nonconfidential practices you've seen elsewhere or read about. There are scores of economic buyers in most organizations. You can reach out to them while implementing in a professional and helpful manner.

25. It is better to do something pro bono than to do it for a lower fee. When there is a significant fee problem and there is no middle ground, consider doing a small project on a pro bono basis to build goodwill, rather than be seen as a consultant who will accept virtually any amount of money. However, here is my ironclad guideline: I'll do pro bono work for nonprofits, but never for profit-making organizations.

26. Fees have nothing to do with supply and demand, only with value. Some experts will tell you that you should raise your fees when demand exceeds supply. There are two massive problems with this superficial philosophy. First, demand will never exceed supply, since being employed every working day during a year is both unlikely and impractical. Second, who wants to work that hard? Isn't the idea to work smart, not hard? Raise your fees when your value increases, due to developing expertise, experience, accolades, publishing, unique approaches, references, and so forth.

27. Find out what consultants are charging and what clients are paying. In your networking, reading, and discussion, determine what the ranges are in the marketplace. Then decide whether you want to be the low-end provider to gain volume, the mid-range provider to compete in a wide spectrum, or the high-end provider to be the "Mercedes-Benz of the business." It's difficult (and self-defeating) to set fees in total ignorance of what the market is currently sustaining, irrespective of whether you seek to be below, at, or above current averages.

28. Psychologically, higher fees create higher value in buyers' perceptions. Buyers don't brag to colleagues that they've managed to hire the cheapest consultant around, who has no other business, and was just waiting by the phone. Their own egos are very much involved. They prefer to say, "Listen to this person. We're lucky to have her, and we're investing a small fortune because of the kind of help she can provide. Do everything you can for her." Higher fees enable the buyer to both fulfill personal ego needs and make a stronger case for supporting your project.

29. Value can include subjective as well as objective measures. Increases in sales, improvements in retention, and more rapid response times are measurable and clearly objective standards. However, a buyer's comment that "Improved teamwork would be invaluable" or "Higher morale would be priceless to me" is also quite powerful. Your fees can be based on a buyer's admission of more confidence, reduced stress, renewed focus, and so on.

30. Introduce new value in existing clients to raise fees within those accounts. Too many consultants agonize over how to raise fees within existing clients, because they want higher fees for doing the exact same thing they're already doing. The client is understandably not interested. However, if you introduce additional value—in the form of integration into business plans, comparisons to best practices, creation of a longitudinal validation study, and so on—then you can raise fees based on the additional value.

31. Do not accept referral work on the same basis as the referent. That means that just because the person who recommended you has accepted client business on an hourly basis doesn't mean that you have to. If the client says, "But your colleague always worked on an hourly rate," simply reply, "I know that, but he and I work differently and I've always maintained that my approach has some unique benefits to the client. Let me explain what they are. . . ."

> **Career Key** Just as clients have policies, so can you. Explain that fee-based projects, or 50-percent-down payments, or expenses paid monthly are your policies, and other clients have no problems with them. Simply assert this as a matter of fact, and don't apologize for it.

32. When forced into phases, offer partial rebates to guarantee future business. Sometimes, justifiably, the client will say, "Our organization needs to take this slowly. Let's begin in one department and then see how it goes." I like to offer a series of phases in these cases where I'll always provide a rebate in the form of a lower subsequent fee if the client agrees to go with phase two before phase one is completed. This is especially helpful when you're forced to begin with a needs analysis prior to embarking on the major project. If you charge $15,000 for the needs analysis, and $45,000 for the major project, offer to do both for $50,000 if the project is accepted at the time the needs analysis is concluded. This could preempt another consultant's being sought at the last minute.

33. At least every two years, jettison the bottom 15 percent of your business. Particularly when entering the profession, you'll be tempted to stay with original clients, interventions that you can do blindfolded, and relationships that are comfortable. The problem is that your early business is seldom representative of the future business you'll need, and unless you consciously abandon the bottom rung of your business you'll have no room to reach out for new business. This is extremely important. Treat the older clients well, provide them with a smooth hand-off to someone who will appreciate the business, but do not continue to service clients who are not paying you well, from whom you are not learning, and who are tying up time that should better be used to penetrate larger organizations and more lucrative markets.

34. Start with payment terms maximally beneficial to you every time. Ask for full payment in advance, with a discount option to make it attractive. Otherwise, demand 50 percent on acceptance, and 50 percent in 30 days. The payment schedule does not have to match the work schedule at all. The faster you are paid, the more valuable your money. Never wait until the project is completed. (When you order something over the phone, you're asked to pay by credit card at the time.) If you start with tough terms, you can at least compromise on pretty good terms (50 percent on acceptance, 25 percent in 45 days, 25 percent in 90 days).

35. Offer incentives to accelerate payments. Fast pay is the equivalent of more money in your pocket. We've discussed offering an incentive for full payment at the outset. You can also offer a one-time fee of X that will include all expenses, thereby removing the need to create more billing and delays. You can offer a 2 percent discount for any fees paid within 10 days of your invoice date. Think about win-win situations that will appeal to the buyer and/or the accounts payable department.

36. Never accept payment subject to conditions to be met upon completion. Many clients—particularly small businesses and family-owned concerns—will insist that final payment be contingent upon a final output or product. Don't do it. The client will often find something wrong and, since you've already done all the work, you have no bargaining chip at all. Inevitably there will be variables that you can't control in any case, sometimes the buyer's own errors. The way to avoid this is never to agree to it at all.[3]

37. Focus on improvement, not problem solving. Anyone can solve problems, including most internal people. There are highly methodical approaches to problem solving, and the result is the restoration of prior standards. Frankly, that has limited value. However, raising the bar—creating still higher standards of performance—is extremely valuable. So, don't merely offer to "fix the performance evaluation process," but suggest that "we will link performance evaluation to succession planning in an integrated manner for the first time."

38. Provide proactive ideas, benchmarking, and best practices. Suggest to your buyer that, if the two of you are going to intervene in the organization anyway, why not do so with the idea of becoming industry or market leaders? Stretch the buyer's imagination and goals. Any change involves some risk, so why not plan for a higher return based on that risk?

Sober Fact to Remember: If you leave money on the table by undercharging, you can never regain it. Therefore, if you're undercharging in the cumulative amount of $50,000 per year, after 10 years that's a half million dollars *that should have been in your bank account but isn't and can never be regained or retrieved.* How would you like an additional half million in your bank account today? You can make it happen in the future if you charge for your value.

39. Practice stating and explaining your fees. Do this alone until you're completely confident stating, "I'm not sure what the fee will be until I learn more, but typically these projects have required an investment of between $35,000 and $65,000. Does that present any difficulty?"

40. Always be prepared to walk away from business. Ironically enough, few behaviors will tend to secure business as much as your readiness to walk away from it. If the buyer realizes that you're serious in your approaches, and are intent to protect the client's and your best interests even to the point of refusing the business, your credibility will soar. So expect at times to have to say, "I just can't take this project on within these constraints, and I'd rather be considered for future projects on better terms than take this on unfairly to you. But I do appreciate the opportunity to have discussed this with you." The buyer will often reply, "Well, wait a minute, let's talk some more. . . ."

SUMMARY

You control the education of the buyer insofar as your fees and value are concerned. Many consultants are performing excellent work for $15,000 when they might have done the same work for $45,000 without any protest from the buyer. However, they've now pegged themselves at a certain level that will stay with them forever within that organization, and probably references from that organization.

The ideal project is one after which the buyer says, "That was a bargain," and you say, "I was well compensated." If you follow the advice in this chapter, that reaction can occur every single time.

Final thought: You deserve your fees in return for the value you are providing. If you don't perceive your own value, you will never demand high fees. The sales start with you.

NOTES

1. Although you'll note that the best and most lucrative recruiting firms generally charge a set fee that is equal to about a third of the new hire's first-year total compensation, meaning that a first-year salary and bonus of $250,000 for a vice president will immediately net the search firm almost $85,000, or about the full year's earnings of a typical attorney.

2. I'd also like to point out that no one with a serious illness goes shopping for the most economical surgeon. What they say is, "Get me the best heart specialist in the East and we'll figure out how to pay for this later."

3. And by the way, if any client is not conforming to your payment schedule and/or is seriously in arrears, stop work. It's your only leverage, and some clients will continue to pressure you with "just one more month" during which you'll be throwing good money after bad. The time to deal with late payments is as soon as they're late.

Chapter 9

Moving to the Next Level

How to Grow Your Business Dramatically

My unscientific estimate is that only one in five people who enter the consulting profession as independent practitioners make it to the point where they are supporting themselves in a comfortable lifestyle (in excess of $150,000 of annual income) within two years. And only one in ten establish a long-term, viable practice, meaning that the business continues to grow, the principal can take time off, more prospects call than have to be called, and so on.

Most of the experts in entrepreneurialism and small business start-ups tell me that the three-year mark is the critical milestone. On average, people beginning their own business have run out of contacts, friends, and luck by three years, and must have forged independent marketing channels and attracted new business sources to survive beyond that point. If they've done that, then they probably have what the accountants refer to as a "going concern." If they haven't, then they will probably go back to work in a corporate setting or return to whence they came.

Add to this the fact that almost everyone beginning a solo-practitioner consulting practice is an experienced veteran of the workforce—in many cases, a refugee from a large company—and is unwilling to spend five or ten years building a career. Consequently, people entering consulting not only have to hit the ground running and create clients during the first year of operation, but also have to establish a thriving business. (Many people who enter my mentoring program tell me that they are consultants, not business people. I tell them they *are* business people, but just lousy ones.)

Here are the hallmarks of the successful transfer from acquisition of initial clients to the building of a practice.

Ten Characteristics of a Successful Consulting Practice

1. More business comes to you via referral and passive marketing than you actively pursue and solicit.

2. You have a fully funded retirement plan that grows every year.

3. You are taking at least two vacations of one week each per year, and they have no tie-in to business or business travel.

4. You have the appropriate and modern equipment that you need, and you are not merely making do until you can afford something more advanced.

5. The practice does not require your 24-hour attention. You have procedures, people (albeit subcontractors or temps), and resources to accommodate normal needs.

6. About 75 percent of business is repeat business, and about 25 percent is new business.

7. You are personally growing each year, learning new approaches, gaining new experiences, and helping to achieve new results.

8. You control your travel to the extent that less than 25 percent of it is on-demand, unpleasant, or outside of your influence.

9. You control your client composition, so that you reject work you do not want or like, periodically end unproductive long-term relationships, and are selective about the projects you accept. Stated succinctly: You can turn down business without threatening your business or lifestyle.

10. You contribute to the profession in some way (e.g., with trade association leadership, publishing, speeches, interns, etc.).

> **Career Key** Always think of the fourth sale first. This is a relationship business, which means building *and nurturing* relationships with key buyers.

FINDING RESOURCES: THE PROS AND CONS OF STAFFS

Some practitioners (I among them) have done just fine with no full-time staff and precious little subcontracting or temp use. My philosophy has always been to maximize the profit I keep; otherwise what I make is irrelevant. And I've mentored too many people who generate well into six figures (and even seven figures) of business but who have to personally barely scrape by because they are supporting a corporate welfare system of staffers who must be paid, housed, and cared for.

However, there are consultants who will accurately make the case that they could never be as productive as they are without a few well-chosen and carefully placed staff members who free them up for both the professional accountabilities that are theirs alone and the personal time that they would otherwise sacrifice.

As the French would say, *chacun à son goût*, which

basically means for you, "Now what do I do?" But no matter which side of the debate you favor, there are some unequivocal rules for hiring people, which can serve as an objective template when you're ready to make that decision.

Rule #1: Implementers Are a Dime a Dozen

If you need people to deliver or implement, then pay them by the project as subcontractors (do not hire them), because the need for this ability is situational and in abundant supply. This category includes training, interviewing, surveys, computer work, assessments, coaching, and so forth. Some of the large seminar companies have successfully hired appropriate talent for as little as $300 per day, which is close to indentured servitude. Any time you need another pair of hands, simply rely on a cadre or network of capable people that you can easily develop amid your professional dealing and travels. They will be grateful for the work, since they cannot do what you are doing: find, solicit, and acquire the business.

Rule #2: One and One Must Equal at Least 64

Anyone whom you hire or collaborate with must provide a synergy that creates an exponential degree of business. In other words, if you and the other party could each generate $50,000 independently, it makes no sense to collaborate to generate $100,000 (or even $125,000) together, because the relationship is going to require energy and resources to manage. Don't team up with people who have the same skills that you already possess (that's duplication, not growth), who must rely on you before they can do something (that's support, not synergy), or who are simply friends and great people (that's loyalty, not strategy). If you're going to partner on a formal, business basis, or collaborate on an informal, trusting basis, begin with a clear piece of business on the table. Otherwise, you're leaving the landing lights on for Amelia Earhart. It's a nice gesture, but it won't help.

Rule #3: Hire the Help That Provides for Abilities and/or Interests You Do Not Possess

I would never take the time to learn the software that would enable me to develop slides or computer-generated presentations from my own computer. I have zero interest in this level of geekiness. I prefer to spend my time on more interesting pursuits (such as playing with my model trains), and I have absolutely no affinity for learning that software. I've gladly paid as much as $3,500 for a visual presentation for a major piece of business, because it would have required $50,000 of my precious time and made me impossible to live with had I tried to do it myself. Similarly, I don't do my own taxes or attempt to balance the books, since I can't begin even to understand the instructions. Your time is valuable. Don't do the difficult or the painful. Find people who will. (This work is almost always situational, meaning you don't need staff, but merely contract help. My bookkeeper costs about $180 per month for a few hours' work. Yet I know consultants with smaller practices who employ bookkeepers part-time for $25,000 a year, simply because they don't believe they should be sending out their own invoices or writing their own checks.)

Rule #4: Demand That Any Service You Pay For, Full- or Part-Time, Be Constructed Totally in Your Self-Interest

When I first interviewed bookkeepers 18 years ago (and you should interview many candidates and make careful choices, so that you can then forget about it after the selection), I found one who manually posted all entries and charged by the hour. "Let me get this straight," I blurted out. "You refuse to use a computer, which makes you slower than those who do use one, and then you penalize me for your slowness by charging by the hour??!!"

She replied, "Yes, and no one has ever questioned me about it before."

I told her that her streak had just ended, and that

she ought to begin considering another kind of work, perhaps calligraphy.

I want my tax estimates done far in advance of year-end, so that I can make adjustments in my favor before it's too late. I want my design work completed in a week for my review, and my printer to give me top priority when I have an infrequent emergency request. I treat my clients with great care and responsiveness; I expect people I pay to see me as that kind of client.

> **Career Key**   Try not to hire, collaborate, or otherwise entangle yourself with staff and external help for at least the first six months and, preferably, the first year of your practice. After that, you'll have an accurate assessment of where you need help, to what degree, and what it would be worth to you.

Rule #5: Don't Confuse Ego with Business Needs

Many consultants can't bear to tell a prospect that their office is at home, they have no staff, they don't have six Ph.D.s and five MBAs, and so on. Get over it. First of all, few prospects ever ask. Most of the time, the poorly prepared consultant is busy spilling all of this irrelevant information all over the carpet. Secondly, most prospects don't care. They want to know what you can do for them, not how many phone lines you have and how many assistants are standing by to answer them.

Having an office, a staff, a payroll, and an accountability to employees does not make you a professional. It simply makes you a supporter. If you need skills and resources beyond your personal abilities, then subcontract for them, and hire only if you need them 100 percent of the time.

Some final thoughts on hiring a staff:

- ✔ I've built a seven-figure business without one.
- ✔ Managing people is not a sign of expertise or maturity.

✔ Staff must enable you to grow your business dramatically, not cause hardship through gobbling
up precious resources.

✔ Think about those people sitting there, with a secure salary, mandatory benefits, and commuting
to their homes, while you're on an airplane missing your family and also about to miss your con-
necting flight on a dank February night.

✔ You have to be able to fire them if economic circumstances dictate.

✔ Under many benefit plans, you can't take certain
advantages unless you extend them equally to
every employee. (This may limit retirement funding, for example.)

BUSINESS PLANNING

I have this to say about planning: Don't do it.

I'm not kidding. Plans have an invidious aspect
about them, in that sometimes you hit them, which is
horrible. I'll explain.

I've had a lot of clients who have plastered their
business plans on every available wall: We will grow by 7
percent in the Northeast next year. Every secretary, sales
manager, marketing director, and visitor knows clearly
what the plan is. And through constant repetition, undi-
minished focus, and fanatic dedication, the organization
indeed hits the unprecedented 7 percent growth mark in
the Northeast.

The problem is that the business should have grown
by 22 percent, given the robust economy, poor competitive services, and unique demographic shifts. But it wasn't
geared to do that. It was geared to grow by 7 percent,
which it inefficiently did.

I had a conversation once with Marsh Carter, the
former CEO of State Street Bank, which is one of the
largest and most successful custodial securities operations in the world. We were discussing the feasibility of a
new project.

"We've grown by over 20 percent compounded annually for five straight years," said Marsh. "That's almost unprecedented. A lot of people would kill to achieve that kind of growth."

"That's true enough," I said. "I just have one question."

"What's that?"

"How do you know it shouldn't have been 34 percent?"

Marsh developed a small twinkle in his eye, paused, and then replied simply, "We don't."

The project was approved.

Don't make business growth plans, no matter how grand—because they are inherently limiting. I know that this is counterintuitive. Nevertheless, you are not General Electric, where there are shareholders, Wall Street analysts, budgeting requisites, and governmental regulators staring you in the face. (And even GE had a magnificently simple overall strategy under CEO Jack Welch: To be number one or two in every market it enters, be it light bulbs, appliances, locomotives, or aircraft engines.) What you should do is put the marketing tactics in place, which we've discussed earlier, and try to maximize your business acquisition and development as the year progresses. The harder you work, the luckier you'll get. It's far better to turn down or delay business because you're generating so much than it is to scratch and claw to reach a certain predetermined ideal.

In this profession, you want a pipeline that is always active and, preferably, filled, beginning with leads and prospects, and ending with signed contracts and enduring business. The major mistake that consultants who are initially successful in the profession make is that they separate and compartmentalize "delivery" and "marketing," thinking that they can't do both simultaneously. The fatal result is that a project consumes them, eliminating all marketing activity, so that after completing one or two projects they have to begin all over again generating business. This is a crazy hand-to-mouth strategy that is always feast or famine.

It's far better to have marketing devices always in place and active, be on the lookout for continued market-

> **Career Key**   Never stop marketing. The creation of a long-term successful practice is dependent on marketing, not delivery. You are better off effectively marketing for a month without delivering a project than you are effectively delivering a project for a month without marketing. This is a tough, counterintuitive lesson for most consultants.

ing opportunities even while implementing,[1] and constantly bring on board new business, rather than fitfully starting and stopping. The goal is to develop a long-term, viable business, not to generate individual consulting assignments. A business plan tends to reward the latter and ignore the former. Don't waste your time with one.

Talking to Consultants

Q. If you were starting all over today, but knowing what you now know, what would you do differently?

A. If I were starting over from scratch (I can't believe it's been over three years), the key thing I'd do is focus on internal clarity. As a consultant in the information technology field, I've been able to set myself apart from most consultants by bringing clarity to my clients' projects. With clarity comes clearly defined inputs, processes, outcomes, expectations, and, ultimately, project success. I'm very good at helping others define this clarity. What I'd do differently is focus on clarity when defining the features, benefits, and detriments of my own company. What is it they say about shoemakers' children?

Q. What's the biggest surprise you found in building your practice?
A. The biggest surprise I've found is how easy it is to sell services to people after you've told them how to do it themselves. For instance, our primary customers are chief information officers. With their focus on Y2K, we found ourselves helping them to organize and manage their year-2000

(Continued)

Talking to Consultants (*Continued*)

projects. One of the areas we focused on was top-down contingency planning, where you define how the workers will get their jobs done while the technicians are fixing the problems. It wasn't until we wrote an article that thoroughly described the planning process that we began to get lots of business. And, the sales process was extremely short. In fact, I actually sold a $60,000 contingency planning engagement in five minutes over the phone, because the prospect had read and understood the entire process that would occur if he hired us.

Q. What do you wish you had known better and earlier?

A. The one thing I wish I'd known is the massive difference a subtle change in wording can have. For instance, most IT consultants will tell you that one of the biggest reasons projects fail is a lack of clearly defined requirements. I agree with the "clearly defined" part, but the word "requirements" should not be used, because it creates an adversarial reaction. When you ask the buyer for requirements, the answer is from an "I must have" point of view. It's much better to ask for "conditions of satisfaction," because the answer comes from an "I'll be happy with" point of view. This results in a collaborative effort to define project features, instead of a contest of wills. I use this same wording change in my sales process. The result can be seen almost immediately in the quality of the relationships I establish. If I knew then what I know now . . .

—Gill Wagner, principal, Orbtechprojects.

CREATING PASSIVE INCOME

If value-based fees enable you to deliver consulting expertise without being dependent on labor-intensive practices, products and certain services can create income without the need to show up anyplace at all. When you reach a certain point in your career—and it may be much earlier than you'd suspect—you can create products and services that will generate income while you sleep.

We've spoken earlier about the use of print, audio, and Internet materials for marketing purposes, which may double as products. In moving to the next level and further developing your practice, these credibility items can also become substantial revenue generators.

Career Key After your first year in business, as you've gained clients, experiences, and repute, try to create at least two products a year thereafter. In no time at all you'll have a catalog of products providing passive income.

Here are some examples of products and services to consider, depending on your expertise, comfort, and interests:

- ✔ Booklets and pamphlets.
- ✔ Manuals, guides, templates, and checklists.
- ✔ Audiotapes.
- ✔ Videos.
- ✔ Self-published books.
- ✔ Commercially published books.
- ✔ Newsletters.
- ✔ Licensing your technology or methodology.
- ✔ Testing, assessments, and evaluations.
- ✔ Remote advice and coaching.
- ✔ Combinations of the above to form "albums" or "libraries."

There are others. Simply bear this in mind: If you can create passive income of just $500 per week, *you've generated a quarter of a six-figure income without ever leaving your home.* That amount alone can pay a mortgage, finance private schooling, fund a SEP–IRA (simplified employee pension individual retirement account), pay off significant indebtedness, and so forth.

Here are some shortcuts and secrets to effectively creating products and services that will generate significant passive income:

✔ *Design from the buyer's perspective.* Don't create a tape or booklet with everything you know about strategy formulation and call it How to Set Strategy Using the 14D

Questar Process. Create the product focused on immediate, practical help to the buyer, and use a title such as How to Get Everyone to Support Your Strategy Every Day. People are interested in tomorrow's business improvement, not theoretical excursions that make them work hard.

✔ *Provide choices.* This is our options tactic again, but it works. Try to have a choice of booklets, a choice of print and audio material, a choice of electronic or hard copy. Let people decide which products to buy, not whether they should buy.

✔ *Be contrarian.* Don't be the four millionth person to write about teamwork. Write instead Why Teams Don't Work, and make your points in that context. Stand out in a crowd. Challenge the potential buyer.

✔ *Accept credit cards.* It's easy to arrange for an electronic terminal right on your desk through your local bank and/or American Express. If you accept MasterCard, Visa, and American Express, you'll cover 99.9 percent of the waterfront, which is good enough. The fees for accepting credit purchases are small compared to the dramatically increased business you'll receive. Arrange for your web site to use a secure server, so that people can confidently provide credit information over the Web. Similarly, have a discrete phone line and/or voice mail option for product orders that only you access. Accept orders by mail, voice, fax, Internet, and on-site (e.g., when you speak at a conference). Establish a privacy policy so that people are assured their names and addresses won't be sold or shared.

✔ *Keep audiotapes to 30 minutes per side,* which is approximately auto commuting time for most people. This is by far the most popular tape length. Consider parallel CDs so that you cover all tastes in media.

✔ *Obtain ISBN numbers for all products* and make sure they are carried by Amazon.com, other Internet providers, and as many other sources as you can convince. (For newsletters: ISSN.)

✔ *Take pains to create and maintain timeless products.* Don't use examples with dates, or examples that can easily be dated. Avoid passing fads and temporary buzzwords. The less dated the material appears, the longer shelf life it will have without need of revision.

✔ When you do reprint, *make some small changes and thereby update the copyright date*, so it always is as recent as possible.

✔ If you commercially publish a book, *ensure that the contract contains a reversion of rights clause*, which enables you to publish the book yourself once the original publisher declares it out of print. Even after paying to print it, you'll still make a profit of almost 90 percent on a hardcover, compared with the 10 percent to 15 percent the publisher was paying you in royalties. And the marketing value of keeping a book with your name on it, "as originally published by . . . ," is significant.

✔ *Include product catalogs* as a normal part of your press kit, speech handouts, client information, and other relevant packages. These are often handed around, filed, or otherwise kept, and people will eventually order something. They may ignore your catalog, but they definitely won't order if they don't have one.

✔ *Provide services*—such as business coaching, mentoring, surveys—*that can be done from the comfort of your office at convenient times.* You can't build a business solely on these, because credibility and word of mouth are so important; but you can build a nice source of income from them once you have established something of a reputation.

✔ *Be vigilant for joint venture partners* who will bear the cost of product development and promotion in return for your intellectual property. There is a constantly growing number of Internet training, video production, audio production, and print publishers who are seeking such relationships. In return for a smaller piece of the pie, you are freed of all production costs, fulfillment responsibilities, and bad debts. In addition, these arrangements can usually be fashioned so that you can have your own version of a product that you continue to sell under certain circumstances.

✔ *Keep abreast of what the competition is offering.* Find out what your clients are buying. I consistently browse my clients' bookshelves, internal course offerings, and libraries to find out what's popular and why. I started producing audiotapes when I found out how much clients love to listen to them in their cars.

Product development and passive income sources probably aren't for everybody. But they can be a quite natural investment and by-product of growing your own practice successfully. One thing I know I would have done differently is to have created products much earlier in the life cycle of my own firm.

WORKING INTERNATIONALLY

All businesses are increasingly global businesses, and yours should be no exception. While some consultants prefer never to leave their general geographic area, others realize that maximum learning and business development occur when they are willing to board airplanes.

The best way to work internationally is to work with multinational, U.S.-based businesses, or the U.S. headquarters of an overseas-based multinational. By doing excellent work locally, and by developing relationships with people here, you are relatively well positioned to do business with their colleagues overseas.

Career Key   The international marketplace will continue to grow for the consulting profession, and American consultants enjoy a high reputation abroad. You can begin to avail yourself of that happy dynamic very early in your career if you focus correctly.

An example of a U.S.-based global company would be Merck, or Ford, or Coca-Cola. An example of foreign-based global companies with North American headquarters here would be DaimlerChrysler, Allianz Insurance, or Sony. When you work with such firms locally, you're almost guaranteed to meet foreign nationals who are here on a temporary or rotational assignment. American expertise is highly respected in most parts of the world (in Asia we're often called "the wise men from the East," which is overstated but makes my point), and is an ongoing import of most nations seeking management improvement. It is not unusual for people in their first year in consulting who are in my mentoring program to acquire overseas business commensurate with their U.S. business development.

Here, then, some tips on fostering an international business.

Ten Tips for Generating International Business

1. Use the Internet. Produce a first-rate web site as described previously, and use articles, tips, techniques, and references that have a global appeal (or an appeal to a particular part of the world you'd like to work in).[2]

2. Keep culturally neutral. Don't be xenophobic, and don't focus on strictly U.S. events. There are plenty of international occurrences, from the European Economic Community struggling with a common currency transition to the growing capitalistic mentality in China, to give some variety to your examples and focus.

3. Develop overseas contacts. Subscribe to *The Economist* or the *International Herald Tribune* (both great publications, and in English). Look up the Hong Kong Management Association on the Web, and see what they're doing and offering. Write to colleagues in your trade associations who reside abroad.

4. Market to trade associations that host international conferences. The Young Presidents Association holds meetings all over the world. The Institute of Management Studies has local chairs in London and Amsterdam. Most international

trade associations, from retailing to banking, hold conferences all over the globe.

5. Build your international and cultural knowledge. Read articles from the international sections of *Business Week*, *The Wall Street Journal*, and other periodicals with international coverage. Do some research about your areas of focus and expertise as they apply to other countries (but be aware that much cultural transition information you'll hear is wrong, and perpetuated by people who have never been abroad).

6. Learn to value diversity. The differences in gender, race, ethnicity, sexual orientation, background, and other factors that enrich the American business environment are representative of what you'll encounter overseas. The more practice you have in diverse environments here, the better equipped you'll be to handle diversity there.

7. Seek out consultants who have worked successfully overseas. Network with them and find out how they started and what mistakes they made. Don't attempt to reinvent the wheel. Who knows—they may just need subcontracting help, which is as good a way as any to start.

8. Focus on a single country or locale. Many consultants have focused on primarily English-speaking countries, which greatly reduces initial difficulties. Some focus narrowly on a single country, attempting to get work, say, in England or Australia. In the early stages, barring serendipity, it's a good idea to limit the search in this manner.

9. Try Canada first. We take it for granted too often, but it's a fine place to work and, although English is predominant in the West, the significance of French in the East will get you accustomed to a bilingual environment. It is easier than ever to do business in Canada, and Americans are welcomed across the longest undefended border in the world.

10. Be alert for serendipity. Keep your radar tuned. You may meet someone at a conference who's an officer of a German company, or you may see a request for help in Peru listed in the back of a management journal. You may publish an article and get a request to reprint it in Italian. Respond strongly, and pursue whatever possible areas of synergy may exist.

Career Key Be bold in your marketing plans. Even if you fail to reach the goal, you'll have advanced significantly. Never create modest goals for yourself, out of fear that you'll achieve them and be content.

Most consultants who do not work internationally are those who choose not to pursue such work, either consciously or unconsciously. How far can you go if you pursue it? Well, I've been to 54 countries as of this writing.

INVESTING IN LONGER-TERM POTENTIAL

If you have the attitude, means, and/or determination, there is a variety of things you can do to build your business to the next level in a more aggressive manner. Some consultants prefer to wait until they have some money in the bank from early business success; others feel that life is short and want to accelerate the process. In either case, it's never too soon to at least contemplate the more dramatic ways to grow your business, so that you're always creating some stretch goals for yourself.

Become a Trade Association Leader

I've listed some of the more prominent trade associations earlier in the book, and you'll find more details in

Appendix D. There are also many more local and regional organizations to consider. Most of these trade and professional associations don't exactly have a line of people waiting to run for office. In fact, most are desperate for talented, creative, and energetic professionals to assume key responsibilities, so much so that I know a person who served on three different trade association boards simultaneously, without breathing hard.

Begin by joining the association, attending every meeting, and networking. Then offer to make a presentation to the group, serve on a panel, or coordinate a fundraiser. Volunteer for a committee chair, especially something that no one else likes to do: programming, membership, treasurer, and so on. Then run for a seat on the board. Most of the time, a nomination is as good as an election because the seats are uncontested. That means that the nominating committee is the key, so that's where your networking, volunteering, and support will pay off the most.

Many of these organizations have a progression of president-elect, president, and immediate past president, meaning that you'll have an apprenticeship and a guaranteed three-year stint in a highly influential position.

Leadership in a trade association at the local level affords the opportunity to meet key people on an intimate basis (guest speakers, national officers, etc.), form relationships with other organizations with which yours collaborates, and gain visibility as a leader in the profession. You will also have the opportunity to run for a national office, present at regional and national conventions, publish in association periodicals, and network with an enormous portion of the membership. This is a strong accelerator of learning and visibility that you can begin quite early in your career.

Publish a Column

I have colleagues who are syndicated in business publications and/or metropolitan newspapers. Some publish weekly in 6, some in 36 publications. Other colleagues publish their own faxed column to a subscriber base every week. After publishing a contrarian article early in my career ("Why Quality Circles Don't Work") of 650 words in a training newsletter, the editor asked for another, and I went on to write 72 consecutive columns, one a month for six years. The reprints served for a decade as invaluable marketing tools.

A regular weekly or monthly column—whether syndicated or simply appearing in a single publication—provides for a consistency of visibility and a forum for your philosophy and approaches. Advertisers appear consistently in select media over long periods of time because research shows that people are influenced over time by repetitive exposure. Similarly, your appearing consistently in print, on the Internet, or by newsletter will create a buzz about you.[3]

For years, a consultant acquaintance of mine had the great visibility of writing the end piece in the prestigious *Management Review*, a monthly business magazine once published by the American Management Association. You never know until you ask. Start modestly with a local weekly business newspaper and work your way up if you must. *Hint:* The minimum frequency for effective influence is monthly; quarterly is too infrequently.

A column will provide credibility, leads, reprints, exposure to additional publishing opportunities, the core material for a book, introduction to people in the media, and very high visibility. You can begin pursuing this at any time you have the energy, nerve, and ideas to sustain a continuing column.

Develop into a Professional Speaker

We've discussed speaking as a marketing device, but I'm talking here of becoming a keynote speaker at conventions and business meetings. This is a discipline requiring discrete skills, but it's a lucrative one from three aspects.

First, non-celebrity keynoters demand anywhere from $3,500 to $15,000, depending on the event, for about 45 minutes to an hour of platform time.[4] Second, I have closed huge consulting contracts after addressing virtually every key manager and executive in an organization, establishing credibility and rapport, and suggesting ways that they can improve their condition—all within an hour while being paid five figures. That's not a bad day's work.[5]

Third, clients don't want to have to educate a lot of people, and one person who can do many things is that much more valuable and economical to them. As a consultant who can also address the annual convention, deliver the results of a project to a major management meeting, or address the parent company of the local operation while representing local management's choice well, you provide exponential value to your client.

Professional speaking will create a second source of income, generate incredible visibility, provide for additional products (audiotapes and videotapes are easily created), and raise your stature as a consultant. Just remember, you're a consultant who speaks, not a speaker who consults. The former position holds far more credibility.

At this point we've covered the creation and growth of your business, and how to then raise it to ensuing and higher levels of success. We have one issue left to address: What happens when you get there?

Final thought: Your success is never relative to someone else's, because there's always someone who's making more, running faster, driving harder. Your success is a function of exceeding your life goals, which are uniquely yours. Consulting is a wonderful profession, but it's a means to another end.

NOTES

1. For example, reaching out laterally to additional buyers within the current client, as discussed earlier.

2. This could be something as simple as using soccer instead of baseball in a sports analogy, or citing Mercedes as an example of a large merger. If you wanted to focus on, say, Australia, then use Australian Rules (a type of soccer/football hybrid) and talk about Qantas Airlines.

3. A warning here: *Do not* fall for the blandishments of radio stations that want you to host a program and charge you for the privilege. This is a scam. The audience is not suitable for you, and the radio station is simply playing on ego—yours—to gain some revenue. For some reason, professional speakers are constantly taken by this scam, perpetuated most aggressively by a radio station in Providence, Rhode Island. Don't forget: The talent usually gets paid, not the other way around.

4. I'm talking here of non-celebrity speakers who are not in the news or voracious self-promoters, but who are merely competent, engrossing speakers who do a good job for their clients. See my book *Money Talks: How to Make a Million as a Speaker* (McGraw-Hill, 1998) if you want to pursue the business aspects of making it big on the speaking circuit.

5. One executive vice president who ran up on the stage to thank me during sustained applause said into my still-live mike, "We're hiring you!"—which gained even louder applause, including my own!

Chapter

10

What Do You Do with Success?

How to Continue to Grow by Paying Back

T he wonderful thing about the profession of consulting is that you are paid to learn, which makes you more valuable to the next client, who will pay you even more to learn still more, which makes you still more valuable to the next client, ad infinitum. There aren't too many professions that create a cycle of value that drives fees up and accelerates learning. Lawyers don't have it, nor do physicians, nor do most business executives.[1]

This dynamic means that there isn't a prescribed dues-paying tenure in the profession. Some of you reading this book may become very successful very rapidly, and many of you could become highly successful more quickly than you thought. It's never too early to prepare for success, and the worst condition of all is to be caught in the "success trap," wherein rapid, early success causes you to believe that this is all there is and you're stuck on a relatively moderate plateau forever, no longer learning, no longer increasing your value, and dead in the water at far too early a point in your career. Figure 10.1 shows the plateaus that are the success traps that undermine continued growth.

So, in no special order, here are 10 goals or pursuits to keep in mind to drive you off plateaus and keep you focused on constant growth.

MAXIMIZE RETIREMENT INVESTING

For most of you who have not entered consulting as a second, retirement career, you're not in the position of having a large company or the government taking care of your long-term future. Start a retirement plan immediately, and try to maximize your contribution to it, especially the tax-free incentives.

Most consultants who enter the field at a younger age put off retirement planning as a luxury, and plunge

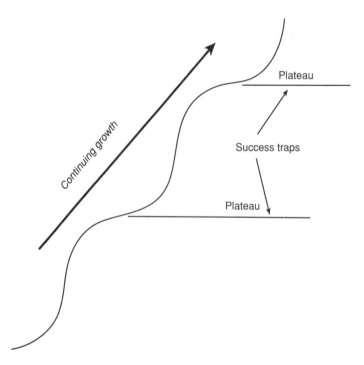

FIGURE 10.1 The success traps.

profits back into the business, or use them to pay off indebtedness, or simply live large. With some intelligent planning, these are not mutually exclusive goals. It's as important, for example, to invest in a tax-free retirement account as it is to pay down debt. The reason is that the younger you are when you begin, the more opportunity there is for the investment to grow and the relatively less you have to put away, since you have the benefit of time and compound interest.

> **Career Key** Spend as much time planning for the long-term future as you do for the short-term future. The long-term is short-term before you know it.

Consult your financial adviser on the best vehicle for your circumstances. But you can shelter an increasing amount of money ($40,000 maximum at this writing, depending on age, but scheduled to increase over the years) in a SEP–IRA (simplified employee pension individual retirement account). This donation is paid by the company in pretax, deductible dollars, and gains interest and dividends from your chosen investments tax-free until withdrawn. Moreover, the investments are determined by you, be they stocks, bonds, or other kinds of qualified investments. A regular IRA, in which you can contribute up to $2,000 at this writing, can be made only with after-tax salary dollars, but all of the subsequent appreciation is tax free until withdrawn, and a nonworking spouse can also make that investment. Roth IRAs are increasingly favored by many financial advisers at the moment. Your firm can create a Keogh or 401(k) plan, subject to your organization and personal situation. These latter plans provide for the company to use pretax dollars to match your own contributions, and also allow for diverse investments.

Some retirement alternatives require that all employees be automatically included, but that is a moot point when you are the sole employee, or your spouse is also an employee of the firm.

At the very least, you should plan to invest the maximum amount permitted by current laws into your SEP–IRA or Keogh or 401(k) plans (usually these are mutually exclusive devices). As an overall guide as you become more successful, try to invest a minimum of 5 percent to 10 percent every year in retirement investments. You want to place yourself in the position that enables you to determine what kind of work you will take on in later years, and not be forced to take on whatever is available because you need the money.

Intelligent retirement planning and investing right from the outset is an important part of your business strategy.

MENTORING

The finest way to learn that I'm aware of is by teaching. I learn more than my clients do every time. Consequently, I've begun a large-scale mentoring program that has now had nearly 400 graduates. This interaction has kept me in touch with all aspects of the profession (and enabled me to authoritatively write books like this one), and has exposed me to many consulting situations through the mentorees that I don't personally experience (e.g., small business, education, government, technology, etc.).

Once you've achieved a modest measure of success (and, remember, this is not time related), you can begin to consider serving as a mentor. You don't have to do it on my scale. Simply offer your help to someone who is currently where you were when you started or were at an earlier point in your growth. The mentoring can be quite informal—"Call me if you need to bounce something off me"—or quite systematic—"Let's meet twice a month to talk about your issues."

When you mentor others, you can't help but learn yourself, you establish a name as someone investing back in the profession, and you might just find some people whom you get to know well who might make significant contributions to your own business as subcontractors or even employees.

Here are some guidelines for effective mentoring:

1. Don't choose someone exactly like you. That doesn't maximize learning. Consider someone of the other gender, different racial background, different consulting focus, and/or different geography (you can effectively mentor by phone and e-mail).

2. Use diagnosis, not prescription. Help the other person to understand the issues and to arrive at solutions. Don't merely provide answers, templates, or your own experiences, which are too easy an outcome (and may be ineffective for others).

3. Use real-time consulting, and encourage the mentoree to contact you when an actual meeting, proposal, or intervention is approaching.

4. Vary the media, so that fax, e-mail, correspondence, phone, and personal interaction are mixed, as issues may require.

5. Create a disengagement point. There will be a juncture at which the learning curves of both you and the mentoree will flatten. It's time for both of you to find new partners.

6. Don't attempt to collaborate. Money will only complicate things. You may choose to take the mentoree along on a call or a project visit if appropriate, but don't attempt to actually work together, which mars the mentoring relationship.

7. Try to provide some leads as well as suggestions. There may be business that you choose not to pursue, or some avenues that were fruitful for you some time ago. Provide substantive help if possible.

8. Make sure the fundamentals are in place. Many people jump the gun and ignore the essentials, such as press kit, networking, and so on. Use

this book as a template to ensure that the basics are in place for the mentoree.

9. Do not reveal confidences. It is unnecessary in your mentoring to provide specific client names, examples, or outcomes. Always observe your duty to your clients first.

10. Have a good time. You don't want to take on someone else's stress. Make sure that discussions are lighthearted and positive. If a mentoree is sapping your energy, simply end the relationship.

Once you've become successful in consulting, you should make it a habit of always having a mentoring relationship with someone.

PROFESSIONAL GROWTH

Most of us who make it big in consulting do so as lone wolves. If that is your situation (or even if you're in collaboration with one or two others), you must take precautions to maximize your professional growth and not become a hermit.

As your success grows, also increase both the number of professional organizations to which you belong and your profile in the organizations. Take on more of a leadership role, to ensure that you are as interactive with others as possible.

Organize a reading regimen that puts you in touch with both contemporary writing on consulting and the classics in areas such as leadership, communication, and other organizational needs. Get to the books you've heard others talk about but haven't yet read. Aside from recreational reading, a growing consultant should read at least one professional book a month in his or her field.

Think about teaching at some level. The local colleges or community colleges may be interested in a course on consulting skills. Or a professional association may be having a convention that lends itself to such a theme. In creating and organizing some kind of course you'll be forcing yourself to critically examine what you do, how you do it, and why it's of value.

Consider acquiring new skills that may require formalized instruction. Many consultants pursue M.B.A.s or Ph.D.s part-time. However, you can also learn about coaching, facilitating, strategic planning, mergers and acquisitions, and a plethora of other fields through seminars, workshops, and courses. Why not deliberately and systematically expand your own competencies?

Finally, use reverse mentoring. That is, find someone to serve as your mentor, someone who will force you out of your comfort zones and demand that you stretch. The key to finding a terrific mentor is not to pursue someone who is at the very top of the profession, but to find someone who two years ago was where you are now. He or she will be most familiar with your current situation, and have relevant, timely experiences and perspective to share.

RETAINERS

At a given level of your success, some clients will just want to have access to your smarts, and will not be so concerned about specific projects and objectives. They will, in essence, want you on call in the event you're needed. Sometimes this will be reactive, in the case of some emergency, and sometimes it will be proactive, in the case of a new initiative being planned.

If you're comfortable with the ambiguity, accept this kind of business gladly, but do so on a retainer basis, not on a per diem basis. Retainers are simply variants of project fees.

Career Key The more you learn, the more valuable you are. Learning and professional growth are investments in your future. Never shortchange your own development, and never assume that you know all you need to know. The only guaranteed condition in the world from inactivity is obsolescence.

Never guarantee a number of days for a retainer relationship (e.g., "I'll be available for one day a week or seven days a month"). Simply promise to be available as a resource, and that actual on-site visits will be subject to mutual scheduling convenience. The client should always pay for travel expenses, so that is not an issue in determining your fee.

I recommend a minimum of 90-day retainers. I like to structure them this way: "I will be available to you as a general consulting resource for a fee of $7,500 per month.[2] The minimum period is three months, and the fee is to be paid at the beginning of the period. Thirty days before the end of the period, both of us will determine whether to extend it for another, similar period."

This arrangement means that you are paid, in my example, $22,500 at the beginning of the first month. You don't have to worry about how many times you show up, and you needn't worry about how many times the client calls on you (on-site visits are subject to your schedule and the client pays the expenses). If the client committed to six months of this arrangement, I might lower the fee to $6,500 per month (now I'm being paid $39,000), and for a year, perhaps $5,000 ($60,000).

Clients virtually never abuse retainer relationships; the work can often be accomplished over the phone and by e-mail; expenses are protected; your scheduling is protected; and the money is in hand. If you can establish two or three of these annually as you become more successful, you'll find that you're making more and working less. I guarantee it, if you use my system.

SELECTIVE PROJECT ACQUISITION

As you become better known and the gravity of your marketing approaches draws more and more interest to you, you can begin to selectively choose your projects and clients. At the outset, we all tend to take on whatever we can to put bread on the table and create some momentum, but too many of us continue in that vein long beyond the need. For several years I accepted full-day training assignments, which I loathed, but which paid well and kept me active in attractive clients. But as soon as I could afford to, I gracefully left those assignments and declined similar, new ones, which allowed me to reach out to better and more fulfilling opportunities.

There is nothing wrong in being selective about the work you accept. Here are some guidelines that may be useful in determining which work you accept and under what conditions:

✔ Do you enjoy the work? Will you have a good time and be happy? Or will you be stressed, miserable, and regret it later?

✔ Does the work force you to grow? Will you learn new techniques, operate in new environments, meet a new type of person? Or can you do this blindfolded and it's the same old same old?

✔ Does it pay well? Are you making money commensurate with the value you are delivering? Or are you accepting this because the client is accustomed to an old price, or you might as well get something rather than nothing?

✔ Will it contribute to life balance? If you want to travel more, does it provide for it? Or if you want to travel less, will it allow you to stay local? Will it intrude on your personal life, or will it enhance your personal life?

✔ Is it high-visibility work? Will you become better known for having done this work? Does the client offer greater recognition? Or will you labor in obscurity? Does the project require that you immerse yourself solely with this client for a prolonged period?

✔ Will the work provide a springboard? Can you gain entry into other divisions, related organizations, industry trade associations, and additional opportunities? Or is the work a singular, one-time experience that offers no leveraging or affiliations?

✔ Would you be proud of it? Is it ethical, proper, and important work that could boldly appear on the front page of *The Wall Street Journal*? Or is it rather marginal, shady, and questionable, like downsizing or multilevel marketing, where you'd just as soon have no one know that you were involved?

✔ Is it cutting edge? Are you in a position to take a role in industry-leading change? Or is it hackneyed and stale, and something that everyone has done a thousand times?

✔ Will it contribute to publishing? Can you incorporate it in a book or in an article, or collaborate with the client to write about the experience? Or is it humdrum and tiresome, or so secretive that you're precluded from mentioning it?

✔ Will the relationship endure? Can you think of the fourth sale? Might this create an annuity for years to come? Or is this simply a one-shot, singular event with no longer-term potential?

Once you're in the position to be selective, apply some template or criteria to your new business opportunities so that you can mold the future of your firm and of your own growth. That's a wonderful position to be in, but one that many consultants either can't see or choose to ignore.

TRAVEL

Let me admit to a bias here: I think that travel is fulfilling and educational, particularly when you can control or influence it. If you have a spouse or partner whom you can bring with you, it can become absolutely invigorating, and build even better relationships.

I've had the good fortune to have visited 54 countries and 49 states, as of early 2003. I plan to build on my country list (although I don't know about finally getting

Talking to Consultants

Q. What do you do differently today from when you started?

A. Long gone are the hourly and per diem rates! That approach truly diminishes how clients perceive your value. Today I assess how I can solve the client's particular need and provide a project fee that is based on the value of the solution. I now take on more focused assignments, with shorter time frames. I've learned that clients have more respect for consultants who expediently solve problems. (And if you're good, they'll be calling again for help.)

Q. What was your biggest surprise?

A. The really huge value of a good reputation. Throughout my career I've always gone the extra distance, whether it's been helping clients think through issues unrelated to my assignments, like their next career move, or spending extra time with employees to help them accelerate their careers. Honesty, frankness, helpfulness, intellectual curiosity, integrity, and plain niceness have always been my mantra. Yet at some points of my career I saw more politically astute and ruthless colleagues surge ahead, and I wondered if I were the fool. Yet today, I can tell you I'm way ahead. Almost all of my assignments come from referrals and a reputation for being both smart and rich in integrity.

Q. What one piece of advice would you provide to other consultants?

A. Dig very deep into your soul to find out not only *what* you like to do, but also *how* you like to work. In my case, I've found that I'm invigorated by short-term assignments (less than three months) in which I work intensely with the CEO and her or his executive team on critical, deadline-driven needs.

—Lois Kelly, president, Meaning Maker, Inc.

to North Dakota). When I visited South America frequently, I learned to speak some Spanish. Recently, I was able to converse in Spanish with the concierge at the Wyndham Palace Hotel in Orlando, and we established a wonderful rapport. There was no request I could make that was inconvenient or burdensome. Travel and its by-products constantly increase our depth and our appeal.

Someone asked me once why travel was so important when current media allow you to view the world from your home. I told them it was the difference between seeing it in black and white and a million colors.

Once you're on a roll of sorts, begin to think about where you'd like to go for vacations and how you can build business around those areas. If your children are grown and living elsewhere, or your own parents are in a distant city, you may want to schedule periodic business in those locales.

Career Key   At the right time for you, begin to steer your marketing toward geographic locations that are appealing to you. Generate your leads and create your gravity from those areas you want to visit.

As you travel for business, you'll amass a bewildering assortment of frequent flier points, hotel points, credit card points, and a myriad of variations on those themes. My advice is to restrict your purchases and travel to those suppliers who offer the best deals, and build sizable bankrolls of these perks. (Some sources, such as American Express and Diners Club, allow you to transfer points to any number of travel partners.) Don't use them for frivolous trips or business trips, or fritter them away for minor upgrades. Save them so that you and a partner can fly significant distances in first class, stay in suites in fine hotels, rent cars for free, and enjoy other benefits. When you combine the trips with business, the client will offset most of your remaining costs.[3]

How can you focus your marketing to reach places you'd like to visit? Here are some ideas:

✔ Publish in those localities.
✔ Offer to do some pro bono work for expenses only for nonprofits in those areas.

✔ Contact the local chapters of trade associations you belong to and ask if they would entertain the prospect of you as a guest speaker.

✔ Contact local trade associations to determine what the local business climate is and who the top prospects may be.

✔ Tear articles out of the newspapers and magazines you read about the area so that you can create a targeted strategy.

✔ Find out whether your existing clients have offices or facilities in the area, and investigate how you might work for them.

✔ Use the Internet to research the area, and find out what prospects might be closest to your ideal buyer.

✔ Investigate subcontract work with firms you know are doing business in the area.

✔ Arrange for business beyond that point, and arrange for a stopover on the way out or back.

✔ Identify a local hotel and offer consulting services in barter for room nights.

Too many consultants view travel as an inescapable evil of the profession. After you've established yourself, travel can actually be a rich enhancement to your job and your life.

CELEBRITY STATUS

There are celebrities and there are celebrities. Some people are well known for exploits in their field (e.g., Colin Powell), and some are well known for, well, being well known (e.g., author and speaker Harvey Mackay). However, some people become well known within more limited bounds for their expertise and competence. And therein lies your possible celebrity.

I'm going to define *celebrity* for our purposes as "that status which confers upon you a credibility and competence

 celebrity that status that confers upon you a credibility and competence that is spoken about by others and readily accepted without further proof or validation by those who do not know you.

that is spoken about by others and readily accepted without further proof or validation by those who do not know you."

> **Career Key**   There is nothing illegal or immoral about creating a certain public persona for yourself. Don't be shameless, but don't be bashful, and if you have to choose one over the other, be shameless. If you don't toot your own horn, there is no music.

You need to be proactive about creating celebrity for yourself, but it's not as difficult as it might sound once you have some successful projects under your belt and your gravity has been effective for a while. No one else is going to do it for you, and the harder you work at it, the luckier you'll get.

Here are some techniques that might be useful to establish a celebrity about yourself.

1. Have a presence on the Internet in all forums and discussions that touch upon your chosen field of celebrity. Aggressively go after the editors and sponsors to make your case for inclusion.

2. Publish articles that are contrarian, innovative, and different, so that you are seen as an original thinker in the field. Don't simply reinforce the chosen path.

3. Write letters to the editor whenever publications print articles or interviews about your field, either pro or con. Make sure that people know that you are the large fish in that pond.

4. Solicit testimonials that endorse the fact that you are the person to see when a particular issue or topic is being addressed.

5. Speak on your topic or field at major public forums, conventions, and meetings.

6. Offer your services in that field, pro bono, to local government, charities, and nonprofits.

7. Contact local newspapers, radio shows, and television shows about your expertise, offering your services if an expert commentator is ever needed on the subject in light of breaking news.

8. Start a newsletter with a subtitle such as "The foremost publication on the subject of . . ." and write the editorials, as well as soliciting articles for it.[4]

9. Host breakfasts or luncheons on the topic, and include a guest speaker and an opportunity for participants to network. Be a gracious host and an assumed expert; don't attempt to do it all yourself.

10. Send out congratulatory notes to people who achieve things in your field, showing them that you appreciate the contribution they are making to your area of expertise.

11. Establish a course on the topic at a local school or extension program.

12. If appropriate and applicable, establish a small scholarship for people studying the field, and run a small competition to determine whom it is awarded to, using outside evaluators as the judges.

Celebrity is not difficult to achieve if you establish your playing field and assiduously pursue the limelight. Once you've grabbed it, it's fairly simple to stay within the focus of others.

LIFE BALANCE

As successful as I've been in consulting, and as passionate as I am about the work, I've always viewed it as a means to an end. In my case, the end is the success of my family in finding fulfillment in life; my personal learning and growth; our ability to contribute back to society; and the flexibility that comes from security and independence. Your life goals may be different, but your perspective on your chosen career must be a balanced one.[5]

> **Career Key**   You don't refuel yourself from within the business. You do so by stepping outside of the business and recharging your batteries on life, interests, and relationships. The most successful consultants are those who have rich and diverse lives.

As you become more successful, you'll have the opportunity to transfer some of the intensity, passion, focus, time, and perseverance that you've invested in your business—and necessarily so, to launch and sustain it successfully—to your private interests, family, community, and friends. Ironically, that transfer to a greater balance of life and work will actually accelerate your business growth still more. The reason is that no one can sustain a 100 percent focus on their business for too long, or they become burned out, or bored, or bereft of ideas. The fuel is not in unlimited supply, but must be restocked and restored.

The ability to pursue nonbusiness passions, to engage in quality family time, to atone for the lost days and perhaps distant travel incurred in a business start-up is a valuable asset. The problem is that too many consultants ignore it or never see it. They believe that the route to more business growth is simply to do more and more of the same things that got them to where they are. But businesses mature in the same way that people do, and changes are required.

I've found that the truly successful consultants are those who appreciate life balance, to the extent that they significantly change their professional habits once their business becomes successful.[6] Here are some attributes and habits of those who understand and exploit the opportunities posed by business success to maximize personal growth and fulfillment:

✔ *Planned, sacrosanct vacation time once a quarter.* This might be a trip or a week spent locally, but it's totally nonbusiness and relaxing.

✔ *Personal education.* Consider non-matriculated courses, reading, membership in courses and fields of study that are personally fulfilling or have been lacking, be they art, music, cooking, architecture, or other subjects.

✔ *Reduction of work hours.* My personal bias is that consultants can make a fortune working—truly working—about 20 hours a week. If you want to double that, it's up to you, but working beyond 40 hours is seldom necessary and always stressful.

✔ *Health and well-being.* Join a gym or participate in regular sports or exercise. Keep your weight under control.

✔ *Quality, sacrosanct time with partner, children, and/or friends.*

✔ *Attention paid and time spent on investments and financial security.* Periodically reevaluate your long-term retirement and financial goals.

✔ *Intellectual breadth and diversity of interests.* You become an object of interest to others.

At some point you'll realize that you don't have a professional life and a personal life, but that you only have a life. Once the compartmentalization is overcome, and you've blended your talents, passions, and abilities into an integrated pattern of growth and success, you've achieved true life balance.

THE FIRM'S FUTURE

Because of the life balance issues, the firm's future is not the key consideration in your long-range planning. While this may seem counterintuitive, consider the fact that your business has served as a means for your individual ends. The business is not an end in and of itself.

If the firm grows to the extent that it employs people, owns significant assets (buildings, property), and has a client base along with goodwill that transcends the individual principal (you), then it is clearly an asset of value that is part of your financial planning. The firm can be sold, for example, or passed on to children. However, be careful when selling the firm to outsiders. The only thing worse than expending blood and sweat for your own equity is to do so for someone else's equity, and management contracts that bind the seller into employment for a transition period that is often several years are like indentured servitude. You haven't come this far to be someone else's employee again, so any sale of the business should be clean, with no lingering affiliations or attachments. I've seen too many once-happy former owners become embittered over what new ownership has done to "my company." Cut the strings and move on.

However, in most circumstances we are talking about solo practices with no employees and, deliberately, no major assets. In these cases, you can consider the following eventual options.

> **Career Key**   You need never retire in this profession. You can reduce the amount of assignments you accept and limit your travel, but you can continue to consult—and to write and speak—for as long as you feel able and interested. In other words, this career can continue as long as you do.

✔ Simply maintain the business ad infinitum, but with diminishing activity. The only costs will be some annual filing fees, reports, and taxes. This allows you to do some work within the corporate entity when the spirit—or the opportunity—moves you, even though you are retired.

✔ Dissolve the firm. Your attorney can do this efficiently and inexpensively. You can still retain trademarks, copyrights, and patents, as the situation merits.

✔ Sell the practice for a nominal fee to someone who has subcontracted, has interned, or is a contact from networking. This person might just enjoy taking on a known name in the field, and you can serve as an unofficial adviser. The buyer can pay you out of future profits (don't forget, your intent is not to make money from the firm's sale in this case, so anything you get is gravy).[7] Some consultants take on an associate a few years prior to their planned retirement for this very purpose. (It's quite a common technique in medical practices, for example.)

✔ Pass the business on to children, if there are any and if they are interested in the profession. What greater gift could there be for an energetic grown child than a thriving consulting practice with strong gravity and a solid reputation?

✔ Sell or merge the business with another consulting firm of similar nature, so that your clients can continue being served and the firm gains from your repute. However, beware of the need to disassociate yourself and not become someone else's employee.

GIVING BACK

When you've reached the points on the climb up the mountainside when your goals are being met, you are financially successful, and your prospects are plentiful, be sure to contribute something back to this wonderful profession. If those of us who approach the summit don't leave handholds and pathways for those further below, then we've abrogated a trust and a professional and ethical responsibility.

Ask yourself what you could have used earlier in your career, and provide it for someone you meet while networking or in a trade association. Establish a section on your web site For Consultants Only to share your insights and experiences with colleagues. Take on leadership positions in trade associations. Debunk and refute articles and commentary in the media that unfairly castigate the profession. Provide pro bono help to those organizations that need your expertise but can't afford it, not for the publicity but for the public good.

Establish a scholarship for consultants to attend conventions or further their learning. Provide resources for a local chapter of a professional trade association. Play a role in the debate on national licensing, or codes of ethics, or governance.

Make your voice heard and your presence felt. You've launched your practice, built your career, and improved the profession. Others are looking up to you. Let them hear you.

Final thought: Success is never final, and failure is seldom fatal. It's courage that counts.

—Winston Churchill

NOTES

1. All of this assumes that you are charging based on value, not time, which is why I've made that strategy so vivid in this book. Consultants who charge for their time diminish their learning and, consequently, their value.

2. This is, of course, an arbitrary example. Establish your fee based on your value or potential value to the client, your uniqueness, your past history, and so on.

3. In case you're wondering, there is absolutely nothing wrong with using a free ticket to travel to a client destination, and charging the client for coach airfare reimbursement, which should be built into your proposal in any case. The fact that you've used a free ticket or hotel room is your decision, but the client is still responsible for reimbursement of normal expenditures.

4. A colleague of mine did this many years ago and the newsletter evolved into a major magazine on executive strategy.

5. For a lengthy discussion about life balance, see my book, *Life Balance: Converting Professional Success Into Personal Happiness,* Jossey-Bass/Pfeiffer, 2003.

6. I publish a free, electronic, monthly newsletter for such people: *Balancing Act: Blending Life, Work, and Rela-*

tionships. To subscribe, simply send an e-mail to join balancingact@summitconsulting.com, or visit our web site (www.summitconsulting.com) and click on the subscription button.

7. For the record, consulting firms are difficult to evaluate for sale, and solo practices are virtually impossible. The beauty and the worth are in the eyes of the beholder. However, many valuation companies have traditionally used one to two times annual sales, or six to eight times annual profits. Others look at excess cash generated after all operating expenses, including principal's salary, are paid. Since the idea is not to leave excess profit in the business, all of these measures are suspect.

11

The Quick Start

How to Hit the Consulting Ground Running at Full Speed

This chapter is intended as a turbo-charged start for those of you seeking to enter the consulting profession both rapidly and effectively. It is not meant for people easing in while they hold current jobs, nor for those considering a part-time focus. It is designed for those who have carefully considered the profession, have read the prior chapters in this book, and who passionately seek a bold and focused entry.

Ideally, the people who will best profit from the approaches described in the following list will have these characteristics:

✔ A minimum of six months of basic living and professional expenses put aside in readily available funds.

✔ Full-time focus on entering the profession with minimum distractions.

✔ Access to resources who can accelerate the process (e.g., designers, printers, equipment suppliers, lawyers, etc.).

✔ Prudent risk takers who are willing to move forward when 80 percent ready and fine-tune the remaining 20 percent as needed.

I assume that you're starting with a tabula rasa—a blank slate—and take you through the Quick Start process from square zero. If, in fact, you've already begun to assemble your practice, then you can pick up at the appropriate point (or undo what you've done and start again with more momentum).

We deal with two basic dimensions: setting up your infrastructure and reaching out for business. They must occur in that order.

FIRST DIMENSION: CREATING INFRASTRUCTURE

Phase I: Incorporate Your Business

Don't listen to anyone who tells you not to incorporate, even if that person is an attorney (many attorneys don't understand professional services firms, believe it or not). You must incorporate immediately to create a legal entity that provides a firewall between your professional and personal assets.

Step 1: Find an attorney who specializes in incorporating professional services firms and solo practices. If you don't know of any, ask someone already incorporated for recommendations. (This is a good reason for professional networking.)

Step 2: Create a name for the business. Don't spend months on this, or even days. You can name it after yourself or use a name that's more descriptive (my company is Summit Consulting Group, Inc.). You should create several names or derivations so that the attorney can do a search to find what's legally available.

Career Key Names are overrated, in that they seldom make much of a difference in closing a sale. Consider using a "tag line" to refine understanding of what you do, for example, The Sales Acceleration Specialists or The All-Star Coach.

Step 3: Form a Chapter S, Chapter C, or limited liability company (LLC). Any of these will suffice. I favor Chapter C since that is what most major organizations use and it affords a few more deductions than do the other alternatives. But these laws change frequently, so confer with your attorney.

Step 4: Set up separate business checking and savings accounts at your bank. Have checks printed. Try to obtain at least a minimal overdraft protection on the account. If you haven't yet done so, meet the branch manager and explain that you're starting a new business and have chosen the bank as your partner.

> Cost estimate: $300 to $750, depending on state regulations. You do not have to be incorporated in your state or residence.

Time estimate: One or two weeks.

Phase II: Set Up Your Office

Whether working at home or elsewhere, you need a private and inviolate space of your own. I've worked out of my home continually for nearly 20 years.

Step 1: Alert the phone company that you'll need at least two lines in addition to your home phone line: one for a business line, and one for a fax. (You may need a third for a computer modem—see the next step—or you may choose to share your fax line for that purpose. *Never* share your computer modem line with your home or business phone line.)

Step 2: If there is a cable company in the area, seriously consider a cable connection rather than a modem. (If you already have cable television, this is an easy and cost-effective addition). If you can't obtain cable—which is lightning fast—then consider an ISDN or other more rapid form on Internet connection than a modem. This will save you over 100 hours a year, easily. (Cable is continuously connected to the Internet, for example, obviating the need for dialing anything.)

Step 3: Obtain a post office box. You can use your street address for courier service, but it's helpful for your company to have a separate address from your business.

Step 4: Create accounts with FedEx and UPS. You'll need these sooner or later and the ease and expense are improved with standing accounts. FedEx is simply the best overnight delivery service, period, even though others may be somewhat less expensive.

Step 5: Secure at a minimum the following equipment:

✔ Desktop computer and laser printer. A scanner and color printer are optional.

✔ Laptop computer for use when traveling and as a backup should your desktop crash or the dog dump coffee on it. (I favor Apple products. They are intuitive, idiot-proof, compatible with virtually any PC software, and rock-solid performers.)

✔ Two-line phone with speaker, auto-dial, and headset.

✔ Copier with decent speed and the ability to shrink or enlarge copies. (Xerox makes the most reliable one I've ever owned.)

✔ Postage meter with electronic scale. Meters are usually leased. Lease one that allows you to refill it over the phone, avoiding trips to the post office and allowing you to obtain postage around-the-clock.

✔ Fax machine with decent speed. Many people use their computers for this purpose, which is fine. I prefer a separate fax so as not to create more complications or warring applications than I need on my computer. Fax machines are very inexpensive. Most come with memory files for frequently used numbers.

✔ Combination VCR, television, and radio. You're going to need entertainment, the ability to follow some breaking news events, and the option to watch some tapes. (You may want to include DVD while you're at it.)

✔ Files for clients, prospects, research, paid bills, and so on.[1]

Cost estimate: $7,500 to $15,000, assuming you're starting from scratch with no equipment or, intelligently, you want to replace your existing personal equipment.

Time estimate: One to two weeks.

Phase III: Create Your Logo and Image

Step 1: Find a designer who will create a logo and look for your letterhead, business cards, promotional material, labels, web site, and so on. Ask people whose materials you admire for recommendations.

Career Key   An excellent source of artistic resources is an art school, school of design, or similar program. You'll find very gifted students who will work quite inexpensively and who are very responsive. The schools will sometimes have a resource list available with samples of work.

Step 2: Explain your company's purpose, audience, and the image you want to convey. Ask for several different approaches for your review. Consider a tag line if your company name needs more explanation, for example, Developing Tomorrow's Leaders Today.

Step 3: Ask for assistance in selecting the stationery, business cards, labels, and so forth, so that the paper quality, color, and formatting are of the highest quality. Do not skimp on your professional image, and do not listen to anyone who tells you that you need only electronic materials. High-level buyers like to see, touch, feel, and pass around hard copy, and aren't always technologically literate.

Step 4: Trademark, copyright, and/or register any names, phrases, or logos that may qualify. Your attorney can help you determine if these routes are applicable. You may need to consult a trademark attorney.

Cost estimate: $500 to $1,000 for graphic design, $250 to $600 for trademark and registration investigation.

Time estimate: One to three weeks.

Phase IV: Create Your Press (or Media, or Presentation) Kit

Step 1: Select a presentation folder. You can find them in stores such as Staples, in business catalogs, or online. Choose the highest quality you can afford (e.g., better finish, superior die cuts, etc.). Make sure there is a die cut for a business card consistent with the one your designer has created, and that there are two large pockets to hold promotional material.

Step 2: Either have your contact information and logo printed on it, or have that information printed on a self-adhesive label that can be placed on the kit. The former alternative is superior to the latter.

> **Career Key** Create minimum numbers of materials to start, despite inducements of lower price in higher quality. This makes it easier to change ineffective or inaccurate materials. But have no more than 100 presentation folders, and print no more than 500 sheets of letterhead, envelopes, business cards, and so on.

Step 3: Create the following basic documents for inclusion. Print them on uniform, high quality paper:

- ✔ Typical client results that accrue during your projects.
- ✔ A brief biographical sketch (not a resume).
- ✔ A list of five to ten references (it's probably too early to have testimonial letters, so use character references).
- ✔ A list of the array of services you offer.

✔ At least three "white papers" or position papers, of two to five pages each, dedicated to your value propositions (e.g., Ten Keys to Successful Leadership or Five Reasons Why Coaching Often Fails).

Put your copyright and contact information on all position papers. Separate the position papers on one side and the rest of the material on the other side of the presentation folder.

Cost estimate: From $100 to $300.

Time estimate: From two to three weeks.

Phase V: Create Your Web Presence

Some people believe that your web domain name should match your company name, but at this point, with so many names already in use, I don't believe you should subject your corporate name to web availability (hence, I didn't recommend this previously when you're incorporating to explore domain name options). My domain matches my company (http://www.summitconsulting.com) but not exactly—there is a summitconsultinggroup.com somewhere, and also a summitconsulting.net.

The key, in any case, is choosing the proper words and phrases on search engines to drive interested parties to your pages. It is, however, important to have *your own domain* and not to use generic providers such as aol or yahoo or compuserve as your home base. Therefore, your e-mail can be directed to your domain site (e.g., Alan@summitconsulting.com), which is the professional way to do it. (I've often regarded use of aol as a home site and/or e-mail source as amateur online.)

Step 1: Find professional services web sites that you admire and ask for the designer. Sometimes your graphic designer might also provide these services. However, it is not important to be geographically proximate to your web guru. I've used the same person since the inception of my site, and have never met him.

Career Key   The power in a web site is not in number of hits. It's in offering compelling reasons for (1) visitors to return repeatedly and (2) visitors to tell others to visit repeatedly.

Step 2: Of those designers whose work you admire, ask for cost estimates and references, and then check the references. These people are notorious for poor follow-up and lack of attentiveness, sometimes despite the quality of their eventual work. Avoid headaches later—after you're committed and waiting for the site to be completed—by assuring yourself now that you're in professional hands.[2]

Step 3: You write all the copy and leave the technical bells and whistles to the designer. Never allow the web person to write or alter your copy.[3] See the box for criteria you should insist on for an effective web site.

Criteria for Highly Effective Consultant Web Sites

✔   Provide value to the buyer immediately. Offer typical client results on the front page. *Do not* go on at length about your methodology. That's a sleeper.

✔   Provide testimonials or character references early. People want to know what's in it for them and what assurances they have.

✔   Provide incremental value. Post a new article, set of techniques, self-tests, or useful links every month. This will do the most to attract repeat visits.

✔   Ensure it's easy and fast to download. Many people work from laptops on the road and/or relatively slow modems. If you want to offer complex graphics, audio, or video,

Criteria for Highly Effective Consultant Web Sites (*Continued*)

> then make it optional to download and not a prerequisite for accessing the site.

✔ Ensure ease of navigation. Don't force people to use the "back" or "forward" browser controls. Provide options on every page to readily reach every other page.

✔ Break up text with simple graphics or photos. People will not sit and scroll down screens of text, no matter how fascinating you believe it to be.

✔ Make it easy to contact you. Have *all* of your contact information easily available, including street address, fax, and so forth.

✔ If and when you're ready, consider an electronic newsletter subscription on the site.

✔ Have some friends test every aspect of the site and read through everything. Even with the best of designers, broken links and blank screens aren't uncommon. Quality control checks are needed (including whenever you make changes).

✔ Always be pragmatic, not cute. No one wants to sit through lengthy start-up screens, despite the photos of your kids or of a sailing ship.

Step 4: Have your designer register your domain name annually, provide comprehensive coverage on search engines, and optimize the pages so that they are most likely to turn up in others' searches.

Step 5: Access a site such as namesecure.com to see if you can reserve your own name so that people who seek it will be forwarded to your site. For example, if someone knew of me only by name and searched for AlanWeiss.com, which is a natural attempt to find me, they would automatically be forwarded to summitconsulting.com, my home site.

Estimated cost: $2,500 to $7,500.

Estimated time: Two to four weeks.

Phase VI: Optimize Your E-mail

Step 1: With your web site complete, set up e-mail accounts with convenient providers using your domain name. I advise that you also create a backup or secondary e-mail account for emergencies in case your provider goes down. For example, you can reach me at Alan@summitconsulting.com, or astonmartin01@ earthlink.net.

Step 2: Create a signature file on your e-mail (virtually every e-mail program allows this) that includes on every e-mail your name, title, company, full address, phone, and fax. You can also provide a brief advertisement, such as Visit Our Web Site at XXXX.com for Free, Indexed Articles on improving team work in any environment.

Step 3: Begin an electronic address book, diligently inserting everyone who may be of even remote importance to you. Most programs allow you to create categories within the address book (e.g., clients, prospects, networking partners, and so on).

Estimated cost: $0 to $250.

Estimated time: One day.

Total cost: $10,900 to $24,800. AVERAGE: $17,850.

Total time: 7 weeks to 14 weeks.

If you're exceptionally aggressive (and/or a smart shopper or already well-equipped), you may beat the averages or even the minimums. For most people, from a standing start and following these criteria, however, it's reasonable to expect to be totally in business in about two months with an expenditure for all new equipment in the neighborhood of $15,000.

Case Study: Lesson Learned the Hard Way

In the game of craps (dice for the hoity-toity), you can place a high-risk bet that the number to be rolled will be made the hard way, meaning a six would require a three on each die, an eight would require two fours, and so on. It's the hard way because there is only one way to make it (as opposed to a four and a two, or a five and a one, on either die also creating the six).

I responded to a major insurance company with generic charts and graphs, and very vanilla ideas about their issues. I literally dumped my graphics file into my response to the client. They were neither impressed nor amused.

I should have taken longer to isolate the key prospect issues, done some homework, and created some approaches and visuals *exclusively prepared for them and their situation*. I was too anxious, not prepared, and much too cavalier.

Don't market until you can professionally support your marketing. Don't try to do it the hard way. With two dice, you can roll a ten with six different combinations, instead of just one combination the hard way.

SECOND DIMENSION: REACHING OUT FOR BUSINESS

You can't reach out for business unless you have your infrastructure in place. But once you have the rudiments of press kit and web site, it's time to start soliciting business.

The techniques that follow can be employed together or singly. While an aggressive approach may seem to promise the earliest new business, it's actually more productive to engage in a manageable and prudent volume of prospecting. This allows you to follow up more assiduously, learn from mistakes, and correct new efforts accordingly in real time, and generally get your feet wet without drowning altogether.

Keep in mind these four principles of rookie marketing:

1. This is the marketing business more than the consulting business. Yet you're probably far better at implementing than you are at selling. Consequently, strive to hone your business acquisition skills far more than your consulting skills at this point.

2. Quality trumps quantity. A few highly promising and high potential leads are far better than a flood of ultimately useless and pointless inquiries.

3. Rejection is the byproduct of marketing. If you're not being rejected, turned away, and otherwise impeded, you're just not trying!

4. You must schedule and implement your marketing on a disciplined basis, every day and every week, just as you would plan a project or tend the plants. Marketing doesn't happen by itself, even serendipity demands attention, and you'll find that it's magical how much it's true that the harder you work, the luckier you get.

Career Key You must view your marketing activities as your honest and diligent attempt to help bring value to people who need it, and not to separate people from their money, or as a zero-sum game that others must lose in order for you to win. Selling is a noble profession, Arthur Miller and Willy Loman notwithstanding.

MARKETING TECHNIQUE 1: CALL EVERYONE YOU KNOW

Make a list of everyone you know, no matter how distantly or casually. The list should include:

✔ Colleagues from former jobs.

✔ School alumni.

✔ Past clients and customers.

✔ Vendors and store owners you've patronized.

✔ Extended family.

✔ Mentors, coaches, and therapists.

✔ Professional providers, such as doctors, accountants, lawyers.

✔ Friends, locally and removed.

✔ Professional association colleagues.

✔ Civic association colleagues.

✔ Neighbors.

✔ Sports and recreational colleagues.

✔ Elected representatives at local and regional levels.

If in doubt at all, include people, do not exclude them. Create a computer list with as much information as you have about them. You can use sophisticated software such as Act, Goldmine, or other such as Microsoft File-Maker Pro, which I've found works fine and is much simpler to use.

If you can average 10 people per category in this list, you'll have 130 people; if you average 20 people, you'll have 260. You get the idea. Dig up the directories, old address books, phone book, and other sources of names and locations. Ask your spouse, significant other, and family members to contribute. With some perspicacity, you can probably create a list of 250 to 500 people with this assistance, depending on your age, experience, and length of time in the community.

You're going to contact every one of these people by e-mail, regular mail, fax, or phone. You can segment them into categories by communications type (e.g., close acquaintances receive a phone call) or you can randomly select.

The reasoning here is that you've referred people to your doctor, attorney, dentist, CPA, designer, hairdresser, and others, but they haven't necessarily reciprocated *because they really don't know what you do.* You're going to remedy that. There is every reason to believe that your dentist might have a general manager in his or her chair

Sample Letter or E-mail

Dear Ralph,

I'm writing to apprise you that I've created a new business called Theresa Dailey, LLC. My purpose is to provide small businesses and nonprofits with strategic direction and growth formulas, which these enterprises often overlook in the course of frantic daily business concerns.

If I can be of help to you directly, please contact me using the various addresses on this letterhead (or in the signature file below). In addition, if you know of anyone who could benefit from the value I'm delivering, I'd greatly appreciate your passing on those names to me.

If you'd like to learn more, please visit my web site: http://www.tdaily.com. I'll probably be in touch with you again in the near future as I continue to increase my customer base and add new services. Thanks in advance for your support and help.

someday who has a need to improve teamwork in the company and, that being your value proposition, the dentist can put you two together *if the dentist is aware of that value proposition.*

Note that the sample letter or fax or e-mail is brief, to the point, and asks for two favors: the opportunity to do business with this individual if appropriate, and the opportunity to receive referrals from individuals whom the recipient believes might be able to use your services. *If you have a mailing list of 300 names, and 20 percent of the recipients pass your name on to two additional people, you've now reached 420 people! Add any referrals you receive to your database, irrespective of whether they agree to see you immediately.*

The phone call would be interspersed with some small talk and responses to questions, of course, but the

> ### Sample Phone Call, including Voice Mail Message
>
> Hello, Gloria, this is Tom Wright. I worked with you on the School Board campaign a few months ago. I'm calling to let you know that I've founded a new business, and I'm concentrating on improving leadership skills for front-line supervisors and mid-managers. The company is called Walk the Talk, Inc., and I know that you may be aware of some opportunities where you work at Boeing that may be appropriate. So I want to ask two favors: If you do know of opportunities for consultants in that general area, could you point me in the right direction? Second, are there any people whom you would recommend I contact, at Boeing or elsewhere, who could use this kind of help?

basic message is nevertheless succinct and to the point. If you're leaving a voice mail message, the script above will serve nicely. Simply add to it your return phone number and/or e-mail address.

If you diligently and methodically call everyone you know over a period of about two weeks, and your beginning list is about 200 people, you should receive positive comment, help, and/or meetings from at least 25–40. And that will create a fine buzz to establish your presence, new venture, and value. Moreover, you may well just land your first piece of business.

MARKETING TECHNIQUE 2: TARGET TWELVE

This technique allows you to identify high potential targets of opportunity in a very cost-effective and logistically convenient manner.

Choose 12 organizations (or 10 or 14, but keep the

number manageable for effective follow-up) within a reasonable distance of your home. If you're in a metropolitan area, that would mean a car ride. If you're in a more remote area, it may mean a quick overnight trip.

Criteria for Choosing the Organizations

✔ Apparently have a need for the value that you deliver. You determine this from local newspapers, networking, local television and radio reports, friends who work there or know people who work there, history, library research, scanning the annual report, and so on.

✔ Operate relatively well. They needn't be all-stars, but you don't want to try to get into organizations in dire straits, about to file for bankruptcy, in the midst of massive layoffs, and so forth. (You won't get their attention and you may well not get paid even if you do.)

✔ Are within your target group, that is, small business, large business, financial services, education, and so on.

✔ Preferably have a history of using external help, which means there is a precedent for consultants and one less hurdle for you to negotiate.

Once you identify the target, make an educated guess as to whom the likely buyer would be. If you're dealing with improving sales skills, for example, the buyer would obviously be the vice president of sales; if you help with innovation, it might be the director of R&D; if you provide succession planning and career development improvement, it may be the vice president of human resources. (Note that the smaller the business, the more likely the buyer will be the president, owner, or CEO. The larger the business, the more likely there are appropriate buyers scattered throughout the ranks.)

Call the switchboard and ask for the name of the person in the position you've identified as the economic buyer. Then craft a specific letter to that person, using the issues you've identified, offering value, and asking for the opportunity to meet.

Sample Targeted Letter

Dear Ms. Hayward:

My impression is that you are facing an unprecedented challenge in finding and retaining talent in this labor market, especially without entering a bidding war with organizations far larger than yours.

My firm specializes in the efficient and effective identification, attraction, acquisition, and retention of top talent without the need to violate existing compensation guidelines or human resource practices. We can provide you with advantages in the marketplace, which include:

- ✔ Techniques that drive attractive candidates to your firm.
- ✔ Behavioral interviewing skills to quickly arrive at hiring decisions.
- ✔ Noncompensation retention and motivation methodology.
- ✔ Hit the ground running orientation and development strategies.

I've enclosed one of our position papers, Ten Techniques to Recruit the Talent You Need at the Time You Require. Many of our clients are able to employ these approaches immediately.

I'll call you at 10 on Friday, March 3 to determine if the position paper is helpful, if you would like additional resources sent, and how we might best pursue the discussion. Thanks in advance. I'm looking forward to speaking with you.

Note that in this targeted letter, you've done the following:

- ✔ Focused on a clear and high value need.
- ✔ Included specific techniques and help.
- ✔ Used very little time and asked for very little time.

✔ Suggested additional resources and value.

✔ Cited a specific contact point.

You may choose to enclose your press kit with this letter, or you may merely enclose the position paper. *Never ask the prospect to get back to you.* Always set up a positive point of contact for which you are accountable.

> **Career Key**   Immediate value and brevity are far superior to general promises and verbosity. Whet the buyer's appetite quickly and get back to the kitchen to prepare the main course.

If you call and are connected with an assistant who tells you the person is not there, say, "Well, that happens, but I am calling as promised. When will she be back? At two? Can you write me in the calendar for two and I'll call back then? Thank you." If you receive voice mail, then leave this message: "This is Tom Wright and I'm calling as promised. My phone number is 401-555-5555. If I don't hear from you by tomorrow noon, I'll try calling you again at 2 P.M."

If you target 12 organizations in this fashion and provide the value and follow-up, you are likely to get one or two appointments. If you can "target twelve" every month (only three per week), in six months you will have contacted 72 organizations and probably obtained six-to-twelve appointments with buyers.

MARKETING TECHNIQUE 3: FOCUSED PROSPECTING

You can actually waste time and money by pursuing too many prospects, many of which will be inappropriate for your value and/or unable to meet your fee requirements.

Here is a highly focused prospecting approach to maximize the quality and potential of your marketing.

Step 1: Create a list of the ideal prospect traits. Determine the ideal prospect. I've included an example following, but change this based on your own preferences and needs.

Ideal Traits

✔ History of using consultants.

✔ Within a day's trip of my home.

✔ Services or financial industries.

✔ Minimum of 250 employees.

✔ Financially strong/stable.

✔ Buyer easily identifiable.

Once you identify the traits for the ideal prospect, rate them on a score of 10–1 in terms of priority. You must start with at least one 10, and rate the others relative to the 10. In my model, it looks like this:

Ideal Traits	*Rating*
✔ History of using consultants.	7
✔ Within a day's trip of my home.	2
✔ Services or financial industries.	6
✔ Minimum of 250 employees.	8
✔ Financially strong/stable.	9
✔ Buyer easily identifiable.	10

Next, fill in the actual traits of a prospect that has come to your attention. (You should print out these blank forecasting sheets on your computer or keep a template on your computer.) I've found a prospect called Acme Mortgage Brokers. Let's continue the example.

Ideal Traits	*Rating*	*Actual*
✔ History of using consultants.	7	Use constantly.
✔ Within a day's trip of my home.	2	Overnight trip.

✔ Services or financial
industries.   6   Mortgage
lending.

✔ Minimum of 250
employees.   8   625 people.

✔ Financially strong/
stable.   9   #3 in the
industry.

✔ Buyer easily
identifiable.   10   VP
operations.

Now score the actual profile of your prospect against
the ideal. A perfect fit would gain a score of 10, and a total
misfit would be 0.

Ideal Traits	*Rating*	*Actual*	*Score*
✔ History of using consultants.	7	Use constantly.	10
✔ Within a day's trip of my home.	2	Overnight trip.	0
✔ Services or financial industries.	6	Mortgage lending.	10
✔ Minimum of 250 employees.	8	625 people.	7
✔ Financially strong/ stable.	9	#3 in the industry.	8
✔ Buyer easily identifiable.	10	VP operations.	8

Next, multiply the rating times the score for a rated
score.

Ideal Traits	*Rating*	*Actual*	*Score*	*R/S*
✔ History of using consultants.	7	Use constantly.	10	70
✔ Within a day's trip of my home.	2	Overnight trip.	0	0
✔ Services or financial industries.	6	Mortgage lending.	10	60

✔ Minimum of 250 employees.	8	625 people.	7	56
✔ Financially strong/stable.	9	#3 in industry.	8	72
✔ Buyer easily identifiable.	10	VP operations.	8	80

Finally, arrive at a total rated score by adding the final column.

Ideal Traits	Rating	Actual	Score	R/S
✔ History of using consultants.	7	Use constantly.	10	70
✔ Within a day's trip of my home.	2	Overnight trip.	0	0
✔ Services or financial industries.	6	Mortgage lending.	10	60
✔ Minimum of 250 employees.	8	625 people.	7	56
✔ Financially strong/stable.	9	#3 in the industry.	8	72
✔ Buyer easily identifiable.	10	VP operations.	8	80
Total Rated Score:	338			
Total Possible Score:	420			
TRS %:	80%			

In my example, the maximum R/S possible (all scores of 10 in every category) would be 420. The actual candidate scored 338, which is 80%, or a B. My advice is to submit every single prospect to my template so that you are ensuring that you are following up on mostly A and B prospects, filling in with C prospects when there is time, and *ignoring all other prospects*. This system will serve to ensure that you focus on the most promising areas of potential business, and that you are selecting and not settling for your prospects. (And if you don't have sufficient information to make the determinations, this means you need to find it before spending time and energy pursuing the prospect.).

QUICK START, FULL-SPEED MILEPOSTS AND DANGERS

I believe that a focused, disciplined individual can set up a highly professional consulting practice within 60 days and for less than $12,000. From a standing start, using the marketing techniques described previously, that person should have consulting income flowing within six months of start-up, and should be able to produce income that can sustain one's current lifestyle within one year.

During the overall first year, all the other aspects of this book—such as marketing gravity—should be implemented, and the start-up materials (e.g., press kit and web site) should be evolved and improved.

All of this can be done well within a 40-hour week, though you may well decide to apportion the hours in nontraditional allocations, eschewing the stereotypical nine-to-five day (one would hope). One of the great advantages of this career is being able to watch your kids play soccer at two in the afternoon and write material at seven in the morning if the spirit moves you.

If business does not occur within six months, or if the pipeline is absolutely barren after only three, don't wait longer to analyze your efforts. Not everyone makes it in this profession. Here are the likely causes of lack of business in the early going, assuming you've followed the advice provided in this chapter assiduously.

Eight Areas to Examine If You Lack Traction

1. *You have overestimated the market need.* Ask yourself if anyone else is making a living in your chosen market segment. Competition doesn't close markets; it opens and expands markets, which is why Burger King builds outlets across the street from McDonald's—they know that people go there to buy hamburgers. Is there any evidence that people are interested in buying your service?

2. *You aren't good enough at what you do.* If there is sufficient market need, are others offering more, better, or faster alternatives? Do you suffer competitively? It's hard to compete against someone with an entrenched brand, a respected book, or unique technology. Do you need additional skills?

3. *You're taking rejection too personally.* The profession requires resilience and swift recovery from setback and rejection. Some people aren't cut out for sales. If you find yourself procrastinating about picking up the phone, following-up on overdue commitments, and/or extolling your value to others, you may not be a comfortable marketer.

4. *Your support system isn't helping.* You need others—family and/or friends—to support your efforts, provide constructive feedback, serve as a sounding board, and provide solace. It's extremely tough to operate in a vacuum, but even tougher to operate in a negative environment. One of the greatest causes of start-up failure is a nonsupportive and negative spouse, for example.

5. *You're spending too much at too great a rate.* There are allures that you need to forgo and ignore. A formal office, a new car, another vacation, top-of-the-line equipment when less expensive alternatives will suffice—all of these can sap your resources and therefore attenuate your marketing efforts. Be frugal with nonessentials to the growth of the business.

6. *You are too restricted geographically.* While it makes sense to focus around your home base, this can be difficult if you're not near population centers and/or the markets most suitable for your value propositions (even New York City would be hopeless for someone who's expert in petroleum exploration). You may have to invest more to travel farther.

7. *You have insufficient contacts and/or business acumen.* Some people do create initial meetings, but nothing ever results and no business ensues. You have to walk and talk like a business person. You may be too young, or too inexperienced, or too removed from business pragmatics (a common problem for academics and human resource professionals seeking to enter consulting). Sometimes, more seasoning merits delaying your entry.

8. *The timing is really poor.* Poor timing is generally an excuse, but a catastrophic event, outbreak of illness, international turmoil, soaring unemployment, and other traumatic factors can adversely impact any start-up.

Your choices here are to wait it out or restart at a later date.

SUMMARY

This is a fabulous profession. Not everyone can make it— that is, build a sustainable practice that can provide for a superb lifestyle while creating tremendous value for clients. But for those who can, there are few better ways to make a living.

I don't guarantee success merely by following the tenets in this book or within this final chapter. But I do guarantee that by adhering to these principles you will have maximized your prospects for success and given yourself the best possible opportunity to build your career.

And that's not a bad way to get started in consulting.

NOTES

1. I've found that discount office supply stores such as Staples or even Wal-Mart offer excellent value and quality, and catalogs such as MacWarehouse provide excellent service and delivery.

2. An outstanding feature of web designers is that they are ridiculously cheap by almost any standards. They compete by undercutting each other's prices, don't under-

stand value-based pricing, and are too stubborn to change. That's fine for us, and I advise them never to read my books.

3. For those of you considering designing your own site, even if you're technically adept, forget about it. You'll use $50,000 of your time and energy to do what a good web person can do for $3,500. If you want to accelerate your entry into consulting, do not become embroiled in technical execution.

Appendix A

Business Plan to Attract Investment

Note: This is a general outline that can be filled in with your particular content. Steps 7 and 8 are usually the most important for a potential investor, and should contain considerable detail and analysis.

1. Company particulars: Name, address, legal entity (corporation, subchapter S corporation, limited liability company, etc.), phone, fax, e-mail, web site.

2. Officers and stockholders: names, addresses, positions.

3. Brief description of the firm (e.g., Acme Corporation is a consulting firm for midsize organizations, specializing in succession planning, benefits, and compensation.

4. History: When founded, under what circumstances, results to date if any.

5. Core values: What the company stands for and its purpose (e.g., respect for employees, integrity of financial systems, assisting in corporate growth through greater productivity of individuals, etc.).

257

6. Vision/mission: What you are trying to accomplish (e.g., to provide more productive workforces through intelligent pay-for-performance systems that benefit both employer and employee).

7. Market analysis: What value do you provide, who is likely to buy it, how do you plan to reach them, who is the competition, why are you superior to other approaches, what uniqueness do you bring to the market?

8. Projected revenues and expenses for the next five years: What are the sources of income, what is the probability of each source, what compensation will be paid to whom, what other expenses will be incurred, is there any other debt, is there any other source of income (e.g., royalties, interest, etc.)?

9. Other assets/uniqueness of the venture: Is there a large and assured contract with a former employer, are you publishing a book, do you speak before large audiences, do you utilize a proprietary model, is there a favorable collaboration in place, will you have passive income from products?

10. What you are seeking: How much investment are you seeking, under what conditions, with what type of reimbursement/equity/ownership, at what time, with what frequency?

11. References/credentials: Testimonials, character references, awards, public acknowledgments, basis of credibility, degrees, publications, appearances, interviews, and so forth.

Sample "To Do" Lists

N*ote:* Shorter-term lists tend to be more activity-driven, while longer-term lists tend to be more results-driven.

Daily

✔ Call three prospects:

Acme Corporation
Beta, Inc.
Omega, LLP.

✔ Write position paper for press kit.

✔ Send web designer copy for site.

✔ Set up new database for prospects.

Weekly

✔ Call 12 prospects.

✔ Write one position paper.

✔ Write one article for web site.

✔ Talk to web designer about progress.

✔ Enter all contacts into new database.

✔ Request two testimonial letters.

✔ Meet with lawyer about retirement plan.

✔ Network at association meeting.

✔ Pay bills.

✔ Research new consulting topic on Web.

✔ Call two trade associations about speaking.

Monthly

✔ Call 45 prospects.

✔ Write three position papers.

✔ Add hot topics and techniques to web site.

✔ Begin an electronic newsletter.

✔ Use database to send mailings to all contacts.

✔ Finalize press kit.

✔ Have six testimonial letters for press kit.

✔ Have retirement plan decided.

✔ Have tax estimates for year completed.

✔ Attend and network at two association meetings.

✔ Complete one-sheet for publicity.

✔ Begin literature on new consulting approach to team building.

✔ Contact six trade associations for possible speaking.

✔ Volunteer for one pro bono project locally.

Appendix C

Office Equipment Recommendations

*N*ote: While virtually all of these items can be purchased through catalogs and discount dealers, it is often worthwhile to pay slightly more at a local retailer if technical help and/or local repair capability is provided. While warranties are often not worthwhile from an investment standpoint, you should always acquire lengthy warranties for copiers and printers, since they are most apt to break down and their absence can seriously undermine productivity.

Phone

Musts: Two lines, one for business, one for home. Storage, redial, and speaker features, hold button.

Desired: Speed dial, conference call, call waiting, caller ID, headset.

Facsimile

Musts: Plain paper, memory, redial.

Desired: Storage for frequently called numbers, audible alarm for paper jams, paper out, cartridge empty, headset for use as backup phone line, copier feature for emergencies, maximum tray capacity, bin or holder for incoming pages.

Copier

Musts: Minimum 99 copies ordered at a time, accommodation for regular and legal sizes, adjustments for contrast.

Desired: Enlargement and reduction capability, single-sheet rapid feed, multiple paper trays, long-lasting cartridge, capacity to copy pages from books and manuscripts, ability to print onto transparencies, easy access to all parts to clear paper jams.

Shredder

Musts: Automatic start, minimum capacity five sheets at a time, reverse feature to unclog jams.

Desired: Can accommodate staples and other soft fasteners.

Postage Meter

Musts: Electronic (now required by law), capacity to handle at least 20 letters a day, optional feed for mailing tapes.

Desired: Electronic scale (10-pound capacity) that triggers meter with correct postage, heavy volume capability, replenishable via phone.

Computer

Musts: Maximum affordable storage and memory, access to help via phone, compatibility with external backup drive, CD-ROM, internal floppy or zip disks.

Desired: Internal modem, internal backup drive, highest possible speed; cable access.

Modem

Musts: 56K built into machine or 56K external equipment.

Desired: Internet access via cable company providing highest possible speed.

Printer

Musts: Laser jet, high-quality printing, maximum pages per minute.

Desired: Multiple trays, separate envelope feed, ability to print transparencies, easy access to all parts to clear paper jams.

Other Computer Peripherals

Logical: Scanner, color printer, trackball (requires less room than conventional mouse).

Luxury: Laptop computer, infrared connector between laptop and desktop, voice recognition system, digital camera.

Software

Musts: Word processing, spreadsheet, database management, basic graphics, Internet access.

Desired: Sophisticated graphics, calendar, road maps, contact management, secondary Internet access.

Other Office Needs

Musts: Cassette deck, television with VCR playback, radio, calculator with tape, clock, personal calendar/diary, pens/pencils/markers, packing tape with dispenser, stapler, adhesive tape with dispenser, paper clips, padded envelopes in various sizes, appropriate furniture (desk or tables, comfortable chair, lamps).

Desired: Label maker, recording device for phone, minicassette recorder (for car), laser pointer, wall scheduler, bookshelves, intercom (if living with family in a large house).

Appendix D

Trade Associations, Professional Groups, Publicity Sources

American Management Association
1601 Broadway, New York, NY 10019
212-586-8100
Publishes the excellent *Management Review*, has a fine research library service, and provides seminars, books, and even meeting space.

American Society for Training and Development
1640 King Street, Alexandria, VA 22314
703-683-8100
Probably a must for those focusing on training and related human resources issues. Publishes *Training and Development*, a monthly magazine. Hosts national events and local chapter meetings.

American Society of Association Executives
1757 I Street, NW, Washington, DC 20005-1168
202-626-2723
If you are looking for an association appropriate for your profession and interests, or want to speak to associations, this may be a logical starting point.

Communispond
300 Park Avenue, New York, NY 10022
212-486-2300
Individual or group participation to hone speaking and presentation skills, whether in meetings or with the media.

Institute of Management Consultants
Dept. 3045, Washington, DC 20041-3045
202-857-5334
The largest and best known of the consulting trade associations for solo practitioners. The IMC provides national conferences, local chapter meetings, insurance, and other benefits, and can bestow the Certified Management Consultant designation. Some local chapters are barely functional, while others are quite active, sponsoring breakfasts, monthly meetings, and educational programs.

National Bureau of Certified Consultants
2728 Fifth Avenue, San Diego, CA 92103
619-297-2207

This group awards the Certified Professional Consultant to Management (CPCM) designation, and is smaller and less well known than the IMC. It provides various publications and networking opportunities. Unlike the IMC, the NBCC is actively engaged in a movement to require licensing of consultants, not unlike CPAs or attorneys.

*National Trade and Professional Associations
of the United States*
Columbia Books, Inc.
1212 New York Avenue, Suite 330, Washington, DC 20005
202-898-0662

An excellent source to find professional associations related to your profession or specialty, how to join, location of conferences, local chapters, and so on.

Society for Human Resource Management
1800 Duke Street, Alexandria, VA 22314
703-548-3440

This society for human resources executives and managers provides extensive benefits and offers, and publishes the monthly *HRMagazine*. Hosts national events and local chapter meetings.

NEW!
Society for Advancement of Consulting
Box 746, East Greenwich, RI 02818
800-825-6153 (401-886-4097)

An organization founded by Alan Weiss specifically to advance the business and image of solo practitioners. New consultants welcome as affiliate members. Visit http://www.consultingsociety.com.

Society for Professional Consultants
Box 785, Westford, MA 01886
978-692-6950

This is a New England-based organization that has shown signs of growing professionalism in its offerings. If you're in the area or visiting, you may want to make contact. The web site is www.spconsultants.org. This is a small group that organizes monthly meetings featuring successful consultants and others of importance to professional development and marketing.

Writer's Digest Books
1507 Dana Avenue, Cincinnati, OH 45207
513-531-2690

Books and magazines for those who want to be published. May be useful if you'd like to achieve greater visibility through print, or if you're called on to contribute in the course of your work.

The Yearbook of Experts, Authorities and Spokespersons
(also now known as yearbook.com or Expertclick.com)
Broadcast Interview Source
2233 Wisconsin Avenue, NW, Washington, DC 20007
202-333-4904

A good source to find consultants, speakers, trainers, facilitators, and others who may be appropriate for buyers' needs, but most important as a source for interviews in all media.

Appendix E

Sample Biographical Sketch for a New Consultant

Joan Smith is the president of Acme Consulting Group, Inc., a firm specializing in human performance and productivity.

Joan is a former assistant general manager for ambulatory care at Mercy Hospital in Cleveland, Ohio. She has managed both line and staff functions, and has overseen both mergers and divestitures in the health care industry. She has been a featured speaker at several industry conferences, and has had articles published in *Health Care Today* and *Professional Women*.

The Cleveland chapter of the American Society for Training and Development named her professional manager of the year for an unprecedented two consecutive years in recognition of her "outstanding and innovative work in maximizing the potential of human resources." She has served as a board member for the Development Agency of Greater Cleveland, the Audubon Society, and the Ohio Youth Orchestra.

She is a member of the Institute of Management Consultants and the Society for Professional Consulting, as well as the American Management Association. Her written work has included articles in *Training* magazine and *Cleveland Business News*.

The facilitation of strategic retreats, conducting customer focus groups, training in conflict resolution, and coaching in creative thinking skills have been numbered among her work.

She once taught herself to play the saxophone, and found herself at a political rally playing alongside then-candidate Bill Clinton. He told her she had no future in music, but then again, neither did he.

Sample Position Paper

Accepting Equity for Your Services: Or Why the Craps Tables Suddenly Look Good

Consultants (and a raft of other professionals, including carpenters and plumbers) are increasingly considering equity participation in place of old-fashioned cash on the barrelhead. Sometimes it's because the clients can't (or claim they can't) come up with the cash, and sometimes it's because the allure of the client's potential payoff is so great that thoughts of vast riches clog the consultant's synapses.

Equity offers exist in two basic situations: In the first, the company is a start-up, usually high-tech but not always, which is so cash poor that it can apply only the precious venture capital for R&D and marketing. Anything else is superfluous, so everyone from accountants to gardeners is offered a stake. In the second case, a legitimate going concern offers a consultant the chance to participate in the fruits of his or her advice, usually because the client thinks the chances of reaching the goal are slim, doesn't want to pay for anything but tangible performance, or is simply cheap.

In either case, there is a strong and rare potential upside, and a strong and frequent absolute downside. Let the equity seeker beware (*caveat equitus*, or something).

WHAT YOU NEED TO KNOW

Before you jump to accept an equity position, you should make sure that you possess the basic information about the client and about yourself. In any given instance, equity can make sense for you and not a partner, or vice versa. In other words, this is like driving a Ferrari: It seems like a great idea and you know you'll look good, but not everyone can handle it and there are some places you just can't take it.

Is It Light of Day or an Approaching Train?

You have more of a chance of hitting a roulette number during an evening at the tables than you do of hitting the big time with an equity start-up. Even in established organizations, where you're taking equity on increased sales or growing market share, there are hazards.

You'll have to get a reading on the likelihood of key talent's staying the course. That means that you'll also have to be absolutely confident about management's ability to lead and to retain key people. Look at the culture. Is it one of relatively low turnover (no turnover is not good, since it fails to clear deadwood), fun, challenge, and collaboration? Are people talking about the excitement of the enterprise or about the potential for jumping ship?

Is the initiative capitalized sufficiently? Are resources and knowledge readily available and shared? Are people running full speed to gain momentum or to flee a fire? Ask yourself whether the operation in which you are considering taking an equity position is one that you would enjoy working in and/or managing. Ask yourself whether you would invest $50,000 of discretionary funds in this opportunity, because that's precisely what you're doing.

Do you like these people and do you trust them?

Who's in Charge?

Your deal about equity must be clear-cut and as unambiguous as possible. The chief executive officer (CEO) and the chief financial officer (CFO) of the client should sign off on the agreement, which itself should be created by your attorney. If the client insists on his or her own attorneys, then agree only with the provision that your attorney will then review their work. Sometimes seemingly trivial matters, such as the state in which legal disputes will be adjudicated, can make a huge difference later (some jurisdictions have laws that could make your position untenable and your contract worthless under certain conditions).

Use as much cement as possible to seal the deal. For example, if there is a board of directors, have the agreement approved by the board and read into the minutes. If key personnel change—especially likely in start-up companies—then have the new officer acknowledge and sign off on the old agreement, even though technically it is binding even without that signature.

What's Your Stress Level?

Evaluate the opportunity not in terms of an individual investment but in terms of your overall cash flow and financial picture. Can you support yourself and your business adequately without the equity position's paying off? If not, then you're creating a huge gamble. If so, then you're taking a prudent risk. Determine whether you can simply let this run its course, albeit with you contributing as a consultant, or if you'd be up during the night and distracted during the day trying to worry this venture over the finish line.

There is no sense getting sick over a piece of business. You have to be careful that, even if the equity position pays off, it doesn't totally undermine all of your other marketing and delivery efforts, which may suffer by comparison.

WHAT YOU NEED TO DO

There are some very specific things you can do to protect yourself in equity relationships. They don't always work, just like fire protection doesn't always work, but at least it's better than simply depending on the sprinkler system.

Evaluate Your Conflicts of Interest

The absolute toughest factor in taking equity is that it can color your judgment and blunt your effectiveness as a consultant, ironically causing you to become detrimental to your own interests. For example, you might come upon a manager whom you know is toxic and ought to be fired. But will you recommend firing him or her, even though it's essential for long-term success, if the position won't be filled for months and you desperately need a body in it to make this year's plan? How much of the future do you sacrifice to guarantee your short-term equity stake?

The answer, of course, is that you have to do what's in the best long-term interests of the client, and not the best short-term financial interest of the consultant. Understand this and evaluate the potential for conflicts of interest at the outset. If you anticipate them, either don't take the job or refer all such decisions to a consultant or insider who doesn't have the conflict, and abide by their decisions.

Establish What You Can and Can't Control

You may do everything humanly possible within your accountabilities, and the contribution should have led to success. But the unanticipated resignation of three top salespeople, the competition's breathtaking new technology, or the government's unexpected regulatory interference might send a torpedo into your best efforts. Try to clarify what you can and can't control. You won't be able to collect if the goals aren't met no matter what your contribution (because there will be no equity to share), so if you find this potential high, don't get into the water.

You may also find that there are managers or highly influential contributors who are rewarded, directly or indirectly, for the exact opposite of what you are trying to accomplish (e.g., a marketing vice president wants to incorporate sales into his unit, and would love to see the expansion in Europe fail so that he can make a case for the integration). If those turf battles are present, you're going to get killed in the crossfire.

Set an Example of Proper Conduct

Throughout the project, act as you always should—as an independent, objective, and decisive adviser. Don't allow yourself to be persuaded by short-term scares, and never enter into discussions that might indicate your judgment is suspect (or can be bought). Make some tough calls early, if possible, to show that your only objective is to improve the client's condition for the long term.

If you're working with a start-up, confront management often and early. These entrepreneurs are the chronically narrow. They can see their technology and its implications, and can rarely see the market, the buyer, or the elusive profit goals (known as spending less than you take in). If you're working with a large organization in a specific initiative (for example, the sales force and its business growth), then make sure you become very familiar with every key player. Never simply accept someone's word about someone else's performance or morale. See it for yourself.

Review Each Situation, Well, Situationally

If someone at IBM wants to offer you IBM stock in return for your consulting efforts, that's far different from someone at silverware.com wanting you to take equity in their new electric fork. Equity in a blue-chip company is like investing in the best market stocks and funds: If you hold on without panic, the market ultimately rewards you. But do you want to either invest in a high-tech start-up or take your chances with factors you can never completely control with a more mature organization? It depends on your tolerance for risk, your eye for opportunity, and your consulting expertise. And on luck.

Don't be afraid to take equity, but don't do it in lieu of cash you need to support your loved ones and your business.

NOTE

This position paper was eventually printed as an article on www.Guru.com.

Appendix G

Sources for
Listings and Advertising

The Directory of Memberships and News Sources
National Press Club of Washington
529 14th Street, NW, Washington, DC 20045
202-662-7500

Circulated to editors, assignment editors, reporters, producers, talk show hosts, and related media people.

*National Trade and Professional Associations of the
    United States*
Columbia Books, Inc.
1212 New York Avenue, Suite 330
Washington, DC 20005
202-898-0662

An excellent source to find professional associations related to your profession or specialty, how to join, location of conferences, local chapters, and so on.

Radio and TV Interview Reporter
Bradley Communications
135 East Plumstead Avenue, Lansdowne, PA 19050
610-259-1070

An advertising source for radio and television talk shows, published twice a month. The staff will help you format and design your ad.

The Yearbook of Experts, Authorities and Spokespersons
    (also now known as yearbook.com or
    Expertclick.com)
Broadcast Interview Source
2233 Wisconsin Avenue, NW, Washington, DC 20007
202-333-4904

Similar to the National Press Club directory, but more aggressively marketed; also has a web site, options for press releases, and so on.

Appendix H

Sample Magazine Inquiry Letter

Jack Gordon
Editor, *Training* magazine
50 South Ninth Street
Minneapolis, MN 55402

Dear Mr. Gordon:

    I'm proposing an article for *Training* on the myths of doing business globally, tentatively titled: "Global Doesn't Mean 'Foreign' Anymore." The article will focus on my trips to 13 countries in Europe and Asia over the past nine months for various clients.

    For your readers, the article will:

- ✔ Debunk the common myths of doing business internationally (e.g., cultural awareness is the most sensitive issue).
- ✔ Describe how even small businesses can readily obtain global work.
- ✔ Provide the essentials for effective global business (e.g., obtaining payment in U.S. funds drawn on U.S. banks).
- ✔ Detail how the Internet can be used for cost-effective marketing.

    I've traveled to 51 countries, and have consistently been able to leverage U.S. global clients into non-U.S.

multinational business. I've found that the mythology is often an unfair disincentive to Americans trying to do business around the world.

I can provide the article within 60 days of your approval. An SASE is enclosed. Thanks for your consideration.

Sincerely,

Alan Weiss, Ph.D.
President
Summit Consulting Group, Inc.

Appendix 1

101 Questions for Any Sales Situation You'll Ever Face

AN OVERVIEW

This material is intended to provide questions to ask in virtually any sales situation, thereby:

✔ Maintaining a conversational and nonsales approach.

✔ Keeping the other party talking in order to learn.

✔ Avoiding deselection by volunteering very little yourself.

✔ Finding the buyer, building a relationship, and closing business.

✔ Accelerating the entire sales process.

You might choose to take these questions on calls, to keep them by the phone, or to use them as the basis for printing out your own questions to keep in your briefcase or calendar. The copyright is intended to protect the work

279

as it is presented, and to avoid resale or unethical use. However, you should feel free to incorporate the generic questions and the derivations that flow from them into your personal routine and support materials.

The questions are deliberately overlapping, and stop just short of duplicative. Essentially, you want to elicit the same information in as many diverse ways as possible.

A Few Guidelines for Use

✔ Don't interrogate people. It's seldom necessary to ask even the majority of questions in any one category.

✔ Employ follow-up questions. The questions contained herein are triggers that may engender a response that demands further clarification.

✔ Trust is essential for candor. The other party will be most honest and responsive when trust is established (e.g., they believe you have their best interests in mind).

✔ Never be content with a single question, no matter how satisfying the answer appears to be. Some people will attempt to deceive you to save their ego, and others will inadvertently deceive you because they misunderstood the question. I recommend that you use at least three questions per category if the answers are consistent, and six or more if the answers appear to be inconsistent.

These questions are rational, objective, and most of all, based on common sense and simple discourse. Try not to be distracted or to digress until the answer you're seeking in any given category is forthcoming. For example, it's dysfunctional to ask questions about objectives if you haven't asked the questions to satisfy you that you're talking to an economic buyer. Discipline is best.

Ironically, the longer you take to find the right answers, the more you accelerate the business.

Good selling and good luck!

— Alan Weiss, Ph.D.

QUALIFYING THE PROSPECT

This is the process of determining whether the inquiry is appropriate for your business in terms of size, relevance, seriousness, and related factors. In other words, you don't want to pursue a lead that can't result in legitimate—and worthwhile—business.

Questions

1. Why do you think we might be a good match?
2. Is there budget allocated for this project?
3. How important is this need (on a scale of 1-10)?
4. What is your timing to accomplish this?
5. Who, if anyone, is demanding that this be accomplished?
6. How soon are you willing to begin?
7. Have you made a commitment to proceed, or are you still analyzing?
8. What are your key decision criteria in choosing a resource?
9. Have you tried this before (will this be a continuing endeavor)?
10. Is your organization seeking formal proposals for this work?

Key Point: You want to determine whether the potential work is large enough for your involvement, relevant to your expertise, and near enough on the horizon to merit rapid responsiveness.

FINDING THE ECONOMIC BUYER

The economic buyer is the person who can write a check in return for your value contribution. He or she is the ONLY buyer to be concerned about. Contrary to a great deal of poor advice, the economic buyer is virtually *never* in human resources, training, meeting planning, or related support areas.

Questions

11. Whose budget will support this initiative?

12. Who can immediately approve this project?

13. To whom will people look for support, approval, and credibility?

14. Who controls the resources required to make this happen?

15. Who has initiated this request?

16. Who will claim responsibility for the results?

17. Who will be seen as the main sponsor and/or champion?

18. Do you have to seek anyone else's approval?

19. Who will accept or reject proposals?

20. If you and I were to shake hands, could I begin tomorrow?

Key Point: The larger the organization, the more the number of economic buyers. They need not be the CEO or owner, but must be able to authorize and produce payment. Committees are never *economic buyers.*

REBUTTING OBJECTIONS

"Obstacles are those terrible things you see when you take your eyes off the goal," said philosopher Hannah Arendt. Objections are a sign of interest. Turn them around to your benefit. Once you demolish objections, there is no longer a reason not to proceed in a partnership.

Questions (in responding to an economic buyer's objections)

21. Why do you feel that way? (Get at the true cause.)

22. If we resolve this, can we then proceed? (Is this the sole objection?)

23. But isn't that exactly why you need me? (The reversal approach.)

24. What would satisfy you? (Make the buyer answer the objection.)

25. What can we do to overcome that? (Demonstrate joint accountability.)

26. Is this unique? (Is there precedent for overcoming it?)

27. What's the consequence? (Is it really serious or merely an annoyance?)

28. Isn't that low probability? (Worry about likelihoods, not the remote.)

29. Shall I address that in the proposal? (Let's focus on value.)

30. Why does it even matter in light of the results? (The ROI is the point.)

Key Points: Don't be on the defensive by trying to slay each objection with your sword, or you'll eventually fall onto it. Embrace the buyer in the solutions, and demonstrate that some objections are insignificant when compared with benefits (e.g., there will always be some unhappy employees in any change effort).

ESTABLISHING OBJECTIVES

Objectives are the outcomes that represent the client's desired and improved conditions. They are never inputs (e.g., reports, focus groups, manuals) but rather always outputs (e.g., increased sales, reduced attrition, improved teamwork). Clear objectives prevent scope creep and enable a rational engagement and disengagement to take place, resulting in much greater consulting efficiency and profit margins. (Note that the fourth, fifth, and sixth—objectives, measures, and value—are the basis of conceptual agreement.)

Questions

31. What is the ideal outcome you'd like to experience?

32. What results are you trying to accomplish?

33. What better product/service/customer condition are you seeking?

34. Why are you seeking to do this (work/project/ engagement)?

35. How would the operation be different as a result of this work?

36. What would be the return on investment (sales, assets, equity, etc.)?

37. How would image/repute/credibility be improved?

38. What harm (e.g., stress, dysfunction, turf wars, etc.) would be alleviated?

39. How much would you gain on the competition as a result?

40. How would your value proposition be improved?

Key Points: Most buyers know what they want but not necessarily what they need. By pushing the buyer on the end results you are helping to articulate and formalize the client's perceived benefits, thereby increasing your own value in the process. Without clear objectives you do not have a legitimate project.

ESTABLISHING METRICS

"Metrics" are measures of progress toward the objectives, which enable you and the client to ascertain the rate and totality of success. They assign proper credit to you and your efforts, and also signify when the project is complete (objectives are met) and it is proper to disengage.

Questions

41. How will you know we've accomplished your intent?

42. How, specifically, will the operation be different when we're done?

43. How will you measure this?

44. What indicators will you use to assess our progress?

45. Who or what will report on our results (against the objectives)?

46. Do you already have measures in place you intend to apply?

47. What is the rate of return (on sales, investment, etc.) that you seek?

48. How will we know the public, employees, and/or customers perceive it?

49. Each time we talk, what standard will tell us we're progressing?

50. How would you know it if you tripped over it?

Key Points: Measures can be subjective, so long as you and the client agree on who is doing the measuring and how. For example, the buyer's observation that he or she is called upon less to settle turf disputes and has fewer complaints from direct reports aimed at colleagues are valid measures for the objective of "improved teamwork."

ASSESSING VALUE

Determining the value of the project for the client's organization is the most critical aspect of conceptual agreement and pre-proposal interaction. That's because when the buyer stipulates to significant value, the fee is placed in proper perspective (ROI) and is seldom an issue of contention. Conversations with the buyer should always focus on value and never on fee or price.

Questions

51. What will these results mean for your organization?

52. How would you assess the actual return (ROI, ROA, ROS, ROE, etc.)?

53. What would be the extent of the improvement (or correction)?

54. How will these results impact the bottom line?

55. What are the *annualized* savings (first year might be deceptive)?

56. What is the intangible impact (e.g., on repute, safety, comfort, etc.)?

57. How would you, personally, be better off or better supported?

58. What is the scope of the impact (on customers, employees, vendors)?

59. How important is this compared to your overall responsibilities?

60. What if this fails?

Key Points: Subjective value (stress alleviated) can be every bit as important as more tangible results (higher sales). Never settle for "Don't worry, it's important." Find out how important, because that will dictate the acceptable fee range.

DETERMINING THE BUDGET RANGE

Too much guessing takes place in the absence of a general understanding about how much the prospect intends to invest (prior to understanding the full value proposition). In many cases, the budget is fixed and entirely inappropriate, and in others it represents a better understanding of the ROI than that of the consultant! (Don't forget, this presupposes you're talking to an economic buyer.)

Questions

61. Have you arrived at a budget or investment range for this project?

62. Are funds allocated, or must they be requested?

63. What is your expectation of investment required?

64. So we don't waste time, are there parameters to remain within?

65. Have you done this before, and at what investment level?

66. What are you able to authorize during this fiscal year?

67. Can I assume that a strong proposition will justify proper expenditure?

68. How much are you prepared to invest to gain these dramatic results?

69. For a dramatic return, will you consider a larger investment?

70. Let's be frank: What are you willing to spend?

Key Points: There is nothing wrong with exceeding the budget expectation if you muster a strong enough value proposition. But don't even proceed with a proposal if the prospect has a seriously misguided expectation of the investment need, or simply has an inadequate, fixed budget.

PREVENTING UNFORESEEN OBSTACLES

As comedienne Gilda Radnor used to say, "It's always something." Inevitably, it seems, the best laid plans are undermined by objections, occurrences, and serendipity from left field. Fortunately, there are questions to establish some preventive actions against even the unforeseen.

Questions

71. Is there anything we haven't discussed that could get in the way?

72. In the past, what has occurred to derail potential projects like this?

73. What haven't I asked you that I should have about the environment?

74. What do you estimate the probability is of our going forward?

75. Are you surprised by anything I've said or that we've agreed upon?

76. At this point, are you still going to make this decision yourself?

77. What, if anything, do you additionally need to hear from me?

78. Is anything likely to change in the organization in the near future?

79. Are you awaiting the results of any other initiatives or decisions?

80. If I get this proposal to you tomorrow, how soon will you decide?

Key Points: Make sure that your project isn't contingent upon other events transpiring (or not transpiring). If the buyer is holding out on you, these questions will make it more difficult to dissemble. Build into your proposal benefits to outweigh the effects of any external factors.

INCREASING THE SIZE OF THE SALE

Once conceptual agreement is gained, it makes sense to capitalize on the common ground and strive for the largest possible relationship. Most consultants don't obtain larger contracts because they don't ask for or suggest them. You can't possibly lose anything attempting to increase the business at this juncture.

Questions

81. Would you be amenable to my providing a variety of options?

82. Is this the only place (division, department, geography) applicable?

83. Would it be wise to extend this through implementation and oversight?

84. Should we plan to also coach key individuals essential to the project?

85. Would you benefit from benchmarking against other firms?

86. Would you also like an idea of what a retainer might look like?

87. Are there others in your position with like needs I should see?

88. Do your subordinates possess the skills to support you appropriately?

89. Should we run focus groups/other sampling to test employee reactions?

90. Would you like me to test customer response at various stages?

Key Points: If you don't ask, you don't get. Don't throw everything including the kitchen sink into your proposal in an attempt to justify your fee. Instead, unbundle what you're capable of providing and add them back in an additional fee.

GOING FOR THE CLOSE

Home stretch, but not across the finish line. Runners who slow up at the approaching tape lose to someone else with a better late kick. Run through the tape at full speed by driving the conversation right through the close of the sale and the check's clearing the bank.

Questions

91. If the proposal reflects our last discussions, how soon can we begin?

92. Is it better to start immediately, or wait for the first of the month?

93. Is there anything at all preventing our working together at this point?

94. How rapidly are you prepared to begin once you see the proposal?

95. If you get the proposal tomorrow, can I call Friday at 10 for approval?

96. While I'm here, should I begin some of the preliminary work today?

97. Would you like to shake hands and get started, proposal to follow?

98. Do you prefer a corporate check or to wire the funds electronically?

99. May I allocate two days early next week to start my interviews?

100. Can we proceed?

Key Points: There is never a better time than when you're in front of the buyer and he or she is in agreement and excited about the project. Even without a proposal, beginning immediately pours cement on the conceptual agreement and greatly diminishes the possibility of being derailed by surprise.

THE MOST VITAL QUESTION

All of the preceding 100 questions are actually based on the reaction to one question, which we often fail to ask of the most difficult person of all. And unlike most of the prior inquiries, it's a simple binary question, with a clear "yes or no" response.

Question

101. Do you believe it yourself?

Key Point: The first sale is always to yourself.

Glossary

acceptance   that part of the proposal that the buyer signs indicating agreement with all details, terms, and provisions included. An acceptance can also be oral, or can be in the form of a payment when you've indicated that a payment will indicate acceptance of the terms.

biographical sketch   a brief (one page or less) description of the consultant's accomplishments, credentials, and credible background. *Note:* This is not a resume.

brochure   a bound booklet that describes your firm's services, client results, and approaches; provides testimonials; and contains other relevant information for a prospective buyer. You are better off with no brochure than a cheap foldout version. Wait until you can afford a decent one of four to a dozen pages.

buyer   that person who can write a check (expend budget without further approvals) for the consultant's products and services; also called economic buyer or true buyer.

C corporation   traditional corporate configuration, which I believe offers more advantages than an S corporation, though either is appropriate for a consulting practice.

celebrity   that status that confers upon you a credibility and competence that is spoken about by others and readily accepted without further proof or validation by those who do not know you.

client   an organization or individual that engages the consultant to achieve certain results in return for agreed-upon compensation.

commercial publishing   producing print or recorded material through a third party, which pays you a royalty for the intellectual property but controls all production and distribution (as opposed to self-publishing).

conceptual agreement   the oral agreement with the buyer that the objectives, measures of success, and value to the organization are accurate and acknowledged.

consulting   the application of talents, expertise, experiences, and other relevant attributes, which results in an improvement in the client's condition.

content   the work of the business (e.g., health care or producing cement).

contingency fees   fees paid only upon achievement of some predetermined goal. As a rule, this is not an attractive fee arrangement.

domain name   your firm's address on the Internet (e.g., summitconsulting.com).

equity   ownership of an enterprise. In this case, it is sometimes offered in place of cash compensation for services rendered. Equity can be attractive as a portion of compensation, but should never represent total compensation, especially for new consultants.

feasibility buyer   that person who is responsible for determining whether a consultant may fit certain criteria or otherwise be acceptable, but who cannot buy the services and can only recommend alternatives to the real economic buyer.

fees   those payments, usually in cash but sometimes in equity, bartered services, or other forms, which compensate the consultant for the value delivered to the client.

gatekeeper   that person who is not a buyer but advertently or inadvertently stands between the consultant and buyer.

inputs   tasks and activities required to generate outputs.

ISBN   "International Standard Book Number," which should be applied to all your printed and recorded products that you wish to sell. This is how all bookstores and online sources order your material. ISBNs are available from R. R. Bowker.

lead   a prospective client's name and contact information, from any source.

limited liability company (LLC)   a form of incorporation increasingly popular, and very appropriate for consulting practices.

marketing   the creation of need for your services among potential buyers.

measures of success   those indicators of progress (metrics) that tell the consultant and the buyer whether the project is meeting the agreed-upon objectives.

methodology   the systematic, procedural approaches that a consultant uses to implement a project (e.g., surveys, training programs, competitive analyses, etc.).

networking the activity of meeting others in a systematic manner, particularly those who can buy, recommend, or otherwise support your services. The best networking is accomplished one-on-one by providing value to the other party first.

objectives those end results whose achievement will indicate project success. Objectives should always be stated as business outcomes.

one-sheet a single sheet in black and white (for faxing) and color that succinctly describes the consultant's accomplishments, clients, results, and credibility. The one-sheet is particularly important for speaking engagements.

options alternative approaches to reach the client's objectives, which provide the client with the ability to determine *how* to use the consultant, rather than *whether* to use the consultant; also called a "choice of yeses."

outputs results that have a demonstrable impact in improving the client's condition. These are always business-related.

press kit a formalized, professional set of documents assembled in a folder that is used for promotion and credibility. Press kits typically include references, testimonials, a biographical sketch, client lists, articles, interviews, and related materials; also called "media kit," "publicity kit."

pro bono work work undertaken deliberately for no compensation, for the purposes of marketing, charitable contribution, longer-term visibility, networking, and other such purposes.

process techniques to run a business that can be applied to any content (e.g., decision making or conflict resolution).

proposal the document that summarizes conceptual agreement, and also details timing, accountabilities, terms, and conditions of the engagement.

reference a source, usually a client, serving as a contact for prospective clients to ascertain the quality of your work, veracity of your claims, and so on.

referral a prospective client's name provided by another source. The best referrals include an introduction of some kind. The barest are those that simply provide a name of someone who may be interested.

relationship the interaction created between consultant and buyer based on mutual trust, candor, respect, and a perception of peer-level credibility.

retainer a set fee paid for access to the consultant's expertise and support without regard for specific projects or objectives. Retainers should be paid in one sum or in installments at the beginning of each designated period.

S corporation   form of incorporation designed for small businesses, wherein the profits flow through the owners' personal tax returns.

search engine   those functions on the Internet that provide information about web sites by keywords, topics, subjects, and so on. Your web site and firm should be listed with the major search engines and updated periodically.

self-publishing   producing your own printed or recorded material by contracting for all technological and logistical assistance (as opposed to commercial publishing).

situation appraisal   a summary of the conditions facing a prospective client that need to be improved as a result of the consulting engagement. This brief description should be the first part of a proposal.

terms and conditions   that part of the consulting proposal that deals with fees, payment schedules, expense reimbursement, and related matters.

testimonial   a written endorsement on a client's stationery validating your value and contributions to the writer's organization.

timing   that part of the proposal that deals with start and end dates, and when certain events are scheduled to occur. Timing should always revolve around calendar dates, not relative dates (e.g., "June 1," not "30 days after our agreement").

value   the degree of improvement to the client represented by the achievement of the objectives. These may be quantitative (2 percent increase in sales) or qualitative (there will be much less stress for me).

values   those fundamental beliefs that guide our behaviors, and that should be congruent between the consultant and buyer in terms of the project and the relationship.

vanity publishing   the paying of a third party to publish your material, sometimes including design, distribution, order fulfillment, and so on. It is more expensive than self-publishing, in which you are paying only for actual printing, and is not credible in the marketplace. Eschew vanity publishing.

Index